Sin

A N D

Syntax

Sin

AND

Syntax

HOW TO CRAFT

WICKEDLY

EFFECTIVE PROSE

Constance Hale

FOREWORD BY

Karen Elizabeth Gordon

BROADWAY BOOKS   NEW YORK

Broadway Books titles may be purchased for business or promotional use or for special sales. For information, please write to: Special Markets Department, Random House, Inc., 1540 Broadway, New York, NY 10036.

BROADWAY BOOKS and its logo, a letter B bisected on the diagonal, are trademarks of Broadway Books, a division of Random House, Inc.
Visit our Web site at www.broadwaybooks.com

Library of Congress Cataloging-in-Publication Data
Hale, Constance.
    Sin and syntax : how to craft wickedly effective prose / by Constance Hale ; with a foreword by Karen Elizabeth Gordon. —1st ed.
        p.   cm.
    Includes index.
    ISBN 0-7679-0308-0
    1. English language—Rhetoric.   2 Creative writing.   3. Report writing.   I. Title.
PE1408.H299   1999   99-13591
808'.042—dc21   CIP

FIRST EDITION

Designed by Pei Loi Koay

99 00 01 02 03 10 9 8 7 6 5 4 3 2 1

To Madeleine Carter Mayher,
who gave me her love
of the mother tongue.

Acknowledgments

This book, more than most, reflects the energies not of one author but of many creative misbehavers. My thanks go first to all the writers whose words you'll see within these covers.

In casting my net wide for examples of wicked and winning syntax, I was helped by many language scamps, including Martha Baer, Wallace Baine, Frank Clancy, Alex Frankel, Mark Frauenfelder, Jesse Freund, Sam Kane, Tim McGee, Keris Salmon, Brad Wieners, and Gary Wolf. Wallace Baine, especially, came through in spades.

My researcher, Julie Greenberg, proved she could track down *anything*—even an almost forgotten 1969 Jell-O commercial. She also sent many useful surprises my way. Meri Brin was unbeatable on the Web and BBS beat. I have half a mind to stand in front of the San Francisco Main Library singing the praises of its reference desk—but the competition for a corner of Civic Center sidewalk is so fierce I'll keep my encomiums here. In particular, I thank Renée Tarshis and Peter Warhit, whose unbridled curiosity and unrelenting helpfulness are shared by their fellow librarians.

Friends and colleagues read parts of the manuscript and saved me from most of my own excesses. Gifted wordsmiths all, Jessie Scanlon, Hollis Heimbouch, Emily McManus, Micki Esken-Meland, and Mary Beth Protomastro were especially generous with the juice. I'm not sure which is more dangerous—Jessie Scanlon's withering wit or her purple pen.

Many thanks to my editor at Broadway Books, Suzanne Oaks, who has made me look good, and to Lisa Olney. The book also benefited greatly from the guidance of Matthew Martin and from the attentions of its copy editor, Rosalie Wieder, and its designer, Pei Loi Koay.

I owe a special debt to Karen Elizabeth Gordon. She first sent me spinning in 1984, when I bought her *Transitive Vampire;* in the past year she became mentor as well as muse, offering me an emergency writing table in the hills, Bariani olive oil, and a couple of killer line edits. Not to mention a foreword!

Also in the special-debt department is my agent, Wendy Lipkind. This book would not have happened without her.

My aunt and godmother, Eleanor Mayher Hackett, started giving me books of poetry before I could talk, and she read my manuscript with the kind of unconditional enthusiasm only an aunt can offer. I am lucky to have her.

And finally, I must thank Bruce Lowell Bigelow, who knows all my sins.

Contents

Oh, the sentence! The shuddering, sinuous, piquant, incandescent, delicate, delirious, sulking, strident possibilities of it all! A sentence can loll à l'odalisque, zap, implore, insist, soar, or simply lay out the facts. This handful of words, each with its own humble or brazen function, lies at the heart of every literary genre, every letter, memo, article, thesis, seduction, threat, and retort. In any book you handle, sentences abound. Here, in *Sin and Syntax,* they strut their stuff in all their guises and moods. From this exploration you'll emerge not only a more sharp-witted writer, but also a more attuned reader.

Often when we speak, our ideas fly out half formed, in scattered confessions and pronouncements, in tattered repartee. It is in writing that we have the time and place to shape our sentences and see what we really think, taking ourselves as well as our readers by surprise or storm. We may not know what we're going to say (it's much more fun when we don't!), and the many ways of combining words help us discover meanings hidden in our own minds. The greater our grasp of these structures, the ampler our repertoire and experience in using them, the farther and deeper we can go.

Books about writing not only abound—they are shamelessly on the make, taking up precious space in bookstores where literature and lovingly crafted nonfiction should be holding biblioshoppers in thrall. I have read few of these how-to and hold-your-hand-while-you-try manuals because it was literature that taught me how to write, and my cursory glances in this section found few compelling pages on which to alight and linger. But when I heard that my fellow bad girl of grammar and style was writing a book called *Sin and Syntax*, my nostrils flared, my pulse quickened, my bodice ripped open—I *had* to take a look. My own association with the word *syntax* postdates my vampirical handbook, and links the divine order of a sentence with scandalous, unfettered behavior. A Yugoslav psychiatrist friend in New York, newly acquainted with my grammatical persona and hearing of my gypsy knockabout life, captured the paradox in a linguistic metaphor: "That's not very syntactical." Thus *sin* seemed a perfect bedfellow for *syntax*. Words sleep around, and the tongues of the world are enhanced in the process.

At times I've envisioned language as a body with its own surge and rhythms and whims, other times as a diaphanous garment that both hides and reveals. But always I see grammar as the choreographer of our language, coordinating the movements of our baffling, flummoxed urge to express, to give voice to the ineffable. Familiarity with the rules of grammar tones our mental musculature, expands our repertoire, sets us free to dance. To break the rules consciously or go around them on purpose is a pleasure multiplied: willful violation, defiance, or deviation with a wicked glint in the eye. The sound, the taste, the thrill of language, its rhythms and edges and riffs—which impart another sort of precision—you will also find underscored in *Sin and Syntax*. To me, music *is* the message, and play, the muse and master of all creation, romps across this realm.

Chapter by chapter, Constance Hale's book is about the rigors and romance of sentences, and sharpening one's senses in the reading and the making of them. It shows how a sentence comes together through the dance of words, how one sentence follows another in an effective piece of prose. Here you will see parts of speech in action, make tracks with parallel structure, catch a coquettish phrase at its arc, or curl up with a curvaceous clause. In dens of iniquity you will consort with the demons you once feared; you will dispel misgivings like bubbles of soap. You will return to this very passage and pronounce it overwrought. But flesh and the devil call for flamboyance now and then, and the legitimate haunts of fanfare include prefaces as well as ads. Here you will learn to handle the bones of writing, to articulate a skeleton before it's dressed and adorned and sets out to stir up its chosen mischief. A knowing body you will become.

Karen Elizabeth Gordon
Mas Lafont
St-Hippolyte du Fort

Driven by some combustible mix of passion (for the power and poetry of words) and desperation (so many snags in your sentences!), you've picked up a book called *Sin and Syntax*. What, you're wondering, does *syntax*—that collection of prissy grammar rules dictating how to put words together—have to do with *sin*—the reckless urge to flout the rules and abandon propriety altogether?

Sin and Syntax plays with dynamic tensions in language: The underlying codes that give prose its clarities yet fail to explain its beauties. The sludge and sloth that muddle your writing. The delight in the wicked and the wacky. *Sin and Syntax* is about the skill that allows you, the writer, to harness such complexities, to create prose that thrills.

Are you ready to turn syntax from a minefield into a stamping ground— your stamping ground? Forget schoolmarmish rules. Forget grammar as it was drilled and grilled in grade school. Rest assured, you'll get your grammar here, on the theory that it's better to know rules than to stay clueless. This book *will* show you how to avoid bonehead mistakes, but, more importantly, it'll show you how to make some sinful mischief.

IF ALL THIS SEEMS a bit paradoxical, get used to it. Language *is* paradox.

Sin and Syntax dwells in contradictions, dabbling in the eloquence of tradition, the intelligence of goofy grammars, the decadence of dialects. We'll root around where language is the most playful and plastic: in the pop, the vernacular, the mongrel tongues. We'll look at how the highbrow and the lowbrow define the exciting edges of prose and how the middlebrow dooms it to mediocrity. We'll diss commonplace lingos like legalese and computerese and ditch the lifeless codes of Standard Written English.

We'll also summon the spirit of renegades who ignore taboos and make the language sing, from Shakespeare to Mark Twain to Chuck D. We'll wallow with Walt Whitman, who ridiculed the "dictionary makers," insisting that language had its base "broad and low, close to the ground." We'll look at English as a robust, swarthy tongue, capable of surviving tumult and thriving on innovation.

T. S. Eliot once argued that a language with identical spoken and written forms would be "practically intolerable," since no one would listen to the first or read the second. Eliot was cool, but don't be fooled by false dichotomies. Insisting on literary language, on strict structures and stuffy phrasing, means you may miss the shifting brilliances of the colloquial and the colorful. On the other hand, glorifying the spoken, demanding that people "write as they speak," can put a higher premium on the pedestrian than on graceful grammar, stylistic complexity, and rich vocabulary. A passion for new terms and easy slang is great, but discretion, sensitivity, and masterful metaphor still matter.

In figuring out how to write better, let's look to the ways the spoken and the written crisscross and connect and cross-pollinate. Let's look to texts like the *Book of Common Prayer,* which was written to be read out loud, and to speechmakers like Winston Churchill, who wrote and rewrote and practiced and repracticed before he ever preached. Let's look to the voices of cyberspace and to the rhythms of rap, celebrating the syntax and sounds that make narratives hop.

BOOKS ON PROSE STYLE, of course, are as old as sin—or at least as old as Aristotle, who launched the industry with *Poetics* and *Rhetoric.* You'll see the names of Aristotle's descendants mentioned throughout the book: Hugh Blair, Henry Fowler, Sir Arthur Quiller-Couch, George Orwell, Sir Ernest Gowers. These men have refined the rules of writing over the centuries, their efforts culminating in the terse commandments of William Strunk and E. B. White (*Use the active voice. Omit needless words. Avoid foreign languages*). The most recent god of prose style, William Zinsser, further distilled the wisdom of the ancients into what he called, in his classic *On Writing Well,* "four articles of faith": clarity, simplicity, brevity, and humanity.

Sin and Syntax accepts the high bar set by Zinsser—and uses grammar and syntax to help you clear it. *Sin and Syntax* holds that the flesh of prose gets its shape and strength from the bones of grammar, and that sinfully good writing depends on understanding both the arcana of syntax and the artistry of music.

Adding a little illicit activity to "articles of faith," *Sin and Syntax* offers these new principles of prose:

RELISH EVERY WORD.

BE SIMPLE, BUT GO DEEP.

TAKE RISKS.

SEEK BEAUTY.

FIND THE RIGHT PITCH.

Moving from the most basic to the most sophisticated, *Sin and Syntax* covers the parts of speech and how to exploit them (in "Words"), shows the parts of a sentence and how to arrange them (in "Sentences"), and reveals how voice, lyricism, melody, and rhythm give prose its mystery and poetry (in "Music").

Within these three parts, "Words," "Sentences," and "Music," the book's individual chapters are broken into four sections:

- The **Bones** section is the grammar sermonette. It gives you simple keys to grammar, one at a time. Learn the sensible system, if only to know how to escape it in flights of creative fancy (it's more flexible than those English teachers would have you believe). We won't linger on every arcane point—you Marian-the-Librarian types who find your appetite whetted for more can consult Appendix 3 for a hefty list of grammar guides.

- The **Flesh** section contains the lesson on writing. Linking grammar to prose, it shows how the parts of speech, the syntax of sentences, and the techniques of music give us the best stories. It also includes samples of prose by writers who exploit grammar in every graf.

- **Cardinal Sins** catalogs true transgressions: errors made in ignorance. Exposing the disaster that lurks in mangled syntax, this section also debunks those horrid myths that often substitute for a real understanding of the underpinnings of language. (*Don't split infinitives. Don't start a sentence with a conjunction. Don't end a sentence with a preposition.*) Cardinal Sins sets you straight.

- **Carnal Pleasures** shows how, sometimes, writing works because it hews exquisitely to the underlying codes of language. And how, sometimes, writing works because it defies the codes—or seems to. Carnal Pleasures contains playful, riotous, sometimes subversive pieces of writing, and shows how breaking the rules can lead to breakthrough prose.

Sin and Syntax is designed so that the novice can march from chapter to chapter in an orderly fashion, learning how to sync the parts, one at a time. But it is also designed so that the prose veteran can head directly to troublesome areas for a refresher course in grammar and a reliable list of do's and don'ts.

Straightening out grammar and syntax is not the be-all and end-all of writing. But you need a command of language as much as you need a commanding idea. When style complements substance, when technique is put into the service of a good tale, prose can plunge deep and pulse with life.

PART I

The French mime Etienne Decroux used to remind his students, "One pearl is better than a whole necklace of potatoes." What is true for that wordless art form applies equally to writing: well-crafted prose depends on the writer's ability to discriminate between pearls and potatoes. Only *some* words are fit to be strung into sentences.

Great writers are meticulous with their pearls, sifting through piles of words and stringing only perfect specimens upon the thread of syntax. The careful execution of beautiful, powerful prose through beautiful, powerful words is guided by these principles:

RELISH EVERY WORD.

True prose stylists carry on an impassioned, lifelong love affair with words, banishing bad words like so many banal suitors, burnishing the good ones till they shimmer. Be infatuated, be seduced, be obsessed.

But be smart about words, too. "All words are pegs to hang ideas on," wrote nineteenth-century essayist Henry Ward Beecher: words not linked to ideas are not worthy of writing— or reading. Once you've committed your words to paper (or to the screen), test each term. Does it carry your idea? Does it express, exactly, that once inchoate thought?

Sensitize yourself to denotation and connotation. *Denotation,* the dictionary definition of a word, refers to its explicit or literal meanings. *Connotation,* the suggestive power of a word, refers to its implicit or latent meanings. The denotations of *peach* (a single-seeded fruit with tangy yellowish pulp and downy skin that goes from yellow to red) and *mango* (a single-seeded fruit with a tangy yellowish pulp and firm skin mottled with greens, yellows, and reds) differ only slightly. But where *peach* summons up hot summers in Georgia and the cheeks of a Southern belle, *mango* conjures images of India and Mexico—and the paintings of Gauguin. The two fruits may be interchangeable in cooking, but wouldn't it be a mistake to swap in *mango* when writing about, say, the dusty peach *chambres* of a grande dame with a thing for Louis XVI?

Beyond the sense of a word is its sensuousness: its sound, its cadence, its spirit. In turning a phrase, let the words build like a jazz riff, allowing the meanings and melodies of one word to play off the meanings and melodies of the words around it.

BE SIMPLE, BUT GO DEEP.

The exquisite "cutouts" of Matisse and elegant line drawings of Picasso came late in long careers of painstaking work and wild experimentation. In writing as in painting, simplicity often follows considerable torment. "People used to call me a good writer," mused John Ruskin, giant of the nineteenth-century essay. "Now they say I can't write at all; because, for instance, if I think anybody's house is on fire, I only say, 'Sir, your house is on fire.' . . . I used to say, 'Sir, the abode in which you probably passed the delightful days of youth is in a state of inflammation.' "

Verbose is not a synonym for *literary*. A member of the British Parliament once commented that if a bureaucrat had tried to express Lord Nelson's "England expects every man to do his duty," posterity would have been left with *England anticipates that as regards the current emergency personnel will face up to the issues and exercise appropriately the functions allocated to their respec-*

tive occupation groups. Bureaucrats and business writers too often prefer big words when they're naming little things. Let's not forsake short, common words that name big things—*hope* and *pride,* for example—or simple couplings that leave concrete impressions, like *the red wheelbarrow.* Shakespeare's "sleep that knits up the ravell'd sleeve of care" uses simple words to go deep. No big-shot words, but a big idea.

It's not enough, though, to be just simple. "Nine pounds where three are sufficient is obesity," said Frank Lloyd Wright. "But to eliminate expressive words in speaking or writing—words that intensify or vivify meaning—is not simplicity. It may be, or usually is, stupidity."

Henry David Thoreau pored over *Walden,* revising it again and again to find words that "intensify or vivify meaning." This journal entry left him unsatisfied:

> I have travelled some in New England, especially in Concord, and I found that no enterprise was on foot which it would not disgrace a man to take part in. They seemed to be employed everywhere in shops and offices and fields. They seemed, like the Brahmins of the East, to be doing penance in a thousand, curious, unheard-of ways.

Setting upon those sentences, clearing the unnecessary words and repetitions, Thoreau crafted a single sentence with greater power:

> I have travelled a good deal in Concord, and everywhere, in shops and offices and fields, the inhabitants have seemed to me to be doing penance in a thousand curious ways.

Thoreau manages to make his idea more specific by panning right in on Concord, paring down his repetitions *(they,* initially repeated twice, is swept away by the stronger *inhabitants),* and cutting more quickly to the final, stirring phrase.

TAKE RISKS.

After having suffered the hyperactive red pens of schoolmarms and the hypercorrect rules of inflexible pedagogues, too many of us have retreated to the realm of the safe, the standard, and the vague. A "mixture of vagueness and sheer incompetence is the most marked characteristic of modern English prose," wrote George Orwell in "Politics and the English Language." "As soon as certain topics are raised, the concrete melts into the abstract and no one seems able to think of turns of speech that are not hackneyed: prose consists less and less of *words* chosen for the sake of their meaning, and more and more of *phrases* tacked together like the sections of a prefabricated hen-house."

Hidden in such prefab prose is a fear of going to the edge. But it's romping around on the fringes of language that gives writing its frisson. The right word might be snagged off the street, snatched from another language, or hatched in the sand tray of the imagination. Dive into the polyglot English tongue, taking a cue from Walt Whitman, that high priest of the rambunctious:

> I like limber, lasting, fierce words. I like them applied to
> myself—and I like them in newspapers, courts, debates,
> Congress. Do you suppose the liberties and the brawn of These
> States have to do only with delicate lady-words? with gloved
> gentleman words? Bad presidents, bad judges, bad clients, bad
> editors, owners of slaves, and the long ranks of Northern
> political suckers (robbers, traitors, suborned), monopolists,
> infidels, . . . shaved persons, supplejacks, ecclesiastics, men
> not fond of women, women not fond of men, cry down the
> use of strong, cutting, beautiful rude words. [But] to the manly
> instincts of the People they will be forever welcome.

Whitman's American English scarfs up words from other languages with a vengeance. If someone's bugging you, you can go the Anglo-Saxon route and *shun* her; or you can *avoid* her (Latin);

or you can *eschew* her (French). Or you tell her to *get outta your face*. Don't shun slang, especially when it's vivid and musical and fills a gap in the lexicon. Think of the words Shakespeare invented: the adjectives *long-haired, lackluster, unqualitied, green-eyed, heartsick,* and *hot-blooded,* the nouns *want-wit, vinegar aspect,* and *wit-snapper,* and the verbs in lines like "You *unlace* your reputation thus" or "The tears that *spanieled* me at heels." More modern neologists have kept up the mischief, giving us gems like *snafu, snarky, muckety-mucks, chump change, copasetic, airhead, hacker,* and, oh, *babelicious.*

A word not in the dictionary is not out of bounds. Isn't the newly popular noun *bloviator* perfect to describe that dude who can't get enough of his own voice? H. L. Mencken carried on about coinages bubbling up out of the American experience; one of his favorites, *rubberneck,* he called "almost a complete treatise on American psychology . . . [conveying the] boldness and contempt for ordered forms that are so characteristically American . . . the grotesque humor of the country, the delight in devastating opprobriums, and the acute feeling for the succinct and savory."

You tell 'em, H. L.!

SEEK BEAUTY.

Brevity isn't everything. Winston Churchill, who generally endorsed short and simple words, chose *flocculent* over *woolly* in describing the mental process of certain people in his treatise *The Second World War.* Why? *Flocculent* carries an edge of contempt, echoing words like *flop, flap, flaccid, flimsy,* and *flabby.* Winston knew that sounds can make words sing.

In our media-driven age, when the succinct sound bite and the skeletal headline push us to ever more elliptical expression, we need to make space for meaning. The constrictive columns on the newspaper's front page make *probe* a popular synonym for *investigation, inquiry,* or *hearing,* but check out the unintended ambiguities of this abominable headline: "City's Housing Chief Probed."

(Did he say "Ouch"?) Journalist G. K. Chesterton once quipped that when it comes to such headlines, brevity, "so far from being the soul of wit, is even the death of meaning." Don't cede to the city editor who insists on *cure* "because no one knows the meaning of *palliative.*" The reporter writing a humorous story on commemorative parties as a palliative for "the earthquake willies" should adamantly refuse to swap in *cure*—because there is none for the fear of earthquakes!

Tight deadlines, TV tastes, small screens, easy shortcuts—we should never let any of these cramp our meandering search for the beautiful, rich word. For inspiration, go on literary adventures with novelists like William Faulkner, Djuna Barnes, Vladimir Nabokov, and Gabriel García Márquez—none of whom uses lowest-common-denominator diction. Faulkner's *Absalom, Absalom!* delivers non-monosyllabic monologues like this one, by Mississippi spinster Rosa Coldfield. The sixty-five-year-old "widowed virgin" reflects bitterly about her latent "root bloom and urge," which was driven underground when, at fourteen, she fell in love only to be badly jilted. Faulkner's rich words have all the pungency of emotions that have been on low simmer for half a century:

> Once there was (they cannot have told you this) a summer of wistaria. It was a pervading everywhere of wistaria (I was fourteen then) as though of all springs yet to capitulate condensed into one spring, one summer: the spring and summertime which is every female's who breathed above dust, beholden of all betrayed springs held over from all irrevocable time, repercussed, bloomed again. It was a vintage year of wistaria: vintage year being that sweet conjunction of root bloom and urge and hour and weather; and I (I was fourteen)— I will not insist on bloom, at whom no man had yet to look— nor would ever—twice, as not as child but less than any female flesh. Nor do I say leaf—warped bitter pale and crimped half-fledgling intimidate of any claim to green which might have drawn to it the tender mayfly childhood sweetheart games or

given pause to the male predacious wasps and bees of later lust. But root and urge I do insist and claim, for had I not heired too from all the unsistered Eves since the Snake? Yes, urge I do: warped chrysalis of what blind perfect seed: for who shall say what gnarled forgotten root might not bloom yet with some globed concentrate more globed and concentrate and heady-perfect because the neglected root was planted warped and lay not dead but merely slept forgot?

FIND THE RIGHT PITCH.

Prose is a human exchange between writer and reader. Everything consigned to the page needs to ring true. Keep your audience in mind, especially when you are setting style and tone; don't talk to readers as if they are strangers, or as if they are beneath you.

The creator of Sancho Panza showed perfect pitch with "How excellent a thing is sleep; it wraps a man round like a cloak"; the pitch would be ruined by a writer fond of pompous words: "among the beneficent qualities of sleep its capacity for withdrawing the human consciousness from the contemplation of immediate circumstances may perhaps be accounted not the least remarkable." (That parody of Panza was penned by Sir Arthur Quiller-Couch.)

Many lawyers perpetuate such pretentious diction and alienate their readers, not to mention their clients. No attorney goes home and says at the dinner table, "Please pass the green beans. Said green beans are excellent." Pompous phrasing often serves no purpose other than to puff up the speaker.

Jargon—the technical words and code phrases that professionals use with one another—can keep a lay reader in the dark. When one computer programmer tells another to "type 'hash bang slash user slash local slash bin slash perl' " (i.e., "#!/usr/local/bin/perl") that coders' jargon is serving its proper purpose, helping two people work efficiently. But when marketing mavens promote hardware and software to the public, their words are softer than software: *implementation, functionality, interoperability,* and even *ease of use* are just a bunch of junk words. Jargon can reflect institutions and industries more than it does the real humans who banter within them. Let the CEOs sit behind their desks and yammer on about *brand identification, market capitalization,* and *shareholder value.* If you want to write eloquently as a professional, you need to do it with good words. Universal words.

To find the right pitch is to be human, to have a sense of the street, while still reaching for the lofty. It means resisting the kind of language that suits cogs in a machine better than sentient beings. George Orwell concocted this impenetrable sentence to show what happens when we lose an ear for our own voices:

> Objective consideration of contemporary phenomena compels the conclusion that success or failure in competitive activities exhibits no tendency to be commensurate with innate capacity, but that a considerable element of the unpredictable must invariably be taken into account.

Orwell's sentence, with its inflated abstractions, makes a mess of a statement that started out as the epitome of simplicity, clarity, and humanity. The sentence comes from Ecclesiastes, and shows how well the seventeenth-century scholars who translated the Bible into English understood the notion of pitch:

> I returned and saw under the sun, that the race is not to the swift, nor the battle to the strong, neither yet bread to the wise, nor yet riches to men of understanding, nor yet favor to men of skill; but time and chance happeneth to them all.

Every word in that sentence is a pearl, and every word helps set a pitch that is at once humble and universal.

Bones

What would a grammar book be if it didn't lounge around in a little Latin? Let's take the word *noun,* which derives from *nomen,* for "name." This is useful Latin trivia (granted, a rare thing), since it tells us exactly why nouns exist: to name people, places, and things. "Things" can be tangible (objects that you can see or smell or hold or hear) or intangible (feelings, ideas, and abstract concepts).

In *Prisoner Without a Name, Cell Without a Number,* Jacobo Timerman creates an indelible image of the cell in which he was imprisoned for criticizing the official cruelty of Argentina's military.

Timerman's nouns are unadorned, naked, stripped of attention-grabbing adjectives, as hard as the cell itself. In fact, his description is *powered* by nouns, and he draws amply from each of the four noun classes:

- People: guard, guards
- Places: cell, corridor, house
- Concrete things: door, arms, body, knees, ceiling, walls, names, messages, floor, mattress, blanket, shoulders, crack, air, watch, cigarette, wife's lighter, gold Rolex watches, Dupont cigarette lighters, Argentine security forces

NOUNS

- Intangible things: luck, encouragement, vestige, testimony, time, semi-penumbra, semi-air, temptation, obsession, sensation, freedom, entire universe, Time, time, Time, existence, duration, eternity

Choosing common, generic words, Timerman uses their dreariness to his advantage: the scene is painted plainly through *the cell, the floor, the mattress, a blanket,* as is the narrator, with his *arms, body, knees, shoulders.* The few proper nouns Timerman adds—*Rolex* watches,

The **cell** is narrow. When I stand at its **center,** facing the steel **door,** I can't extend my **arms.** But it is long, and when I lie down, I can stretch out my entire **body.** A **stroke** of **luck,** for in the **cell** I previously occupied—for how long?—I was forced to huddle up when seated and keep my **knees** bent while lying down.

The **cell** is quite high. When I jump, I'm unable to touch the **ceiling.** The white **walls** have been recently painted. Undoubtedly they once had **names** on them, **messages, words** of **encouragement, dates.** They are now bereft of any **vestige** or **testimony.**

The **floor** of the **cell** is permanently wet. Somewhere there's a **leak.** The **mattress** is also wet. I have a **blanket,** and to prevent that from getting wet I keep it on my **shoulders** constantly. If I lie down with the **blanket** on top of me, the part of my **body** touching the **mattress** gets soaked. I discover it's best to roll up the **mattress** so that one **part** of it doesn't touch the **ground.** In time, the top **part** dries. This means, though, that I can't lie down, but must sleep seated. My **life** goes on during this **period**—for how long?—either standing or seated.

The **cell** has a steel **door** with an **opening** that allows **part** of a **face,** a minimal **part,** to be visible. The **guard** has

Dupont cigarette lighters, *Argentine* security forces—give the piece an eerie specificity, though not enough to detract from the sense that the main character is less Jacobo Timerman than Everyman.

In a piece so sparely written, the intangible nouns stand out: words like *semi-penumbra, contaminated air,* and *semi-air* convey Timerman's grim predicament, while others, like *life, light, glow, sensation, freedom, an entire universe, Time, existence, duration, eternity,* attest to his hopes. Such intangible nouns, when used so expertly,

---

orders to keep the **opening** shut. **Light** enters from the outside through a small **crack,** which acts also as an **air vent.** This is the only **ventilation** and **light.** A faint **glow, night** and **day,** eliminating **time.** Producing a **semi-penumbra** within an **atmosphere** of **contaminated air, semi-air**. . . .

One of the **guards** has my **watch.** During an **interrogation** another **guard** offered me a **cigarette** and lit it with my **wife's lighter.** I later learned that they were under **army orders** not to steal anything from my **house** throughout the **kidnapping** but succumbed to **temptation. Gold Rolex watches** and **Dupont cigarette lighters** were almost an **obsession** with the **Argentine security forces** during that **year** of 1977.

Tonight, a **guard,** not following the **rules,** leaves the **peephole** ajar. I wait a while to see what will happen but it remains open. Standing on **tiptoe,** I peer out. There's a narrow **corridor,** and across from my **cell** I can see at least two other **doors.** Indeed, I have a full **view** of two **doors.** What a **sensation** of **freedom!** An entire **universe** added to my **Time,** that elongated **time** which hovers over me oppressively in the **cell. Time,** that dangerous **enemy** of **man,** when its **existence, duration,** and **eternity** are virtually palpable.

convey an author's themes and offer glimpses into the human condition.

E very noun is either a person, place, concrete thing, or intangible thing. A noun might fall into other categories as well:

- A *common noun* refers generically to people, places, or things and so is written with all lowercase letters (actor, state, movie).

- A *proper noun* is much more specific, referring to one and only one person, place, or thing (Frances McDormand, North Dakota, *Fargo*) and written with an initial capital letter—in the case of some brands, with internal caps as well (PolyGram Filmed Entertainment).

- In *compound nouns,* nouns double up to express a whole that is more than the sum of its parts (film star, silver screen, award winner).

Flesh

As Timerman's passage shows, *plain* nouns can also be *strong:* they can convey vivid images and powerful emotions. Not all nouns need be plain, but they must all be strong. So what's the difference between a strong noun and a weak one? Style coaches like the Fowler brothers and Strunk and White have defined strong nouns in mantras that go something like this:

Prefer the familiar word to the highfalutin.
Prefer the single word to the circumlocution.
Prefer the short word to the long.

Prefer the standard to the offbeat.
Prefer the specific to the general.
Prefer the definite to the vague.
Prefer the concrete to the abstract.

Most of this makes sense. Who wouldn't take a kiss, any day, over a "demonstration of affection"? You keep your "domestic partner"; I'll clutch my lover, my sweetie, my one-and-only. Let's skip town in a little red Corvette, forgetting forever the dreariness of "an automobile" or—heaven forbid—"a sport-utility vehicle."

But in the fever for the fast and familiar, the prose pedagogues can go too far. They canonize "the standard," forgetting that slang and regionalisms are colorful, full of verve, and adopted with alacrity. H. L. Mencken championed New World neologisms like *cloudburst* ("Why describe a gigantic rainstorm with the lame adjectives of every day?") and *roughneck* ("more . . . savory than any English equivalent").

"House" is familiar, it's short, and it's standard, but why ignore the options, which include cottage, duplex, dacha, shack, bungalow, A-frame, Tudor, Victorian, hacienda, manor, and wickiup? (Don't even think about colorless words like *abode, dwelling, domicile,* or *residence.*) Create analogies: is that pile of wood and steel a poor man's Fallingwater? a Tony-Smith-on-stilts? or a Bauhaus mineshaft?

Choosing the right noun means exploring the layers of a word. First, it must be precise, conveying the exact image you are rendering: pick *bungalow* if you're describing a one-story house with a low pitched roof. Second, your noun must be rich, its connotations conjuring a realm of emotion or sensation: stay with *bungalow* if you're capturing coziness, a homey atmosphere. Finally,

Over the centuries, grammar guides and style manuals have favored Anglo-Saxon pedigree. Some style stentorians still cling to the patently ridiculous—not to mention jingoistic—proclamation "Prefer the Saxon to the Roman." This meme started in England in the sixteenth century, when "inkhorn terms" (Latinisms and foreign phrases creeping into the Anglo-Saxon lexicon) were disparaged as a vestige of the Norman invasion. (In 1560, Thomas Wilson, in *The Arte of Rhetorique,* denounced the "long Ciceronian sentences" and "subordinate clauses" larding the language.)

But this is silly. Why should a "foreword" be preferable to a "preface"? Why is "swear" necessarily better than "blaspheme"? In *Grammar and Good Taste,* Dennis E. Baron shows the laughable lengths to which philologists would take this argument: William Barnes, in the nineteenth century, suggested that we replace the Latinate *criticism* with the Saxon *deemster-hood,* *grammar* with *speechcraft,* *botany* with *wortlore,* and *active* with *sprack.*

Ack!

your noun must be apt—its associations, its links to other words and ideas, must complement your meaning: Are the occupants a bunch of frat boys? Then *crash pad* might work better.

Nouns can be playful. When Ferdinand LeMenthe (leader of the Red Hot Peppers) was upstaged by a comedian calling himself "Sweet Papa Cream Puff right out of the bakery shop," the early jazzman rechristened himself "Sweet Papa Jelly Roll, with stovepipes in my hips and all the women in town dyin' to turn my damper down." According to an account by J. L. Dillard in *American Eng-*

lish, LeMenthe was rolling together myriad associations: *jeli* in the African Mandingo language is a minstrel popular with women because of his skill with words and music; in the Caribbean, *jelly* refers to the meat of the coconut when it is still white and viscous, resembling semen; in Harlem, street associations for the gooey pastry have included *lover, vagina,* and *sex* itself.

WITH HIS NEW NAME, Jelly Roll Morton was branding himself for his avid fans. Brand names, when they work, are killer nouns—pithy and packed with meaning. Memorable brands are nouns so evocative that they become synonymous with the thing they name, whether a soft drink (Coca-Cola), a laundry detergent (Tide), or a train line (the Orient Express). Sometimes brands are *jeux de mots.* In 1989, starting with the terms *laptop* and *notebook,* Apple serendipitously hit upon PowerBook, combining the notion of a small product brimming with information and the image of pure computing muscle. Likewise, in 1982, a Texas Instruments spinoff searching for a name combined *comp* (shorthand for computer) with *pack* (small, integral object). Changing the *ck* to a *q* made the name stand out in the gray text of the *Wall Street Journal,* and Compaq packed a nice double entendre.

The automobile industry knows big brands *and* big busts. The best names combine meaning, message, and melody: Acura (conveying precise engineering), Alliance (a joint effort by France's Renault and American Motors), and Caravan ("It's a car! It's a van! No, it's a parade!"). Less successful names try for euphony and end up just phony: Celica, Sentra, Camry, Tercel. Some names are conceived as bursts of testosterone, then bloom into doomed alphabet soups: ES, GXE, STE-AWD, TSi. (OK, OK, an early one, the Datsun 280Z, showed some imagination—a sporty Datsun as dashing as Zorro—but it's been downhill from there.) Then come the boners—betraying an absolute ignorance of the English language: Would *you* have wanted a Dictator to take you for a ride? (Studebaker, ca. 1927.) Wonder why Ford's Nucleon, er, bombed?

SOMETIMES NOUNS PINWHEEL around a subject, giving it a multicolored vitality. An *SF Weekly* profile of Rosalie Sorrels began by calling the folksinger "part poet, part parent, part pioneer, part provocateur." Francis X. Clines, in the *New York Times,* referred to Judge Kenneth Starr's style as "part Garbo, part Inspector Javert."

Descriptions of people, places, or things require powerhouse nouns. Good character sketches focus right in on concrete details, as does this profile of Dizzy Gillespie from the *New Yorker.* The writer, Whitney Balliett, starts with Gillespie's duds, focusing next on the jewelry, the cheeks, the mouth, and, finally, the eyes:

> Gillespie, who is not a **clotheshorse**, was wearing a **Sherlock Holmes hat**, and houndstooth **jacket**, rumpled striped brown **pants**, a navy-blue **T-shirt**, and a couple of **medallions** suspended from a long gold **neck chain**. He hasn't changed much in the last ten years. He has a medium-length grayish **Afro**, and he looks grizzly. His huge and celebrated **cheeks** are **broadsides** in repose and **spinnakers** in action, and he has a **scimitar smile** and a thousand tiny, even **teeth**. He likes to smile and roll his **eyes** in mock **surprise**, but most of the time his **eyes** are narrowed; they take

in much and send out little, and when he puts on his dark-rimmed, two-ton **glasses** they disappear.

Balliett's precise images give us a clear snapshot of Gillespie, and the perfectly pitched metaphors (cheeks that are "broadsides in repose and spinnakers in action") make the portrait breathe.

Andy Warhol, predictably, took a different tack when describing himself in *The Philosophy of Andy Warhol.* He started with intangible nouns (modified by some hefty adjectives) before settling on the hair, the skin, the scars, the cords of the neck, and the Adam's apple:

> The bored **languor**, the wasted **pallor**. . . . The chic **freakiness**, the basically passive **astonishment**. . . . The chintzy **joy**, the revelatory **tropisms**, the chalky, puckish **mask**, the slightly Slavic **look**. . . . The childlike, gum-chewing **naïveté**, the **glamour** rooted in **despair**, the self-admiring **carelessness**, the perfected **otherness**, the **wispiness**, the shadowy, voyeuristic, vaguely sinister **aura**. . . . The albino-chalk skin. The knobby **knees**. The roadmap of **scars**. The long bony **arms**, so white they look bleached. . . . The graying **lips**. The shaggy, silver-white **hair**, soft and metallic. The **cords** of the **neck** standing out around the big Adam's **apple**. It's all there.

In crafting descriptions of people and things, many writers make the mistake of loading up adjectives. But the best concentrate on noun-filled detail. In *Burning the Days,* James Salter goes far beyond the merely generic "West Point cadet's uniform," offering his reader specific, concrete nouns that add up to an anthropology of military culture:

> For parade and inspections we wore eighteenth-century **accessories**, crossed white **belts** and dummy **cartridge box**, with **breastplate** and **belt buckle** shined to a mirrorlike **finish**. In the doorway of the room at night, before taps, we sat feverishly polishing them. **Pencil erasers** and **jeweler's rouge** were used to painstakingly rub away small **imperfections**, and the rest was done with a constantly refolded **polishing cloth**. It took hours. The terrible **ring** of **metal** on the floor—a **breastplate** that had slipped from someone's hand—was like the dropping of an **heirloom**.

Salter gives us not just the glimmering "breastplate and belt buckle," but the "pencil erasers" and "jeweler's rouge" that burnish them. And in one noun—"heirloom"—he conveys an entire, centuries-old legacy.

Cardinal Sins

Nouns were big in Gregory the Great's *Moralia,* which first warned us of the dangers of Pride, Envy, Anger, Lust, Gluttony, Covetousness, and Sloth. Lurking in more contemporary texts are the Seven Deadly Sins committed with nouns: Sloth, Gluttony, Fog, Pretense, Gobbledygook, Jargon, and Euphemism.

SLOTH.

If you can't be bothered to pick up a thesaurus, you are not a prose stylist. You are a hack. Sloth means grabbing the closest shopworn words without so much as a glimmer of guilt, or hastily creating inelegant nouns out of other nouns, or even verbs. Watch out for the slapping

together of prefixes on prefixes, suffixes on suffixes—
don't create more clunkers like *disintermediation, decen-*
tralization, effectualization, finalization, scrutinization,
and that horrid replacement for "use," *utilization.*
William Safire once facetiously hailed the "ugly but necessary new noun" *izationization,* which he defined as "the
creation of lengthy nouns out of shorter words by adding
-ization." Stop the suffix cut-and-paste acts; go on
thoughtful searches for the *right* words.

Clichés—trite phrases blanched of all meaning by
overuse—also signal sloth. They may start life as vivid
metaphors (whoever uttered "It's raining cats and dogs"
for the first time found a catchy way to convey anarchy in
the sky), but over time, clichés become drained of surprise and power, and writers rely on them only because
they're handy and require no thought. Of course, many
clichés never even had metaphorical merit to begin with.
Avoid them all:

> level playing field
> new challenges
> (at) a crossroads
> bottom line
> fast track
> rat race
> old hat
> firm foundation

Even students of prose can't always see the clichés for
the trees. The Graduate School of Journalism at UC
Berkeley once had to warn aspiring journalists against
using "honing my skills" in their application essays; the
phrase was turning up too much for the admissions office to bear.

GLUTTONY.

A close second to Sloth, Gluttony refers to the gourmandish urge to use five words where one would do. The gluttons yammer on about "adverse climatic conditions" instead of calling bad weather just that; rain is rain, and not "precipitation activity" or "a thunderstorm probability situation." When Thomas Hardy wrote "This is the weather the shepherd shuns / And so do I," he wisely did *not* say, "The present weather conditions are causing considerable inconvenience to the sheepfarmer."

Abstractions ending in -*ion*, like "situation" or "condition," are setups. Don't be tempted to prettify a blunt noun like "a drunk" with a staggering noun phrase like "a person in an intoxicated condition." Other words bloated with empty calories include *case, character, degree, element, instance, kind, nature,* and *persuasion*. These will lead you to roundabout prepositional phrases instead of straight nouns and verbs:

"His complaints are of a very far-reaching character." → His complaints ranged from leaky faucets to noises in his head.

"Voters showed a greater degree of interest in the electoral process this year." → Citizens voted in droves.

"The wages will be low owing to the unremunerative nature of the work." → You're a teacher? Don't expect to get rich.

"People of the artistic persuasion require a degree of freedom." → Artists need freedom.

FOG.

Foggy thinking leads to vague and woolly words rather than concrete ones. Sometimes, a writer who hasn't stopped to think about what he or she is trying to say piles up abstract nouns like *phenomenon, element, individual, objective.* "The phenomenon of a health anxiety" should be defogged to, simply, "anxiety about health." Some folks seem to be in the business of manufacturing fog: GreenTree Nutrition, Inc. called its Web site hawking health news, diet tips, and vitamins "a business model focused on content-enabled commerce"; a press release the company put out bragged about the "deep Internet and nutraceutical industry knowledge" of its investors and called its site the "wellness hub people will come to for its deep, consumer-focused content and brand-agnostic wellness product superstore." That sentence could send even the healthy running for aspirin.

Government writing suffers the worst smog levels. Until recently, an Occupational Safety and Health Administration "egress" standard read:

> Ways of exit access and the doors to exits to which they lead shall be so designed and arranged as to be clearly recognizable as such.

Fortunately, OSHA rewrote the rule, coming up with:

> An exit must be free of signs or decorations that obscure its visibility.

But what's wrong with this:

> Only put up signs that make exits stand out.

PRETENSE.

Is it powermongering? Is it insecurity? Is it arrogance? Why do so many professors and professionals resort to pompous, ponderous, or just imponderable nouns?

The worst offenders must be academics—and they're the ones teaching students how to write! Can *you* decipher this beaut from Eric Voegelin's *The New Science of Politics*:

> The problems of an eidos in history, hence, arises only when Christian transcendental fulfillment becomes immanentized. Such an immanentist hypostasis of the eschaton, however, is a theoretical fallacy.

Did you catch the subject-verb disagreement there? (Problems . . . arises?) Even Voegelin lost track of his point!

If the Ivory Tower and the Tower of Babel are converging, it's bad news for us all. Academic writing is on the creep. Check out these program notes from an opera production at Kansas State University:

> A perpetual dualism underlies the production style of this *Susannah*. In the first place, the *mise-en-scène* is not an environment in the naturalistic sense, but a conceptually-defined space intended as a spatial correlative to the elemental action of the opera. Indications of "real" time and place in scenery and costumes point away from abstractionism, rather than toward realism. By the same token, characters are pinned down to a specific historical period, yet their essential *Gestus* is timeless and universal.

Don't those nouns—*"mise-en-scène,"* "spatial correlative," "elemental action," "abstractionism," "realism," *"Gestus"*—make you yearn for some trash TV?

Professionals, unfortunately, have co-opted the professors' tricks (or tics). Go no further than the nearest business memo to find these hollow organization men: *your consideration of this matter, your earliest convenience, the aforementioned point,* and the corporate secretary's favorite, *the above-referenced matter.*

Pretense results when a writer preoccupied with his or her own diction loses sight of the primary goal: communicating with an audience. Choose words that are appropriate for the subject, the audience, and the forum. When a father talking to his child's teacher mentions a "colloquy" with his seven-year-old daughter, he is not being articulate, he's being ridiculous.

Whenever you've got a choice, go with the plain talk, not the pomposity.

GOBBLEDYGOOK.

Will we ever forgive Warren G. Harding for taking the perfectly good noun *normality* and perverting it into *normalcy?* Bureaucratese, of course, didn't end with Harding. Al Gore could be called Mr. Gobbledygook: online citizens, thank God, replaced his "national information infrastructure" with *the Net.* But Gore needed some netizens around at the 1997 press conference where he argued that "no controlling legal authority" deemed his 1996 campaign solicitations illegal. Why didn't Al just say, "I didn't break the law"?

In gobbledygook, a year is "twelve calendar months," orders are "directives," down payments are "capitalized cost reductions," and a weapons wonk is "a specialist in arms control and security issues." A New York State fire officer who wrote this monthly progress report clearly wasn't in a rush to put out any flames:

> FIRE REPORT: Heavy rains throughout most of the
> State have given an optimistic outlook for lessened fire
> danger for the rest of the season. However, an abundance
> of lightning maintains a certain amount of hazard in
> isolated areas that have not received an excessive amount
> of rain. We were pleased to have been able to help
> Nevada with the suppression of their conflagration.

That paragraph was quoted in the Bureau of Land Management's *Gobbledygook Has Gotta Go*. Look how easy it is to edit it down to plain talk and add a few strong nouns and verbs:

> FIRE REPORT: Heavy rains throughout most of the State
> ~~have given an optimistic outlook for~~ lessened fire danger
> for the rest of the season. However, ~~an abundance of~~
> lightning ~~maintains a certain amount of hazard in~~ **threat-
> ens** isolated **dry** areas ~~that have not received an excessive
> amount of rain.~~ We were pleased to help ~~have been able
> to~~ Nevada **fight fires.** ~~with the suppression of their con-
> flagration~~.

Public officials have periodically launched campaigns to eradicate gobbledygook from governmental communications. Jimmy Carter called for "keeping it simple" in 1978, and Bill Clinton signed a similar executive order twenty years later. Things got so bad at the Justice Department in the early '90s that Attorney General Janet Reno urged the nation's lawyers to find "small, old words that all people understand—words like 'right' and 'wrong' and 'justice.' "

JARGON.

Reno may be fighting an uphill battle in taming the Justice Department, but she'd need to clone herself five times over to police the language in the national bar association. Like other professionals, lawyers rely on jargon—agreed-upon argot and technical lingo. A staple of every work conversation, jargon makes for a telegraphic shorthand that lets professionals banter precisely and efficiently. Lawyers' terms like *plaintiff, ex parte, hearsay, felony, prima facie,* and *habeus corpus* are, indeed, precise. But what about all those *aforesaids, hereofs,* and *hereinbelows?* That's not just jargon. It's junk. Legalese. Is it really necessary to say "Now comes the above named John Doe, plaintiff herein, by and through Smith & Jones, his attorneys of record, and shows unto this Honorable Court as follows . . ."? Why not just "For his complaint, the plaintiff says . . ."? Why write "I have received your letter and thank you for the information contained therein," when "Thank you for the information relayed by your letter" does the job?

A parody in a lawyers' magazine once launched the story of "Jack and the Bean Stalk" like this: "Once on or about a time, there was a minor named John or 'Jack' (as he will hereinafter be designated), other name or names to your relator unknown."

WHEN IT COMES TO IMPENETRABILITY, legal writing is only the most notorious. Doctors, lawyers, merchants, chiefs—they've all got their own jargon and they all should avoid it when trying to communicate with clients or write for the lay public. As Steve Mirsky points out in *Scientific American,* the doctor mumbling about "a bilateral digital amputation" should just say a patient "lost two fingers." Computer keyboards might lead to "a diminution of digital dexterity, the end product of same being a severe limitation of your preoperative ability," but the doctor needs to tell the patient, "rest your hands till they heal." The best docs know that a gift for the vernacular helps them communicate well with patients and write memorably about their field. The term "tennis elbow" beats "lateral epicondylitis." "Chauffeur's fracture" sticks better than "a break to the radial styloid"—even if it means explaining that the name for this wrist injury pays homage to those drivers of old who hurt themselves turning a hand crank to rev up the Studebaker.

E U P H E M I S M .

Let's concede that discretion *is* the better part of valor, and that civility, diplomacy, and tact *are* worth cultivating. We all have experienced the compassionate desire to address something unbearably painful or embarrassing— the death of a beloved, say, or a distressing medical condition—without causing someone else even more pain and embarrassment.

But such a concession is not tantamount to an endorsement of euphemism—the description of offensive behavior through inoffensive terms. "Political language is designed to make lies sound truthful and murder respectable, and to give an appearance of solidity to pure wind," wrote George Orwell in "Politics and the English Language." "In our time, political speech and writing are largely the defense of the indefensible. . . . Defenseless villages are bombarded from the air, the inhabitants driven out into the countryside, the cattle machine gunned, the huts set on fire with incendiary bullets: this is called *pacification.*"

Orwell's essay, written in 1946, has done little to discourage the powers-that-be from substituting mild or vague expressions for harsh or blunt ones. An air attaché at the U.S. Embassy in Phnom Penh once admonished reporters: "You always write it's bombing, bombing, bombing. It's not bombing. It's air support." In the 1980s, Ronald Reagan dubbed the MX missile the "Peacekeeper," in hopes of making the controversial nuclear weapon more palatable. The Clinton administration's end to "welfare as we know it" has ushered in "job centers" instead of *welfare offices;* "financial planners" instead of *caseworkers;* and "job seekers" instead of *welfare recipients.*

In the corporate world, euphemism allows boardroom bullies to call massive firings *layoffs, downsizing, rightsizing,* and *reshaping.* (Digital Equipment Corporation once resorted to the patently ridiculous *involuntary methodologies.* One plant shutdown at General Motors was a *volume-related production-schedule adjustment.*) Such euphemism is merely a cowardly attempt by bosses to depersonalize the firing process, a code way of saying "Blame the organization, not me!"

Even salesmen in this age of telemarketing wrap themselves in euphemisms: the Willy Lomans of yesteryear are now *advisors, associates, specialists, consultants, customer service representatives,* and, in the case of United Airlines, *employee owners.* Speaking of airlines, have you noticed how filled with euphemism airlinespeak is? Nothing is free, but everything is "complimentary." Instructions are "friendly reminders." Your buoyant cushion is "a flotation device."

Euphemisms are for wimps. Invented in an attempt to avoid offending others or to pussyfoot around socially prickly subjects, they are the last words you should resort to if you're trying to be clear, concrete, concise, and compassionate. Euphemism conceals reality rather than re-vealing it—which is, after all, what a writer should be doing.

P oke fun of euphemisms whenever you can, as did H. L. Mencken when he was implored to create a euphemism for *strip-teasing*. It all started when Mencken, the author of *The American Language,* received this letter from a Miss Georgia Sothern:

> It happens that I am a practitioner of the fine art of strip-teasing. Strip-teasing is a formal and rhythmic disrobing of the body in public. In recent years there has been a great deal of uninformed criticism levelled against my profession.
>
> Most of it is without foundation and arises because of the unfortunate word *strip-teasing*, which creates the wrong connotations in the mind of the public.
>
> I feel sure that if you could coin a new and more palatable word to describe this art, the objections to it would vanish and I and my colleagues would have easier going. I hope that the science of semantics can find time to help the verbally underprivileged members of my profession. Thank you.

Mencken replied, tongue firmly in—oh, never mind where his tongue was:

> I need not tell you that I sympathize with you in your affliction, and wish that I could help you. Unfortunately, no really persuasive new name suggests itself. It might be a good idea to relate strip-teasing in some way or other to the associated zoölogical phenomenon of molting. Thus the word *moltician* comes to mind, but it must be rejected because of its likeness to *mortician*.
>
> A resort to the scientific name for molting, which is *ecdysis*, produces both *ecdysist* and *ecdysiast*. Then there are suggestions in the names of some of the creatures which practice molting. The scientific name for the common crab is

Callinectes hastastus, which produces *callinectian*. Again, there is a family of lizards called the *Geckonidae*, and their name produces *gecko*. Perhaps your advisers may be able to find other suggestion in the same general direction.

Georgia Sothern cast her fate with *ecdysiast*. And thus—Mencken's facetiousness notwithstanding—was a euphemism born.

W e hate euphemisms, but you gotta hand it to the Mr. and Miss Lonelyhearts in the personals, who in their refusal to be doomed by external reality have created euphemisms for *fat* that are made palatable by a sense of humor:

"very attractive Rubenesque beauty"
"the bigger the better"
"large and lovely"
"big beautiful blonde"
"chubby teddy bear"
"volumes to offer"

Carnal Pleasures

Now, lest you still think nouns are too crisp and concrete to have fun with, lest you think paring down the pap leads only to the stuff of *serious* description, let's turn to Tom Wolfe, a writer who based an entire journalistic career on bending rules. Wolfe found nouns irresistible in a story on supermodel Baby Jane Holzer. "The Girl of the Year," which ran in *New York* in 1964, opened with a breathless noun frolic:

Bangs manes bouffant beehives Beatle caps butter faces
brush-on lashes decal eyes puffy sweater French bras
flailing leather blue jeans stretch pants stretch jeans
honeydew bottoms eclair shanks elf boots ballerinas
Knight slippers, hundreds of them, these flaming little
buds, bobbing and screaming, rocketing around inside
the Academy of Music Theater underneath that vast old
moldering cherub dome up there—aren't they super-
marvelous!

Homely adjectives and prepositions hardly dare to show
their faces in that paragraph; the one verb that sneaks
in—*are*—is practically a wallflower.

Practitioners of the New Journalism aren't the only
ones to flout the rules and flaunt their wit. The flacks at
Cyan Inc., the company that produced the adventure-
game-to-end-all-adventure-games, *Myst,* showed a better
sense of words—and humor—than most PR types,
avoiding the knee-jerk tendency to drown crucial words
in a tide of filler. If all press releases were so funny, editors might actually read them. Here's what landed on the
desk of an editor at *Wired* magazine. The press release
focused all attention on a few key nouns (i.e., the names
of the products being hawked) and poked fun at meaningless PR.

Dear Mr. Frauenfelder,

Blah, blah blah blah blah Cyan blah Blah blah *Myst* blah
Blah. BLAH! Blah blah blah blah blah blah blah blah, blah
blah blah blah. Blah blah blah blah blah blah: blah blah. Blah
blah Cyan blah blah blah blah blahblah blah blah blah *Myst*
blah blah. Blahblah *The Manhole Masterpiece Edition* blah
blah *Cosmic Osmo and the Worlds Beyond the Mackerel.*

The Manhole Masterpiece Edition blah blah blah blah
blah blahblah blah blah blah blah blahblah blah. Blahblah
blah blah blah. Blah blah blah blahblah; blah blah blah blah
blah. Blah blah blah *The Manhole Masterpiece Edition,* blah
blah blah blah blah blahblah blahblah.

Cosmic Osmo and the Worlds Beyond the Mackerel blah
blah blah blah blah blah blah blahblah blah blah blah, blah
blah. Blah blah! Blah blah blah & blah blah blah blah, blah
blah blah blah blah blah blah. Blah, *Cosmic Osmo and the
Worlds Beyond the Mackerel* blah blah blah blah blah blah
blah blah blah blah blah blahblah. Blah blah.

Blah blah Cyan blah blah blah blah blah blah blahblah
blah—blah blah. Blah blah blah blah blah blah blah blah
blah blah blahblah.

Regards,
Rand Miller & Robin Miller
Founders

P.S. Blah blah blah blah Blah blah: blah blah blah!

CHAPTER 2

Pronouns

Bones

Pronouns are proxies for nouns. They stand in willingly when nouns don't want to hang around sounding repetitive. The noun (or noun phrase), whose bidding the pronoun does, is called the *antecedent*—because it goes (*ced-*) before (*ante-*) the pronoun in the sentence or paragraph.

Unlike nouns, a class of words that is forever morphing and mutating, the list of pronouns is finite and predictable, subdividing neatly and changed only slightly since the days of Shakespeare:

- Personal pronouns might be the subject of a sentence (*I, you, he, she, it, we, they*) or the object (*me, you, him, it, us, them*): "*I* come to bury Caesar, not to praise *him.*" Certain personal pronouns (*my, your, his, her, its, our, their*) double as adjectives, since in indicating possession they modify nouns: "Friends, Romans, countrymen, lend me *your* ears."
- Demonstrative pronouns (*this, that, these, those*) direct attention to another word or phrase. They can be nouns: "*This* was the most unkindest cut of all." They can be adjectives: "If we do meet again, why, we shall smile; If not, why then, *this* parting was well made."
- Relative pronouns (*that, what, what-*

*ever, which, whichever, who, whoever, whom, whom-
ever, whose*) introduce a clause that wants to hitch
itself firmly to its antecedent: "The evil *that* men
do lives after them." The antecedent can be a noun,
a phrase, a clause, a sentence, or even a whole
paragraph.

- Indefinite pronouns (*all, another, any, anybody, anything, both, each, either, every, everybody, everyone,
everything, few, many, most, much, neither, no one, nobody, none, one, several, some, somebody, someone,
something, such*) also stand in for people or things, but
not necessarily ones specifically named by an antecedent: "If *any,* speak; for him have I offended." Indefinite pronouns move around sentences with abandon and can also play the role of adjectives. (Take care
to see indefinite pronouns for what they are, because
they make subject-verb agreement quite dicey. But
more on that in chapter 9.)

- Interrogative pronouns (*what, which, who, whom,
whose*) kick off questions: "*What* cause withholds you
then to mourn for him?"

- Expletive pronouns (*it, there*) are less sexy than they
sound, stepping into a sentence as subject when the
juice of the sentence lurks in the predicate: "*There* is
no terror, Cassius, in your threats."

- Reflexive pronouns (*myself, yourself, himself, herself,
itself, ourselves, yourselves, themselves*) allow a person
or thing to be both the subject and the object of a sentence ("I have o'ershot *myself* to tell you of [Caesar's
will]") or add emphasis (Marc Antony *himself* didn't
need emphasis in his famous speech. That should tell
you something.)

Reflexive pronouns deserve a caveat: Sometimes they are absolutely necessary for clarity, distinguishing, for example, in the following non-Shakespearean sentence, between two possible antecedents (May and April): "As May sashayed through the yard, April wondered whether she **herself** would ever again have the upper hand." But novices most often use reflexive pronouns when a personal pronoun would be simpler and more elegant (not to mention more correct): "Jim and **myself,** however, were holding out for June" is hardly a studly sentence; June would prefer "Jim and I."

PRONOUNS MAY SEEM PUNY next to their heftier kin, and some writers might initially view them as too generic, too homely to put much faith in. But sometimes their very simplicity is their strength. Jacobo Timerman shows how powerful they can be in the opening to *Prisoner Without a Name, Cell Without a Number* (see opposite page).

The stark plainness of Timerman's *I* and *He* complements the dreariness of his nouns. He repeats the simple pronoun *I* again and again, giving it the strongest position in the sentence: the subject. This repetition makes the sudden appearance of *He* all the more startling and powerful. Timerman has also exploited the anonymity of *I* and *He*—those bare pronouns, lacking antecedents, fit perfectly in a book about nameless prisoners.

The passage cited in chapter 1 continues with these pronoun-driven paragraphs:

Tonight, a guard, not following the rules, leaves the peephole ajar. I wait a while to see what will happen but **it** remains open. Standing on tiptoe, I peer out. There's a narrow corridor, and across from my cell I can see at least two other doors. Indeed, I have a full view of two doors. What a sensation of freedom! . . .

My entire forehead is pressed against the steel and the cold makes my head ache. But it's been a long time—how long?—without a celebration of space. I press my ear against the door, yet hear no sound. I resume looking.

He is doing the same. I suddenly realize that the peephole in the door facing **mine** is also open and that there's an eye behind **it**. I'm startled: They've laid a trap for me. Looking through the peephole is forbidden and they've seen me doing **it**. I step back and wait. I wait for some Time, more Time, and again more Time. And then return to the peephole.

He is doing the same.

Flesh

Pronouns keep style succinct, allowing us to skirt the needless repetition of nouns. In prose, pronouns also establish the voice of the narrator, offering the writer the opportunity to play with point of view.

The third-person pronouns (*he, she, it, they*) allow the narrator to recede. In the most common point of view in fiction, the "third-person omniscient," the author is allowed to see into the heads of characters, to relay to readers what they are thinking, without necessarily being a character in the story. In nonfiction, the third-person point of view is not so much *omniscient* as *objective*. It's the preferred point of view for reports, research papers, or articles about a specific subject or cast of characters.

It's best for business missives, brochures, and letters on behalf of a group or institution. See how a slight shift in point of view creates enough of a difference to raise eyebrows over the second of these two sentences: "Victoria's Secret would like to offer you a discount on all bras and panties." (Nice, impersonal third person.) "I would like to offer you a discount on all bras and panties." (Hmmm. What's the intent there?)

In today's culture of confession, many writers prefer the first-person point of view. Unabashed subjectivity may be fine for ever-popular memoirs on incest and inside-the-Beltway intrigue, but the third-person point of view remains the standard in news reporting and writing that aims to inform, because it keeps the focus off the writer and on the subject. The following Associated Press report, dictated in 1957 by Remain Morin from a phone booth across from Little Rock's Central High School, shows how the third person can lead to both power and emotion:

> The eight Negroes—the three boys and five girls—were crossing the schoolyard toward a side door at the south end of the school. The girls were in bobby socks and the boys were dressed in shirts open at the neck.
>
> They were not running, not even walking fast. They simply strolled toward the steps, went up and were inside before all but a few of the 200 people at the end of the street knew it.
>
> "They've gone in," a man roared. "Oh, God, the niggers are in the school."

IN CERTAIN SITUATIONS, the first-person point of view comes most naturally and lets the narrator be an integral part of the story. Sometimes it's time to loosen your tie, to get personal. In a 1976 address at the University of California at Berkeley called "Why I Write," Joan Didion made a persuasive case for the first person:

> Of course I stole the title for this talk from George Orwell. One reason I stole it was that I like the sound of the words: *Why I Write*. There you have three short unambiguous words that share a sound, and the sound they share is this:
>
> I
>
> I
>
> I
>
> In many ways writing is the act of saying *I*, of imposing oneself upon other people, of saying *listen to me, see it my way, change your mind*. It's an aggressive, even a hostile act. You can disguise its aggressiveness all you want with veils of subordinate clauses and qualifiers and tentative subjunctives, with ellipses and evasion—with the whole manner of intimating rather than claiming, of alluding rather than stating—but there's no getting around the fact that setting words on paper is the tactic of a secret bully, an invasion, an imposition of the writer's sensibility on the reader's most private space.

In her journalism, Didion packs her reporting with the acute—and indispensable—detail of personal observation, and she uses the self as a mirror on the times. In the title essay of her book *The White Album*, Didion recalls a period—between 1966 and 1971—when, she says, she "began to doubt the premises of all the stories I had ever told myself, a common condition but one I found troubling."

Didion does not use the first person because it's easy, nor does she use it out of a rampantly narcissistic need to write about herself. She puts herself into service to explore a subject very much outside herself: "the summer of 1968." The first-person in Didion's essay is not tantamount to writing-as-confessional; it is a way to link the schism in her own soul to the schism in society. It is an example of what Hemingway called writing "hard and clear about what hurts."

During those five years I appeared, on the face of it, a competent enough member of some community or another, a signer of contracts and Air Travel cards, a citizen: I wrote a couple of times a month for one magazine or another, published two books, worked on several motion pictures; participated in the paranoia of the time, in the raising of a small child, and in the entertainment of large numbers of people passing through my house; made gingham curtains for spare bedrooms, remembered to ask agents if any reduction of points would be *pari passu* with the financing studio, put lentils to soak on Saturday night for lentil soup on Sunday, made quarterly F.I.C.A. payments and renewed my driver's license on time, missing on the written examination only the question about the financial responsibility of California drivers. It was a time of my life when I was frequently "named." I was named godmother to children. I was named lecturer and panelist, colloquist and conferee. I was even named, in 1968, a *Los Angeles Times* "Woman of the Year," along with Mrs. Ronald Reagan, the Olympic swimmer Debbie Meyer, and ten other California women who seemed to keep in touch and do good works. I did no good works but I tried to keep in touch. I was responsible. I recognized my name when I saw it. . . .

This was an adequate enough performance, as improvisations go. The only problem was that my entire education, everything I had ever been told or had told myself, insisted that the production was never meant to be improvised: I was supposed to have a script, and had mislaid it. I was supposed to hear cues, and no longer did. I was meant to know the plot, but all I knew was what I saw: flash pictures in variable sequence, images with no "meaning" beyond their temporary arrangement, not a movie but a cutting-room experience. In what would probably be the middle of my life I wanted still to believe in the narrative and in the narrative's intelligibility, but to know that one could change the sense with every cut was to begin to perceive the experience as rather more electrical than ethical.

During this period I spent what were for me the usual proportions of time in Los Angeles and New York and Sacramento. I spent what seemed to many people I knew an eccentric amount of time in Honolulu, the particular aspect of which lent me the illusion that I could any minute order from room service a revisionist theory of my own history, garnished with a vanda orchid. I watched Robert Kennedy's funeral on a verandah at the Royal Hawaiian Hotel in Honolulu, and also the first reports from My Lai. I reread all of George Orwell on the Royal Hawaiian Beach, and I also read, in the papers that came one day late from the mainland, the story of Betty Lansdown Fouquet, a 26-year-old woman with faded blond hair who put her five-year-old daughter out to die on the center divider of Interstate 5 some miles south of the last Bakersfield exit. The child, whose fingers had to be pried loose from the Cyclone fence when she was rescued twelve hours later by the California Highway Patrol, reported that she had run after the car carrying her mother and stepfather and brother and sister for "a long time." Certain of these images did not fit into any narrative I knew.

Another flash cut:

"In June of this year patient experienced an attack of vertigo, nausea, and a feeling that she was going to pass out. A thorough medical evaluation elicited no positive findings and she was placed on Elavil, Mg 20, tid. . . . The Rorschach record is interpreted as describing a personality in process of deterioration with abundant signs of failing defense and increasing inability of the ego to mediate the world of reality and to cope with normal stress. . . . Emotionally, patient has alienated herself almost entirely from the world of other human beings. Her fantasy life appears to have been virtually completely preempted by primitive, regressive libidinal preoccupations, many of which are distorted and bizarre. . . . Patient's thematic productions on the Thematic Apperception Test emphasize her fundamentally pessimistic, fatalistic, and depressive view of the world around her. It is as though she feels deeply that all human effort is foredoomed to failure, a conviction which seems to push her further into a dependent, passive withdrawal. In her view she lives in a world of people moved by strange, conflicted, poorly comprehended, and above all, devious motivations which commit them inevitably to conflict and failure. . . ."

The patient to whom the psychiatric report refers is me. The tests mentioned—the Rorschach, the Thematic Apperception Test, the Sentence Completion Test, and the Minnesota Multiphasic Personality Index—were administered privately, in the outpatient psychiatric clinic at St. John's Hospital in Santa Monica, in the summer of 1968, shortly after I suffered the "attack of vertigo and nausea" mentioned in the first sentence and shortly before I was named a *Los Angeles Times* "Woman of the Year." By way of comment I offer only that an attack of vertigo and nausea does not now seem to me an inappropriate response to the summer of 1968.

THE FIRST-PERSON PLURAL PRONOUN, *we*, is less common—and certainly less aggressive—than Didion's spearlike *I*. *We* includes the reader in the experience described. In *The Medusa and the Snail*, the physician Lewis Thomas reaches out to his reader by choosing the pronoun *we:*

> **We** are a spectacular, splendid manifestation of life. **We** have language. . . . **We** have affection. **We** have genes for usefulness, and usefulness is about as close to a "common goal of nature" as I can guess at. And finally, and perhaps best of all, **we** have music.

By extending his point of view from *I* (the author/physician) to *we* (all of us), Thomas broadens his subject from biology to the human condition.

It's rare to see the first-person plural in fiction, but Suketu Mehta uses *we* to great effect in the short story "Gare du Nord":

> After **we** left the restaurant, **we** walked around outside the Gare du Nord. It was a Tuesday night, and **we** were the only people out, but **we** were in such good spirits that **we** were a crowd all by ourselves; **we** made the street feel inhabited. The buildings around the Gare du Nord are filled with immigrants; it is as if having come off the train from their distant homes, they were so exhausted by the journey that they put bag and baggage down in the first empty room they saw. It is not a pretty area, and the noise of trains and cars consumes the neighborhood from an early hour. But maybe what keeps the immigrants in the area is the knowledge that the first door to home is just there, in the station, two blocks away. The energy of travelers is comforting, for it makes **us** feel that the whole world, like **us**, is transient.

Mehta never actually reveals who the *we* is, though, clearly, it is less universal than Lewis Thomas's. At times *we* seems to refer to a single person, at times it refers to a couple, at times it refers to the entire expatriate community of Paris.

THE SECOND-PERSON PRONOUN *(you)* lets the author hook the reader as if in conversation. Call it cozy. Call it confiding. *You* is a favorite of the Plain English folks, who view it as an antidote to the stiff impersonality of legalese and urge bureaucrats to write as if speaking to the public.

Pauline Kael, unlike most film critics of her time, frequently used the second person to enliven her reviews:

- From a review of *The French Connection:* "The panhandler in the movie who jostles the hero looks just like the one who jostles you as you leave the movie theatre."
- From a review of *Last Tango in Paris:* "It is a movie you can't get out of your system, and I think it will make some people very angry and disgust others."
- From a review of *Platoon:* "There are too many scenes where you think, It's a bit much. The movie crowds you; it doesn't give you room to have an honest emotion."

The second-person point of view gives Kael's reviews urgency and intimacy. Fellow *New Yorker* writer Adam Gopnik called Kael's point of view the "complicitous" second person, explaining: "It wasn't her making all those judgments. It was the Pop Audience there beside her."

The second-person point of view is rarer in fiction and long-form nonfiction narrative. But Jay McInerney used it in *Bright Lights, Big City,* implicating the reader ("you") in the cocaine-fueled antics of the main character, Jamie:

You are not the kind of guy who would be at a place like this at this time of morning. But here **you** are, and **you** cannot say that the terrain is entirely unfamiliar, although the details are fuzzy. **You** are at a nightclub talking to a girl with a shaved head. The club is either Heartbreak or the Lizard Lounge. All might come clear if **you** could just slip into the bathroom and do a little more Bolivian Marching Powder. Then again, it might not. A small voice inside **you** insists that this epidemic lack of clarity is a result of too much of that already. The night has already turned on that imperceptible pivot where two A.M. changes to six A.M. **You** know this moment has come and gone, but **you** are not yet willing to concede that **you** have crossed the line beyond which all is gratuitous damage and the palsy of unraveled nerve endings. Somewhere back there **you** could have cut **your** losses, but **you** rode past that moment on a comet trail of white powder and now **you** are trying to hang on to the rush. **Your** brain at this moment is composed of brigades of tiny Bolivian soldiers. They are tired and muddy from their long march through the night. There are holes in their boots and they are hungry. They need to be fed. They need the Bolivian Marching Powder.

The longer the creative work, the harder it is to carry off the second-person point of view. Using it might provoke reader revolt: "Hey, dude, I have better sense than to cave to the Bolivian Marching Powder." As *Bright Lights, Big City* progresses and the novelty wears off, the reader identifies less and less with Jamie, and the second-person comes to seem contrived and false; it's definitely Jamie, not "you," who's self-destructing.

Taking advantage of pronouns as a literary device is not a light undertaking: in choosing a point of view, the writer must make sure it's *true,* appropriate to the story being told. Does the presence of the writer in the story add critical color, perspective, and insight? Or is the novice who is tempted to use *I* just being self-indulgent? Don't use pronouns to, in the words of writer Jack Beatty, gratuitously drape your own attitudes onto others "as if they were rhetorical tailor's dummies."

Cardinal Sins

PRONOUNS ON THE LOOSE.

Keeping pronouns straight is as important to writing as keeping a firm hand on the rudder is to sailing. Your biggest problems with pronouns will come if you lose sight of the antecedent: when a pronoun drifts away from its antecedent, the entire meaning gets lost at sea.

When the actress Jane Alexander mused about her tenure as head of the National Endowment for the Arts, she committed the gaffe of the Shifting Pronoun: "I am sure there are always things one could have done differently," she conceded, "but I really think I did at least a couple of things right, mostly out of instinct." Notice how "one" made some missteps, yet "I" chose the instinctually correct course?

The use of *one* to deflect culpability is a classic pronoun cop-out. *One* is also brought in when people feel insecure about an opinion, or just when they want to sound portentous: "One finds oneself unable to abide McInerney's choice of pronoun, not to mention his character's behavior." Nonacademic writers not self-confident enough to use *I* and not presumptuous enough to speak for *we* also take recourse in the neutral, neutered, and nonspecific *one*. But this is fraudulent: it's

W hen Republican speechwriter Peggy Noonan discovered that George Bush was constitutionally unable to use the pronoun *I* and killed sentences or ideas expressed via the first person, she finessed the problem by adopting a construction more palatable to the Prez, "I am one who":

"I am one who is not a card-carrying member of the ACLU."

"I am one who feels it is wrong to release from prison murderers who have not served enough time to be eligible for parole."

"I am one who believes it is right for teachers to say the 'Pledge of Allegiance' to the flag of our country. . . ."

"The speculation among his friends and staff," Noonan writes in *What I Saw at the Revolution,* "was that it was due to his doughty old mom, who used to rap his knuckles for bragging, a brag apparently being defined as any sentence with the first-person singular as its subject." Noonan soon became adept at crafting pronounless sentences: *I moved to Texas and soon we joined the Republican party* became *Moved to Texas, joined the Republican party, raised a family.* On Bush, those sentences sounded natural and relaxed, though the spectre of a president on the Capitol steps raising his hand and saying *Do solemnly swear, will preserve and protect* gave Noonan pause.

a way for people to pretend they're not being solipsistic by being incomparably stuffy.

Another pronoun that will take you straight into the bloviator zone is the royal *we.* In 1990, Vice President Quayle answered a TV interviewer's invitation to come again with "We will." Can anyone explain why a pronoun adopted by British monarchs has been so warmly embraced by candidates in our anti-monarchic, once-Anglophobic democracy?

Editors also use the royal *we* (calling it "the editorial *we*"). Remember all those "Talk of the Town" pieces in the pre-Tina *New Yorker*? Lesser mortals—and writers not yet in *New Yorker* nirvana—might want to heed Mark Twain's advice: "Only presidents, editors, and people with tapeworms ought to have the right to use *we.*"

EATING YOUR *ITS* AND *THEYS*.

Remember, pronouns must agree with their antecedents in number, person, and gender. The most common pronoun-antecedent sin happens when writers use *they* instead of *it* when referring to a singular body. This happens often in speech and, therefore, in quotes—like this one by Senator Patrick Leahy in July 1998, urging independent counsel Kenneth Starr to conclude his investigation of Bill Clinton: "Let the Congress act whichever way *they* want. But wrap this sucker up." With "the Congress" as the antecedent in that first sentence, the pronoun should have been *it*. But who can't forgive Pat for being blunt?

Such pronoun gaffes may be common in speech, but they are *not* kosher in writing. William Safire, in his annual Bloopie Awards column in the *New York Times Magazine,* puts the noose around Madison Avenue goofs in the pronoun-antecedent department:

- "**British Airways** is encouraging any passenger who can say that **their** business class isn't the most comfortable in the air to write and tell **them** why." (The admen started out right, matching *British Airways* with the singular verb *is*. But then they nosedived. A company is one entity, an *it*, not a *they*.)

- "If **the government** thinks it has a role in health re-form, we've got a message for **them**." (Blue Cross blew it. Who, exactly, is *them*? Replace "the government" with "legislators," or "politicians," or "members of the administration.")
- "**Anyone** who thinks a Yonex Racquet has improved **their** game, please raise **your** hand." (As Safire scores it, mixing up the indefinite singular *anyone* with the third-person plural *their* and the second-person singular *your* is a "double fault.")
- "Give **someone** a bottle of Irish Mist and you give **them** hills that roll forever, lakes that radiate light. . . ." (Too much Mist: sober types know that *someone* is singular.)

"DO YOUR CHILD A FAVOR; TEACH THEM GRAMMAR."

Increasingly, writers defend pairing the plural *they* with a singular antecedent. Maybe it's just laziness, maybe it's misguided political correctness. In our dim patriarchal past, the masculine pronoun *he* was routinely used to re-place nouns like "the president," "the CEO," and "the en-trepreneur." In the days of bad-girl businesswomen like Madonna, *he* is a nonstarter.

But solving the problem by pasting in *they* or *them* just invents a new one. Here are some horrid examples plucked from papers around the country:

- **He** or **she** who laughs loudest around the watercooler may not be who **they** say they are.
- Do **your child** a favor; teach **them** grammar.
- Our society has gotten to the point where **each person** does what's right in **their** own eyes.
- A **motorcyclist** has the right to decide if **they** want to wear a helmet.

No real wordsmith ever meets a sentence that can't be gracefully recast. Resist replacing *they* with *he/she*—real people don't speak in slashes. Do make the antecedent plural and use *they* with a vengeance. Don't be afraid of an occasional *he or she,* awkward though it may be. Or take the ultimate judicious approach: some U.S. Supreme Court justices alternate between *he* and *she* when they write their decisions.

LOOSEY-GOOSEY REFERENCES.

"The ladies of the church have cast off clothing of every kind, and they can be seen in the church basement Friday afternoon." This doozy, culled by Richard Lederer from a church bulletin, is an instance of "obscure pronomial reference," or, in plain English, a pronoun without a clear companion noun. Does *they* refer to "the ladies"? Or to "clothing"? Or to "items of clothing"?

You, the author, step into the "obscure pronomial reference" trap when you assume the antecedent is obvious. It may not be to your reader or listener. Often this happens when two separate nouns immediately precede the pronoun, as in this snippet of dialogue from *Arcadia,* a Tom Stoppard play:

> SEPTIMUS: Geometry, Hobbes assures us in the *Leviathan,* is the only science God has been pleased to bestow on mankind.
> LADY CROOM: And what does he mean by it?
> SEPTIMUS: Mr. Hobbes or God?

Although the line draws a laugh from a theater audience, Lady Croom should have just used a proper noun rather than *he.*

It's OK for an antecedent to be supplied by the context of a sentence, so long as clarity isn't compromised. But don't assume the last-named object or idea is the noun the pronoun replaces. An idea or noun implied but not specifically stated can be an antecedent, but referring to it with *it* can send the wrong message: *If I told you that you had a beautiful body, would you hold it against me?*

JUST BETWEEN YOU AND, UH, ER. . . .

When pronouns play the role of subject in a sentence or clause, they appear in the nominative case *(I, you, he, she, it, we, you, they)*. When they play the role of objects in a sentence—objects of a verb or of a preposition—they appear in the objective case *(me, you, him, her, it, us, you, them)*. Mixing the cases is a common blunder. Ernest Hemingway—no doubt so flummoxed by gender issues that he lost track of his cases—erred in writing to Sherwood Anderson in 1922, "Gertrude Stein and me are just like brothers." Hemingway shoulda used an *I*.

It's not uncommon, especially in some regional dialects or street speech, to use the objective pronoun as the subject ("Us girls went cruising"), but it's more common to do what Hemingway did: to flub the pronouns when they appear as part of a compound. Especially common is what the inimitable *Fowler's* calls "the regrettable" *between you and I.* "Anyone who uses that phrase," warns *Fowler's*, "lives in a grammarless cavern."

Put Mark Twain in that cavern: he regularly relied on *between you and I,* as in a letter written toward the end of the *Innocents Abroad* voyage: "Between you and I . . . this pleasure party of ours is composed of the rustiest, ignorant, vulgar, slimy, palm-sing cattle that could be scraped up in seventeen States."

Between isn't the only preposition to get folks in pronoun trouble. In an ad for a bra "for we full-figured gals," Jane Russell was led astray; the preposition *for* also mandates the pronoun *us*. But then, Russell never was known for her pronouns.

WHOMDUNNIT.

When faced with the two-pronged attack from *who* and *whom,* most people start waving the white flag. If they toughed it out, though, they'd learn how easy it is to conquer these pronouns. Use *who* when the pronoun is acting as a subject *(Who is it?)* and *whom* when it is acting as an object (in *For Whom the Bell Tolls* the pronoun is the object of the preposition *for*).

We'll get back to *who* and *whom* in chapter 10, when we discuss subjects and objects, but to tide you over, take these tips from the Wise Old Word Man, Jacques Barzun:

1. Use *who* whenever the verb form that follows could be wrapped in parentheses without changing the sentence: "who (he believed) had been up the mountain."
2. Make it *whom* when you would use *him* and *her* and *them* in place of *whom*. "Oprah knew he?" sounds silly; "Oprah knew who?" should too. Replace *he* with *him* and *who* with *whom*.
3. Go ahead and use *who* when the pronoun starts the sentence: "Who do you love?" sounds more natural to many people than "Whom do you love?"

ME, *NOT* MYSELF, AND I.

Watch your reflexive pronouns. As Patricia O'Conner writes in *Woe Is I,* "In the contest between *I* and *me,* the booby prize often goes to *myself.*" Why do people insist on *myself* when a simple *I* or *me* will do? Adding a reflexive pronoun doesn't necessarily add clarity. This classified ad, reprinted in Richard Lederer's *Anguished English,* goofed badly (or bawdily):

Tired of cleaning yourself? Let me do it.

WHOSE ON FIRST?

Some overly loyal writers cannot give up the grammar myth that the relative pronoun *whose* cannot be used for antecedents that are not human. Such folly leads to unfortunate constructions like this one:

A wonder of the ancient world, the Great Library in Alexandria was an edifice **in the corridors of which** resided the papyrus scrolls that amounted to the sum total of human knowledge.

That sentence might have been elegant had the writer subtly changed it:

A wonder of the ancient world, the Great Library in Alexandria was an edifice **whose corridors** housed the papyrus scrolls that were the sum total of human knowledge.

Speaking of *whose,* the one truly unforgivable sin that haunts the use of pronouns is the confusion of *whose* with *who's* and *its* with *it's.* Pronouns, when they get possessive, act weirdly. We do not say *I's, you's, he's,* or *she's* to indicate possession, so why would we say *who's* or *it's?* Possessive pronouns are all apostrophe-less: *my, your, his, hers, its. Who's* and *it's* are contractions of *who is* and *it is.*

Learn this or die.

Carnal Pleasures

Flubbing pronouns is an easy trick when a writer wants to convey colorful colloquial speech. Combined with other grammatical gaffes, pronoun-case errors smack of the untutored:

> I knowed it was her.
> Me and her was both late.
> If Gomer and them had not of begin kicking.
> Them dogs are us'n's.

Songwriters play fast and loose with their pronouns to give their songs traction—"Just Because She Made Them Goo-Goo Eyes" was a hit in the '30s, and years later Paul Simon crooned about "Me and Julio Down by the Schoolyard."

Intentionally flubbing your *her*'s and *me*'s isn't the only way for a writer to play with pronouns. Earlier in this chapter, you read the warnings about overrelying on the confessional first person. In a piece titled "College Application Essay," which appeared first in *Literary Cavalcade,* then in *Harper's,* and has since circled and recircled the world on the Internet, Hugh Gallagher takes the notion of the first-person-singular point of view to outlandish lengths. Parodying the shameless self-promotion often on display in admissions essays (and, later in life, in résumé cover letters), Gallagher uses *I* to make fun of an entire genre of nonfiction writing.

3A. ESSAY

IN ORDER FOR THE ADMISSIONS STAFF OF OUR COLLEGE TO GET TO KNOW YOU, THE APPLICANT, BETTER, WE ASK THAT YOU ANSWER THE FOLLOWING QUESTION: ARE THERE ANY SIGNIFICANT EXPERIENCES YOU HAVE HAD, OR ACCOMPLISHMENTS YOU HAVE REALIZED, THAT HAVE HELPED TO DEFINE YOU AS A PERSON?

I am a dynamic figure, often seen scaling walls and crushing ice. I have been known to remodel train stations on my lunch breaks, making them more efficient in the area of heat retention. I translate ethnic slurs for Cuban refugees, I write award-winning operas, I manage time efficiently. Occasionally, I tread water for three days in a row.

I woo women with my sensuous and godlike trombone playing, I can pilot bicycles up severe inclines with unflagging speed, and I cook Thirty-Minute Brownies in twenty minutes. I am an expert in stucco, a veteran in love, and an outlaw in Peru.

Using only a hoe and a large glass of water, I once single-handedly defended a small village in the Amazon Basin from a horde of ferocious army ants. I play bluegrass cello, I was scouted by the Mets. I am the subject of numerous documentaries. When I'm bored, I build large suspension bridges in my yard. I enjoy urban hang gliding. On Wednesdays, after school, I repair electrical appliances free of charge.

I am an abstract artist, a concrete analyst, and a ruthless bookie. Critics worldwide swoon over my original line of corduroy evening wear. I don't perspire. I am a private citizen, yet I receive fan mail. I have been caller number nine and have won the weekend passes. Last summer I toured New Jersey with a traveling centrifugal-force demonstration. I bat .400. My deft floral arrangements have earned me fame in international botany circles. Children trust me.

I can hurl tennis rackets at small moving objects with deadly accuracy. I once read *Paradise Lost, Moby Dick,* and *David Copperfield* in one day and still had time to refurbish an entire dining room that evening. I know the exact location of every food item in the supermarket. I sleep once a week; when I do sleep, I sleep in a chair. While on vacation in Canada, I successfully negotiated with a group of terrorists who had seized a small bakery. The laws of physics do not apply to me.

I balance, I weave, I dodge, I frolic, and my bills are all paid. On weekends, to let off steam, I participate in full-contact origami. Years ago I discovered the meaning of life but forgot to write it down. I have made extraordinary four-course meals using only a Mouli and a toaster oven. I breed prizewinning clams. I have won bullfights in San Juan, cliff-diving competitions in Sri Lanka, and spelling bees at the Kremlin. I have played Hamlet, I have performed open-heart surgery, and I have spoken with Elvis.

But I have not yet gone to college.

Bones

Verbs add drama to a random grouping of other words, producing an event, a happening, an exciting moment. They also kick-start sentences: without them, words would simply cluster together in suspended animation, waiting for something to click.

Verbs subdivide into two major classes: Static and Dynamic. The ur-verb, *to be*, is chief among the static verbs, which either express a state of being or quietly link starlet nouns and adjectives without demanding a lot of attention. *To be* crops up in various guises, including *am, are, is, was,* and *were.* The static verbs also include *appear, become, seem, prove,* and *remain,* as well as verbs that define things in terms of the five senses: *look, taste, smell, feel,* and *sound* (as in "the following soliloquy *sounds* serious").

In Hamlet's most memorable speech, Shakespeare expressed the heart of the Dane's dilemma via the ultimate static verb:

> To **be** or not to **be**: that **is** the
>   question:
> Whether '**tis** nobler in the mind to
>   suffer
> The slings and arrows of outrageous
>   fortune,
> Or to take arms against a sea of
>   troubles

> And by opposing end them? To die, to sleep;
> No more; and, by a sleep to say we end
> The heartache and the thousand natural shocks
> That flesh **is** heir to, **'tis** a consummation
> Devoutly to be wished. To die, to sleep;
> To sleep: perchance to dream: ay, there**'s** the rub;
> For in that sleep of death what dreams may come,
> When we have shuffled off this mortal coil,
> Must give us pause.

Stasis certainly has its place—whether expressed by the infinitives in *to be or not to be* or by the less anxious *is* and *'tis*. But remember: static verbs lack punch.

Dynamic verbs, on the other hand, grab you by the lapels. Hamlet's active verbs include *suffer, take, end, die, sleep, wish, dream, come, shuffle,* and *give.* Some of these dynamic verbs are transitive, meaning that they take a direct object (a noun) in expressing a complete action (*suffer* takes *slings and arrows*). Verbs not taking a direct object to complete the action are called intransitive (*die* and *sleep* say it all). Don't fret about these verb castes now; we'll come back to the transitive and intransitive distinction when we get to sentences in Part Two.

In a third, subordinate class, verbs gather around other verbs, acting as accomplices in the action. These auxiliary or "helping" verbs—*may, might, could, should, would, have, can, must, will,* as well as *am, are, is, was, were*—are mere sidekicks, symbiotically attaching themselves to a main verb in a combo called a "verb phrase." Helping verbs exist mainly to conjugate tenses (she *was lurching,* she *had been lurching*) and to indicate volition (*will lurch*), possibility (*can lurch*), or obligation (*must lurch*). They also step in to express a negative (she *may* not *lurch*), to transform a thought into a question

(*Would* she *lurch?*), and to emphasize (She *will lurch, won't* she?).

Because there's much more to say about verbs, two entire appendices are devoted to them. Go there if talking about tenses makes you tense, and if words like *indicative, imperative,* and *subjunctive* put you in a bad mood.

Flesh

More than any other part of speech, it is the verb that determines whether a writer is a wimp or a wizard. Novices tend to rely on *is* and other static verbs and lose momentum by stumbling into the passive voice (more on that in a moment). The pros make strong nouns and dynamic verbs the heart of their style; verbs make their prose quiver.

The first key to exploiting dynamic verbs is simply to *use* them. For some reason, even experienced writers pepper first drafts with forms of *be*. Nothing wrong with that, as long as the writers indulge in many more drafts to go back and season the prose with dynamic verbs. Some writers devote one entire rewrite to verbs, circling every *is* and *are* and trying to replace as many as possible. Eventually, dynamic verbs will start flowing from the get-go.

Another way to tone up prose is to eliminate what's known as "the passive voice," in which the subject of a sentence is being acted upon—by an agent named elsewhere in the sentence or left ambiguous—rather than taking the action directly. Going back to Shakespeare's soliloquy, when Hamlet says "a consummation devoutly to be wished," the subject, *consummation,* is receiving the action; who's doing the *wishing* remains unclear. That's the passive voice. By contrast, in the active voice, the subject of the sentence is the one *acting:* in "we end the heartache and the thousand natural shocks," it is *we* who *end*. The active voice is strong, direct, muscular.

Notice how *Wired* writer Richard Rapaport worked his verbs to transform a description of the setting of the Sandia National Laboratories from a pedestrian catalog of nouns into a landscape shimmering with activity. An early draft of his "The Playground of Big Science" opened with a mixture of static and dynamic verbs, passive and active voice:

> It **is** nearly noon, on a cool (temperature 66°), dry (humidity 21%), high-desert day. The azurescent New Mexican sky **hangs** languidly over a flat, antediluvian landscape. It is **broken** to the East by the glowering granite of the Sandia Mountains and off to the North by the shimmering hills that **lie** past the Rio Grande River, and **mount** up to the Jemez Mountains and Los Alamos beyond.

The final, published version of the paragraph banishes the passive. Rapaport erased the opening *is*, promoted adjectives to verbs, and made the mountains move:

> At noon on a cool, high-desert day, the azure New Mexican sky **hangs** languidly over a low, antediluvian landscape. To the east the granite of the Sandia Mountains **glowers** darkly; to the north, the hills past the Rio Grande **shimmer** as they **rise** to **meet** the Jemez Mountains and Los Alamos beyond.

DELETING *IS* AND *ARE* doesn't suffice. Don't replace versions of *to be* with just any verbs. Be inventive! "She walks through the house" wins points over "She is inside," but why *walks* when the choices include *paces, skips,* and *skedaddles*? Why settle for a verb like *says* when *wail, whisper,* and *insist* are waiting to be heard?

Notice how verbs give verve to "Hoppers," a "Talk of the Town" piece that ran in the *New Yorker* in 1988. Check out the energy and humor that come from the various ways urbanites respond to a puddle in the path:

A hydrant was open on Seventh Avenue above Twenty-third Street last Friday morning, and we stopped on our way east and watched people **hop** over the water. It was a brilliant spring day. The water was a nice clear creek about three feet wide and ran along the gutter around the northwest corner of the intersection. A gaggle of pedestrians crossing Twenty-third went *hop hop hop hop hop* over the creek as a few soloists **jaywalking** Seventh **performed** at right angles to them, and we got engrossed in the dance. Three feet isn't a long leap for most people, and the ease of it permits a wide range of expression. Some hoppers **went a good deal higher** than necessary.

Long, lanky men don't hop, as a rule. The ones we saw hardly **paused** at the water's edge, just **lengthened** one stride and **trucked** on across—a rather flatfooted approach that showed no recognition of the space or occasion. Tall men typically suffer from an excess of cool, but we kept hoping for one of them to **get off the ground.** Most of the tall men wore topcoats and carried briefcases, so perhaps their balance was thrown off. One tall man in a brown coat didn't notice the water and **stepped** off the curb into fast-flowing Hydrant Creek and **made a painful hop,** like a wounded heron: a brown heron with a limp wing attached to a briefcase bulging as if full of dead fish. He crossed Twenty-third looking as though his day had been pretty much shot to hell.

Short, fat men were superb: we could have watched them all morning. A typical fat man crossing the street would **quicken** his step when he saw the creek, and, on his approach, **do a little shuffle,** arms out to the sides, and suddenly and with great concentration *spring*—a nimble step all the more graceful for the springer's bulk. Three fairly fat men **jiggled** and **shambled** across Twenty-third together, and then one **poked** another and they saw the water. They **stepped** forward, **studying** the angle, and just before the point man **jumped** for the curb his pals said something, undoubtedly discouraging, and he **threw** back his head and **laughed** over his shoulder and **threw** himself lightly, boyishly, across the water, followed—*boing boing*—by the others.

The women we watched **hop** the water tended to **stop** and **study** the creek and **find** its narrows and **measure** the distance and then **lurch** across. They seemed dismayed that the creek was there at all, and one, in a beige suit, put her hands on her hips and **glared** upstream, as if to say, "Whose creek *is* this? This is utterly unacceptable. I am *not* about to **jump** a *creek.*" But then she **made a good jump** after all. She **put** her left toe on the edge of the curb, **leaned** forward with right arm outstretched—for a second, she looked as if she might **take off** and **zoom up** toward the Flatiron Building— and **pushed** off, **landing** easily on her right toe, her right arm **raised.** The longest leap we saw was made by a young woman in a blue raincoat carrying a plastic Macy's bag and crossing west on Seventh. She **gathered herself up** in three long, accelerating strides and **sailed,** her coat billowing out behind her, over the water and five feet beyond, almost **creaming** a guy coming out of Radio Shack. He shrank back as she **loped** past, her long black hair and snow-white hands and face right *there,* then **gone**, **vanished** in the crowd. . . .

If you want your writing to hop, try to train yourself to see differently, to watch not just for the puddles but for the action and reaction to them: the zooming, trucking, and sailing. Rich images develop from the capacity to observe subjects in action, even if the action is just breathing.

No one does this better than *New Yorker* writer Roger Angell. Notice the verbs in this signature piece, "In the Fire," on baseball's unseen hero, the catcher, whose many motions go unnoticed as the fans keep their eyes not on him, but on the ball:

Consider the catcher. Bulky, thought-burdened, un-clean, he **retrieves** his cap and mask from the ground (where he has **flung** them, moments ago, in mid-crisis) and **moves** slowly again to his workplace. He **whacks** the cap against his leg, **producing** a puff of dust, and **settles** it in place, its bill astern, with an oddly feminine gesture and then, **reversing** the movement, **pulls** on the mask and **firms** it with a soldierly downward tug. Armored, he **sinks** into his squat, **punches** his mitt, and becomes wary, balanced, and ominous; his bare right hand **rests** casually on his thigh while he **regards,** through the portcullis, the field and deployed fielders, the batter, the base runner, his pitcher, and the state of the world, which he now, for a wait-ing instant, **holds** in sway. The hand **dips** between his thighs, **semaphoring** a plan, and all of us—players and umpires and we in the stands—**lean** imperceptibly closer, **zoom-lensing** to a focus, as the pitcher **begins** his motion and the catcher half **rises** and **puts** up his thick little target, **tensing** himself to **deal** with whatever **comes** next, to **end** what he has **begun.** These motions—or most of them, anyway—**are repeated** a hundred and forty or a hundred and fifty times by each of the catchers in the course of a single game, and are the most familiar and the least noticed gestures in the myriad patterns of baseball. The catcher **has** more equipment and more at-

> tributes than players at the other positions. He <u>must be</u>
> large, brave, intelligent, alert, stolid, foresighted, resilient,
> fatherly, quick, efficient, intuitive, and impregnable. These
> scoutmaster traits **are counterbalanced,** however, by one
> additional entry—catching's bottom line. Most of all, the
> catcher <u>is</u> invisible.

Angell packs his paragraph with thirty active verbs
and—count 'em—four linking verbs. Every writer should
adopt this eight to one ratio. Angell uses the passive voice
twice, with *are repeated* and *are counterbalanced.*

The verbs in "In the Fire" aren't just dynamic, they're
high-octane—from *whacks* and *dips* to *sinks* and *zoom-
lensing.* Angell, a virtuoso of verbs, is at his most inspired
with *semaphoring,* which imagines myriad flag signals as
the perfect metaphor for the catcher's constantly communicating hands.

Angell doesn't even let the reader remain static. "Consider," he demands, "the catcher." Using the imperative
voice, he implores the reader to engage. When he resorts
to the humble *to be,* Angell does so strategically. That
lone *is* in "The catcher is invisible" betrays the craft in the
prose: in the moment he means to convey "invisibility,"
Angell strips the catcher, indeed the sentence, of action.

Angell performs one other verbal sleight of hand: he
lets verbs pinch-hit as adjectives. The form of an active
verb ending in *-ing* or *-ed* is known as a participle; participles give you another way to load up on action. Angell's
participles include *thought-burdened, armored, balanced,
deployed, waiting, noticed,* and *foresighted.*

William Finnegan, in a 1992 *New Yorker* opus on surf-
ing, uses participles to turn waves into swirls of activity.
Each of these images, from "The Sporting Scene: Playing
Doc's Games," depends upon a participle for its drama:

onrushing water
punishing waves
shifting mountains of water
twenty-foot **splitting** tubes
a rocky, **waterfall-threaded** scree
a long, **tapering, darkening** wall
the glassy, **rumbling,** pea-green wall
the first wall of sandy, **grumbling** white water
pulverizing force
a swift, **swooping, surefooted** ride
a vicious, **ledging** wave
the final, **jacking** section
a maelstrom of **dredging,** midsized waves
the thick, **pouring, silver-beaded** curtain

Finnegan doesn't stop at participles. He fills his entire story with sentences that use active verbs to make inanimate things animate, like this one: "The waves seemed to be **turning themselves inside out** as they **broke,** and when they **paused** they **spat out** clouds of mist—air that **had been trapped** inside the truck-size tubes."

Cardinal Sins

WHAT *IS* IS—AND ISN'T.

In speaking and informal writing, we naturally gravitate to *to be* in all its incarnations—present tense and past, active voice and passive. A reliance on *to be* is a sure sign of a novice, like this high-school Miss Malaprop, whose usages were recorded by Richard Lederer in *Anguished English:*

The greatest writer of the Renaissance **was** William Shakespeare. Shakespeare never made much money and **is** famous only because of what he wrote. He lived in Windsor with his merry wives, writing tragedies, comedies and errors. In one of Shakespeare's plays, Hamlet rations out his situations by relieving himself in a long soliloquy. In another, Lady Macbeth tries to convince MacBeth to kill the King by attacking his manhood. Romeo and Juliet **are** an example of a heroic couplet. Romeo's last wish **was** to be laid by Juliet.

A dependence on *is* and its family screams "rough draft"—even if your piece escapes the kind of factual errors rampant in the paragraph above. The best writers, during the many revisions they put every piece through, go back and scrub out every unnecessary *is* and *are*.

THAT BAD, BAD *BEING*.

A first-cousin sin of *is* is *being*. Nine times out of ten, when *being* appears, it makes for an error; the remaining time, it's probably extraneous. Try these sentences by high-school composition students:

- *Being that my brother is obese, I'm embarrassed to go out with him.* This would be less shameful syntax (if an equally shameful sentiment) if written "My brother is obese, so I'm embarrassed to go out with him."
- *My birthday, being April 6, usually falls during Easter vacation.* No need for *being*: "My birthday, April 6, usually falls during Easter vacation."
- *It is a machine which I, being one of the few can operate.* To brag about skill, try this: "I am one of the few who can operate this machine."

• *If I could depend on myself for being aware, all of the time, then a license might add up to its expectations.* Too wordy. Go with "If I could always depend on my own awareness, my driver's license might get me somewhere."

For the record, here's *being* used correctly: "Good writers, *being* aware of the pitfalls of weak verbs, avoid *being* like the plague."

DON'T BE PASSIVE — AND DON'T PASS THE BUCK.

Every style maven since Aristotle has urged writers to use the active voice. Sir Arthur Quiller-Couch may have said it most quaintly in 1916: "Eschew the stationary passive."

This is not hard to do. Almost any sentence can be made active. Take this passive line: *The coiffeuse was being ogled by the guy whose hair was being snipped.* See how easy it is to straighten out this tangle of attentions: *Goldilocks couldn't take his eyes off his coiffeuse.*

Entrepreneurs are, by definition, active types, so how is it that so much business writing sags with the passive voice? No letter should go out with the phrase *It has come to our attention that.* "We notice" is much stronger. Likewise, CEOs and secretaries should recast *every effort is being made* into "we are trying." And business reporters shouldn't let *any involvement has been vigorously denied by the company; a statement will be issued shortly* into their copy. Better to say "the company denied involvement and will comment soon."

The passive voice often crops up intentionally, when the writer or speaker wants to blur the relationship between the person committing an action (the "agent") and the action. Politicians and bureaucrats love the passive voice, because it gets them off the hook. During the Iran-contra scandal of the 1980s, pundits noted that President Reagan was barely able to concede that "mistakes were made" in the implementation of his policies. Then, in his 1987 State of the Union speech, he got radical: "serious mistakes were made." The Great Communicator never did say *who* made the mistakes or whether *his* policy was flawed. Such intentional dodges are harder to make active because the agent (the person who took the action) is AWOL.

HYPERACTIVE EDITING.

Writers and editors can get too literal-minded about "eschewing the stationary passive." They forget that the passive voice does exist *for a reason*. One syntactically challenged slot editor at the *Oakland Tribune,* sticking adamantly to a policy demanding the active voice, changed the screaming, above-the-fold headline "I-580 killer convicted" to "Jury convicts I-580 killer" (which screamed less loudly, since the stretched-out phrase required a smaller type). What do *you* think the public cared about—the jury's role, or the fact that a notorious slaughterer got the slammer?

The *San Francisco Examiner,* on the morning after the death penalty was invoked in California for the first time in twenty-five years, ran a large photo of murderer Robert Alton Harris and a one-word headline, above the fold, in huge type and the passive voice: "Executed." That said it all.

If you want to keep the focus on a particular subject, you may want to keep that person the subject of the sentence, using the passive voice if necessary to do so. Don't let your editor fiddle with sentences like this: "Jerry Brown has never been able to settle for the Zen life. After being defeated in successive presidential campaigns, he set up camp in Oakland and crushed all competition in the mayor's race." The passive voice (*after being defeated*) works, because the agents—Carter and Clinton—are irrelevant to Brown's political resurrection.

Similarly, if your intention is to emphasize a subject's very passivity, use the passive voice, as does Germaine Greer in *The Female Eunuch*: "The married woman's significance can only be conferred by the presence of a man at her side, a man upon whom she absolutely depends. In return for renouncing, collaborating, adapting, identifying, she is caressed, desired, handled, influenced."

COUCH POTATO WRITING.

Drab linking verbs—sure saboteurs of whatever drama lurks in a sentence—do in unsuspecting writers. The worst offenders are *seems* and *appears,* the favorites of reporters unwilling to commit to a strong idea. In a profile of David Geffen, this sentence should have been reverbed:

> Though he preferred to remain above the fray, he didn't seem to have lost his gut for pop culture.

Doesn't "he never lost his gut for pop culture" read better?

The same thing can happen with *feels, looks, smells, sounds,* and *tastes.* Why wimp out and say "my job feels rewarding"? Take a stand. Say "it pays off." (And one more point about *feels*: it is not synonymous with *thinks*.)

Although other miscellaneous wimps—*does, get, go,*

has, put—are (technically) dynamic verbs, they add almost nothing to a sentence. Look out for verbs that convey less action than other words in the sentence, and avoid them:

> Turn "he *has* a plan to" into "he *plans* to."
> Turn "the team *had* ten losses" into "the team *lost* ten games."
> Turn "an accident occurred that damaged my car" into "that teenager bashed my Ferrari."
> Turn "her speech caused me to blush" into "Hearing so many compliments, I blushed."

Finally, avoid those bulwarks of the bad memo: *utilize, prioritize,* and *implement,* which fill business writing with fuzz instead of delivering direct actions and strong statements. When your imagination fails you, grab a thesaurus. And don't gloss over the truth. Why write that the CEO of the high-tech startup "is leaving the company" when you can report the brutal truth: "she quit in protest." Or the "vulture capitalists booted her." Or "her minions ousted her in a corporate coup." Even if you have to check with a lawyer, isn't a kick-ass piece of writing worth the effort?

AIRHEAD ACTION.

Have you ever pondered those verbs that everyone uses but that make no sense? *Revolve around,* for example, and its cousin *center around* usually mark desperate attempts by unimaginative reporters to sound good. Take this from a report on the National Ocean Conference in Monterey, California: "While the issues at the conference revolve around economics and politics, as well as science, the high public visibility of the ocean is a factor, too." The earth may very well revolve around the sun, but what, exactly, do issues revolve around? Don't say "fin-de-siècle corporate innovation *centers around* Silicon Valley"; that makes no sense. Do say "Silicon Valley is the center of fin-de-siècle corporate experimentation."

Sometimes such verbs are called "false limbs," an apt term for meaningless words that a writer grabs onto rather than searching for stronger pillars. Don't pass over strong single words, such as *break, stop, spoil,* and *kill,* in favor of phrases made of a noun or adjective tacked on to some general-purpose verb:

> make contact with → use *call, fax,* or *email*
> exhibit a tendency to → *tend to*
> come to an agreement on → *agree*
> to cause an investigation to be made with a view to
>   ascertaining → *find out*
> will take steps → *will*
> does not see his way to → *will not*
> is not in a position to → *cannot*
> is prepared to inform you → *will tell you*

ACTION, NOT ABSTRACTION.

Linguists estimate that fully twenty percent of English verbs began life as nouns. The best of these conjure vivid images of concrete action—*to audition, to bayonet, to gel, to moralize, to pocket, to stump, to scalp,* and *to white-wash,* for example. NPR language man Geoffrey Nunberg calls this "syntactic switch-hitting," and mentions a brilliant example from a novel in which the writer, Bruce Olds, describes blood that "rooster-tails" from a wound. That invention does what a verb is supposed to do: it gives an image, conveys an action.

But this is not to say that nabbing the nearest noun

beats searching for the *best* verb. Few public figures have engaged in this sin more than Alexander Haig. "I'll have to caveat any response, Senator, and I'll caveat that," Haig said to one politician. To another Haig replied: "Not the way you contexted it, Senator." *Caveat* and *context* are flat-footed ideas, not fleet-footed actions. (When secretary of state nominee Haig appeared at Senate confirmation hearings, a British newspaper heralded the attendant linguistic developments: "verbs were nouned, nouns verbed, adjectives adverbised" and the secretary-designate "techniqued a new way to vocabulary his thoughts so as to informationally uncertain anybody listening about what he had actually implicationed.")

Haigs do it, headline writers do it, managers do it, lawyers do it. Joseph Cammarata, erstwhile attorney for Paula Corbin Jones in her suit against President Clinton, uttered this whammy: "I don't think we should wordsmith this in public." Some verb inventions work because they convey action through strong images: *stonewall* and *launder.* But what's the image in *wordsmith*—beating a word over an anvil? Here's another one: *feedback,* as in "Let me feedback later"? That sounds like the function of a machine rather than a bona fide human activity. Turning people and things, especially abstractions, into acts often invents awkward and imprecise shortcuts that reveal a lack of imagination for verbs, or simply a desire to sound more highfalutin than necessary. It takes only a few seconds to improve upon a bad verb created out of a vague noun:

> Rather than to access → try *to view*
> to author → *to write*
> to finalize → *to finish*
> to impact → *to touch*

to input —→ *to enter*
to interface —→ *to talk*
to prioritize —→ *to reorganize*
to obsolete —→ *to outpace* or *to
  supersede*

IF THE VERB DOESN'T FIT, YOU MUST ATTRIT.

Verbs also enter the language through back-formation, the process that gave us *to rob* from *robber,* *to beg* from *beggar,* *to diagnose* from *diagnosis,* and *to babysit* from *babysitter.* This can make for unbridled originality, as when a senator from Utah proclaimed "I prefer a polyga-mist who doesn't polyg to a monogamist who doesn't monog." Some back-formed verbs work because they are visual and their sounds evoke the action they describe: *crash, hum, plop, poke, splut, swagger, waffle, whoosh, zap.*

But beware of back-formations. They can range from the ugly *(burgle,* from *burglar)* to the awkward *(televise,* from *television)* to the downright dastardly, like *enthuse, liaise,* and *attrit* ("our air strike will attrit their armor"). Just because a verb descends from a legitimate noun does not give it a proper pedigree.

"WHEN I SPLIT AN INFINITIVE, GOD DAMN IT, I SPLIT IT SO IT STAYS SPLIT."

Thank you, Raymond Chandler. He's right to defend his split infinitives, instances in which an overeager adverb or phrase wedges itself mid-infinitive: **to go** is an infini-tive; **to proudly go** is split. Split infinitives are at least as old as the fourteenth century. Scottish poet Robert Burns wrote of those "who dared **to** nobly **sham**"; two centuries later, James Thurber cracked about his *New Yorker* editor,

"Ross wants you **to** for God's sake **stop** attributing human behavior to dogs."

Even though pedagogues trying to apply Latin grammar to our Anglo-Saxon tongue insist the split infinitive is a no-no, they're dead wrong. Copy editors need to back down, lest they earn the wrath of a latter-day George Bernard Shaw. In 1892, the split-infinitive police made the playwright apoplectic. Shaw wrote this to the local paper:

> If you do not immediately suppress the person who takes it upon himself to lay down the law almost every day in your columns on the subject of literary composition, I will give up the *Chronicle*. The man is a pedant, an ignoramus, an idiot and a self-advertising duffer. . . . Your famous specialist . . . is now beginning to rebuke "second-rate" newspapers for using such phrases as "to suddenly go" and "to boldly say." I ask you, Sir, to put this man out . . . without interfering with his perfect freedom of choice between "to suddenly go," "to go suddenly" and "suddenly to go. . . ." Set him adrift and try an intelligent Newfoundland dog in his place.

Carnal Pleasures

Sometimes a writer does without other parts of speech altogether, letting a verb demand your complete attention: *Listen!*

Drivers returning to San Francisco from Lake Tahoe rise through the infamous Donner Pass (elevation 7,239 feet) and then begin a steep decline out of the Sierra and into the Sacramento Valley. An enormous billboard—"Let 'er drift"—tells truckers to use their engines to slow down their big rigs, lest they burn out their brakes. (*Let drift* here is the verb; *'er* is that damn truck.)

Called "the imperative," this form of a verb is bracing and bold. It lets the writer address the reader directly and powerfully.

Jamaica Kincaid, in a story called "Girl," makes the literary device her own, building one long crescendoing run-on sentence out of a lifetime of commands with which a mother tries to shape her daughter. At the heart of this poisonously poignant relationship is the verb:

Wash the white clothes on Monday and put them on the stone heap; wash the color clothes on Tuesday and put them on the clothesline to dry; don't walk barehead in the hot sun; cook pumpkin fritters in very hot sweet oil; soak your little cloths right after you take them off; when buying cotton to make yourself a nice blouse, be sure that it doesn't have gum on it, because that way it won't hold up well after a wash; soak salt fish overnight before you cook it; is it true that you sing benna in Sunday school?; always eat your food in such a way that it won't turn someone else's stomach; on Sundays try to walk like a lady and not like the slut you are so bent on becoming; don't sing benna in Sunday school; you mustn't speak to wharf-rat boys, not even to give directions; don't eat fruits on the street—flies will follow you; *but I don't sing benna on Sundays at all and never in Sunday school;* this is how to sew on a button; this is how to make a buttonhole for the button you have just sewed on; this is how to hem a dress when you see the hem coming down and so to prevent yourself from looking like the slut I know you are so bent on becoming; this is how you iron your father's khaki shirt so that it doesn't have a crease; this is how you iron your father's khaki pants so that they don't have a crease; this is how you grow okra—far from the house, because okra tree harbors red ants; when you are growing dasheen, make sure it gets plenty of water or else it makes your throat itch when you are eating it; this is how you sweep a corner; this is how you sweep a whole house; this is how you sweep a yard; this is how you smile to someone you don't like too much; this is how you smile to someone you don't like at all; this is how you smile to someone you like completely; this is how you set a table for tea; this is how you set a table for dinner; this is how you set a table for dinner with an important guest; this is how you set a table for lunch; this is how you set a table for breakfast; this is how to behave in the presence of men who don't know you very well, and this way they won't recognize immediately the slut I have warned you against becoming; be sure to wash every day, even if it is with your own spit; don't squat down to play marbles—you are not a boy, you know; don't pick people's flowers—you might catch something; don't throw stones at blackbirds, because it might not be a blackbird at all; this is how to make a bread pudding; this is how to make doukona; this is how to make pepper pot; this is how to make a good medicine for a cold; this is how to make a good medicine to throw away a child before it even becomes a child; this is how to catch a fish; this is how to throw back a fish you don't like, and that way something bad won't fall on you; this is how to bully a man; this is how a man bullies you; this is how to love a man, and if this doesn't work there are other ways, and if they don't work don't feel too bad about giving up; this is how to spit up in the air if you feel like it, and this is how to move quick so that it doesn't fall on you; this is how to make ends meet; always squeeze bread to make sure it's fresh; *but what if the baker won't let me feel the bread?;* you mean to say that after all you are really going to be the kind of woman who the baker won't let near the bread?

Bones

Adjectives are consorts, never attending a party alone, preferring to hook themselves on the arm of a sturdy noun. Adjectives modify their companions, defining the qualities of the person, place, or thing they're escorting, and sharing relevant details whenever possible.

In chapter 1, we talked about nouns that might be used in place of *house*. Leaving the party and mixing our metaphors as blithely as we would our cocktails, we can say that adjectives are the words that make the duplex, dacha, or hacienda distinctive, by suggesting the size and shape of the structure (*boxy, sprawling*), the trim around the windows and doors (*Victorian, postmodern*), the color of the siding (*cerise, celadon*), or the overall effect (*elegant, hangarlike, downright dingy*).

"Limiting" adjectives include articles (*a* door, *the* cellar); possessive nouns and pronouns (*Benny's* bungalow, *my* favorite color); demonstrative, indefinite, and interrogative pronouns (*that* closet, *any* bathroom, *which* window?); and numbers (*three* bidets!).

Skilled writers play with strings of adjectives to convey someone's character in the equivalent of one brushstroke (*a mustache-on-upper-lip, black-leather-jacket* type) or to explore an archetype, as in these sentences from that first salvo of '60s feminism, Simone de Beauvoir's *The Second Sex:*

> Woman? Very simple, say the fanciers of simple formulas: she is a womb, an ovary; she is **female**— this word is sufficient to define her. . . . The term "female" is derogatory not because it emphasizes woman's animality, but because it imprisons her in her sex. . . . Females **sluggish, eager, artful, stupid, callous, lustful, ferocious, abased**—man projects them all at once upon woman.

Other parts of speech sometimes dress in adjective-drag. Attributive nouns, for example, modify other nouns, giving them a whole new identity: Marlboro country, Hammer time, wine bar. Modifiers can also double or triple up on a noun, and these compounds are often held together by hyphens, which help distinguish the "adjective" from the noun being modified. Bruce Sterling gave us this pileup in a *Wired* story: "Magor is the perfect model of a Czech hippie-dissident-tribal-shaman-poet heavy dude." Hip-hop's Ice Cube gave us this rap: "Give me a black goddess sister, I can't resist her / No stringy-haired blond-haired pale-skinned buttermilk-complexion-grafted recessive depressive ironing-board-backside straight-up-but-straight-down no-frills-no-thrills Miss-six-o'clock-subject-to-have-the-itch mutanoid Caucasoid white cave bitch."

Generally, adjectives set the stage for the nouns they modify by preceding them, with a few notable exceptions:

- In some established terms—attorney **general**, body **politic**, notary **public**—the adjective follows the noun.

This is why the plurals seem irregular: in attorneys-general and notaries public it's the first word, the noun, that gets the *s*.

- Sometimes, writers take poetic license and reverse the usual order of nouns and adjectives, as in "Trip the light **fantastic**" or "The loving hands of the Almighty cradled him in bliss **eternal.**"
- In sentences, a linking verb can be wedged between the adjective and the noun it modifies (the sentence's subject): "I agree that he's **lusty,** but I never said he was **indiscriminate.**"

Placement is more important than you might think. Sleep deprivation may cause us to ask for "a hot cup of coffee" when we really want "a cup of hot coffee." When a PC somnambulist asks for "an organic cup of coffee," is he being fussy about the kind of mug he wants, or does he mean "a cup of organic coffee"? This placement stuff may seem minor, but look what happened when one classified ad writer tried to save two short words, two spaces, and one letter by turning "a lover of antiques" into "antique lover": "Four-poster bed, 101 years old. Perfect for antique lover." That writer ended up hawking an accoutrement for a creaking Lothario!

Flesh

Are you old enough to remember the 1969 Jell-O commercial by Young & Rubicam that built an entire sixty-second sketch around perfect adjectives? A lonely and somewhat dorky man in a business suit is sitting at a table in a cafeteria-style restaurant. A no-nonsense Laverne look-alike approaches.

SHE: Dessert?

HE: Yes! I'd like something **cool,** like ice cream.

SHE: Ice cream! *(She nods and walks toward the kitchen, writing up the check.)*

HE: But not ice cream.

SHE: *(She returns.)* Not ice cream?

HE: No, I'd like something **smooth,** like pudding.

SHE: Pudding!

HE: Not pudding. *(She returns and bends over him, her hand on the table. She's got his number now.)* Hmmm. Fresh fruit? No. Something **light,** like chiffon pie?

SHE: Uh, but not chiffon pie?

HE: Something **refreshing,** like sherbet, but ... not sherbet. Um. *(He sits, mumbling, drumming his fingers on the table, looking desperately skyward, as she bolts away, returning a few seconds later with a bowl of Jell-O.)*

Your readers may not be as patient—or perceptive—as that early Laverne. Caring about precise adjectives is one key to vivid prose, and it's important to fine-tune your modifiers before you demand the reader's (or listener's) attention.

Why use the generic *yellow,* given the options: *bamboo, butter, canary, chamois, dandelion, jonquil, lemon, maize, mimosa, mustard, ochre, old gold, popcorn, saffron, sauterne, turmeric,* and *yolk?* In a story about golden lion tamarins in *The Rarest of the Rare,* Diane Ackerman shows characteristic creativity in describing that yellowish monkey as "a **sunset-and-corn-silk-colored** creature." Elsewhere she describes one male of the species as having "**sweet-potato-colored** legs, a **reddish** beard and arms, and a chest and belly the **tawny** gold of an **autumn** cornfield."

Every one of Ackerman's adjectives in this description of a monkey named Jenny is carefully crafted:

> **Golden** tufts of fur stick out between her fingers and toes, which have **small round** pads at the base of **each** claw. Her **long, slender** fingers were made for reaching into **narrow** places, where insects may lurk. I have seen **lithe, graceful** hands like these in paintings of **Thai** dancers. Stroking the **dark** pads on her feet, I'm surprised to discover them **soft** and **yielding**. . . . On Jenny's **small** nose, **two thin** nostrils angle away from each other. A **slight, upside-down** curve is the **natural** shape of her mouth, as if she were caught in a **perpetual** pout. **Gold** whiskers sprout from her chin, and a widow's peak of **canary** yellow leads to a **full golden** mane encircling her head. Her **tiny, guitar-pick-shaped** tongue, flicking in and out, has a **deep** groove down the center. Golden lion tamarins give off a **pungent** odor. Burying my nose in Jenny's chest, I inhale deeply the aroma of **hot** gingerbread mixed with **drenched** wheat.

Ackerman's specific—and unexpected—adjectives mark her finesse as a stylist. None of these adjectives are filler words; all enhance her description. They give her passages a lushness perfectly appropriate for a story set in the Brazilian rain forest and populated by "**shy, quick-footed, promiscuous**" plants, by "**swelling purple** bougainvillea," by an "**aphrodisiac** brew" of pollen, by "**clutching**" and "**slime-coated**" vines, by "**gaudy** flowers," and by the "**Saran Wrap–like** crinkling of leaves."

Not all scenes merit lush description, though, and not all adjectives enhance. In a *New Yorker* cartoon, Michael Maslin parodies Madison Avenue's overreliance on empty adjectives: Lying on a porch swing with an iced tea nearby, a poor mensch indulging in a little summer reading hits this patch of adjective-polluted prose: "Night fell over the land like an **L. L. Bean navy-blue summerweight one-hundred-percent-goose-down-filled** comforter covering up an **Eddie Bauer hunter-green one-hundred-percent-combed-cotton, machine-washable king-size fitted sheet**." Ugh!

Simply using more adjectives is not necessarily better. Be selective. George Bush's "kinder, gentler nation" stuck because it was succinct. But it took a skilled speechwriter to distill Bush's idea and turn the phrase: Peggy Noonan recalls that the adjectives were inspired by a cascade of nouns Bush unleashed while brainstorming about the words that carry special meaning for him: "Family, kids, grandkids, love, decency, honor, pride, tolerance, hope, kindness, loyalty, freedom, caring, heart, faith, service to country, fair play, strength, healing, excellence."

That's the alchemy of adjectives: boiling down an excess of ideas to the essence of a thing, with words that surprise.

Cardinal Sins

"When you catch an adjective," Mark Twain once wrote to a twelve-year-old boy, "kill it. No, I don't mean utterly, but kill most of them—then the rest will be valuable." At some point, however reluctantly, all writers must disabuse themselves of adjectives. We must learn to bring in descriptive terms only occasionally, sparingly, and astutely, to avoid the following sins:

DESCRIPTIVE DOUBLERS AND POSEURS.

Adjectives often get hauled in to prop up weak, generic, imprecise nouns when writers are too lazy to do the thinking to find better nouns. The result is imprecision, squared. Don't slap on an adjective that merely repeats what the noun or verb makes obvious. In "the first vote we'll start with," *first* is extraneous. So are the adjectives clinging to these nouns: *free gift, personal opinion, little baby, afternoon matinee, true facts, convicted felon, vast majority, acute crisis, grave emergency, serious danger.* By the same token, pairing an adjective with a noun coined to mean the opposite just leads to confusion: *new tradition, original copy, partial cease-fire, limited lifetime guarantee,* and (a personal favorite) *tight slacks.*

Back in 1783, Hugh Blair admonished his students at Edinburgh to "Beware of imagining that we render style strong or expressive, by a constant and multiplied use of epithets. Epithets have often great beauty and force. But if we introduce them into every Sentence, and string many of them together to one object, . . . we clog and enfeeble Style; in place of illustrating the image, we render it confused and indistinct. He that tells me, 'of this punishing, mutable and transitory world' by all these three epithets, does not give me so strong an idea of what he would convey, as if he had used one of them with propriety." Updating Blair just a tad, let's put his advice this way: strong nouns create a better image than descriptive poseurs. A *luau of fruits and fishes* is better than "a **delicious, inviting, attractive** spread of food."

Seek surprise, paradox, and parody—whether with Shakespearean oxymorons like *brawling love* or more recent inventions like Walter Winchell's *lohengrinned couple* (newlyweds), Betsey Wright's *bimbo eruptions,* or Candace Bushnell's *toxic bachelors.*

SHOW, DON'T TELL.

The most common criticism many writers hear from editors is "show, don't tell." By using this cliché, the editors are usually hinting at an overabundance of frothy, emotional adjectives that fail to convey to a reader the experience the writer had. "It's no use *telling* us that something was 'mysterious' or 'loathsome' or 'awe-inspiring' or 'voluptuous,' " writes C. S. Lewis, reciting the editor's standard lecture to the newsroom novice. "By direct description, by metaphor and simile, by secretly evoking powerful associations, by offering the right stimuli to our nerves (in the right degree and the right order), and by the very beat and vowel-melody and length and brevity of your sentences, you must bring it about that we, we readers, not you, exclaim 'how mysterious!' or 'loathsome' or whatever it is. Let me taste for myself, and you'll have no need to *tell* me how I should react."

Certain adjectives should be avoided altogether if you want to "show." George Orwell railed against "meaningless words" like *romantic, plastic, human, dead, living, sentimental, natural, vital;* these turn art and literary criticism into utter pap. Check out this doozy: "Comfort's catholicity of perception and image, strangely Whitmanesque in range, almost the exact opposite in aesthetic compulsion, continues to evoke that trembling atmospheric accumulative hinting at a cruel, an inexorably serene timelessness."

The cultural elite don't have a monopoly on meaningless adjectives. Orwell also deplored those favored by politicians trying to "dignify the sordid processes of international politics": *epoch-making, epic, historic, unforgettable, triumphant, age-old, inevitable, inexorable, veritable.* Politicians trying to "dignify the sordid processes" of *national* politics sin, too: "As members of the House, you get an opportunity very few times in your career to make a historic vote," said U.S. Representative Martin T. Meehan about the House's doomed 1998 campaign-finance-reform package. Like a candidate who can't get enough of soft money, Meehan couldn't get enough of this soft adjective, adding, "This was a historic vote."

Then there are the staples of the high-school English paper, which stick around to clutter our prose long after we've stopped analyzing *The Great Gatsby* and *Romeo and Juliet*. These ultimate lightweights describe the reaction of the observer rather than the qualities of the thing observed: *unique, interesting, boring, good, bad, important*. Ban these snoozers from your prose, lest you end up sounding as silly and insipid as this writer from *Commerce*:

> Hillary's, a singularly distinctive and unique restaurant, has made a well-planned and suspicious début, bringing a special new flavor and excitement to the North Jersey scene.

Add *singularly distinctive* and *special* to that list of no-brainers. (Oh, and don't you have a slight suspicion that Hillary's début was more auspicious than sneaky?)

PLEASE, SWEAT THE SMALL STUFF.

Get a grip on these adjectival fine points:

- *Less* and *fewer*. Take a stroll through the nearest grocery with its signs screaming "less calories than ice cream" and "Express line: ten items or less." Both phrases use *less* incorrectly. When talking about a

smaller *number* of things (as you are when you're loading your arms with groceries or loading your body with
calories), use *fewer*. When you are talking about a
smaller *quantity* of something, use *less*. (Say, for instance, you need *less* catsup: get the smaller bottle.)
You would also use *less* to refer to degree or extent. (If
you have *less* patience than ever, buy fewer things and
stand in the ten-items-or-fewer line.)

Wanna get more technical? *Fewer* is used with
countable, or collectible nouns (Are your eyes glazing
over? Those would be nouns that take an *s* in the
plural): fewer burgers, fewer buns. *Less* is used with
uncountable, or mass nouns: less mustard, less catsup, less hunger, less indigestion. If you use *many*
with a word, use *fewer* with the same word (*many* cartons of milk, *many* shopping bags, and *fewer* cartons of
milk, *fewer* shopping bags); if you use *much* with a
word, use *less* (*much* food, *much* hassle, and *less* food,
less hassle).

• *Good* and *well* and *bad* and *badly*. It's simple: *good* and
bad are adjectives, *well* and *badly* are adverbs. (You
have an excuse on *well* and *badly*, because we haven't
covered adverbs yet.) *Good* and *bad* modify nouns.
She's a *good* dancer, but a *bad* cook. They don't modify
verbs, so you'd have to say she dances *well* but cooks
badly.

• That elliptical, photo-caption prose. The articles—*a,
an,* and *the*—are becoming forgotten souls in the fast-
moving world of headlines and captions. We would
never speak without these pipsqueaks, yet writers increasingly abandon them. "The very word *article*
means *a little joint*," grammarian Jacques Barzun
writes, noting how these natural links are so "chaoti-
cally applied." In headlines like "Train Rams Car," he

adds, "idiom is flouted for brevity" and "inelegance" prevails. Equally egregious is the cavalier conversion of adjectives into nouns. When "the escaping couple" becomes "escape couple," all meaning escapes the headline. Kingsley Amis, in *The King's English,* recalls competing headlines in two British tabloids that ignored any part of speech other than a noun: "School Coach Crash Drama," screamed one, and "School Outing Coach Horror" the other. Amis awards the prize, though, to a headline that managed five nouns in a row: "School Bus Belts Safety Victory."

MARKETING MADNESS.

The cheap modifiers in this Gump's catalog copy hardly explain why the item they're describing justifies a $115 price tag: "These *extraordinary* flutes . . . bring a *unique* design energy to any setting. *Masterfully rendered* in life-like details in *brilliant* lead-free pewter wedded with European crystal." It's not those empty adjectives that hint at what you're buying, it's the nouns in that last phrase.

In a misguided effort to be "fresh," some writers of marketing copy verge on the ridiculous. Have you ever studied the syntax of women's clothing catalogs? OK, I got it that "aubergine" stockings are gonna make my legs look like eggplants, but will "mist" stockings make them disappear? What, exactly, does Spanish Flesh look like? Or Cold Morn, Pearly Gates, Kitten's Ear, and Folly?

The wine industry may have even textiles beat. With all sympathy for oenophiles trying to describe sensations on the palate, does anyone think these blurbs from a wine magazine help us figure out what a wine will *taste* like? The Chablis Grand Cru Vaudésir 1994, we're told, is "fat, rich, quite heavy, overdone . . . full-bodied and

quite mature, as evidenced by its yellow color." The Al-
beret Boxler Riesling Alsace Grand Cru Sommerberg
1993 is "as fresh and clean as a mountain stream. Aro-
mas of wet stones and herbs make way for a racy palate
of grapefruit and lime. Light but intense, it's a lively
match for food." If you're not racy enough to drink wet
stones, you might try the J-B. Adam Tokay Pinot Gris Alsace 1994: "Thick, almost viscous, yet dry, with herbal
and pear flavors. Big but inarticulate."

Who can't love a wine that doesn't talk back?

Carnal Pleasures

They can be empty, they can be redundant, they can be
fuzzy, they can be silly. But when the right adjective
catches, it can become a cultural icon. Given a brand
name that was, effectively, an adjective, TBWA Advertising (now TBWA Chiat Day) conceived an ad campaign
with endless memorable permutations. Since 1981 the
ad agency has treated us to Absolut Perfection, Absolut
Proof, Absolut Larceny, Absolut Wonderland, Absolut
Joy, Absolut Brooklyn, Absolut Citron, Absolut au Ku-
rant, Absolut Warhol, Absolut Avedon, and a host of
other absolutes.

Since we've so ruthlessly skewered oenophiles enam-
ored of adjectives, let's remember that some grape-
squishers *do* get it right. The winemakers at California's
Bonny Doon Vineyards know how to mix a little wit with
their words. Tongue firmly in palate, the scribes at Bonny
Doon wildly carom between metaphoric parody and
over-the-top gushiness in these bits of bottle copy:

VIN GRIS DE CIGARE: "the thinking person's pink wine"

PACIFIC RIM GERWÜRTZTRAMINER: "neither too tannic nor Teutonic"

BIG HOUSE RED: "full-bodied eclectic pan-Mediterranean blend"

MONTEREY REFOSCO: "rich, plummy with a haunting almond fragrance . . . enriches the world with its unique strangeness"

BARBERA: "alarmingly rich, dense brambleberry fruit . . . the perfect accompaniment to grilled *qualcosa.*"

As for that grilled *qualcosa,* when your adjectives are working for you, who needs nouns?

Bones

Adverbs are more promiscuous than adjectives. They partner loosely, modifying verbs, adjectives, or other adverbs. Sometimes, adverbs even modify an entire sentence.

All adverbs express either Time (*immediately, now, soon*), Place (*here, there,* and *everywhere*), Manner (*boldly, nonchalantly, purposefully*), or Degree (*absolutely, quite, very*). Another way to think of adverbs is in terms of the questions they answer: When? Where? How? or How much? In "Yesterday, all my troubles seemed so far away" the adverb *yesterday* tells When Paul McCartney's troubles seemed so far away. In Ronald Reagan's memorable "Mr. Gorbachev, tear down this wall," the adverb *down* modifies the verb, telling Where the wall will fall. In the *Star Trek* preamble, "To boldly go where no one has gone before," the adverb *boldly* tells How to go. And in Mark Twain's inimitable cable from London, "The reports of my death are greatly exaggerated," *greatly* tells How Much the reports have been exaggerated.

However, thus, nevertheless, and *indeed* are adverb hybrids, sharing the DNA of both adverbs and conjunctions. Called conjunctive adverbs, they juxtapose fully formed ideas, linking muscular independent clauses that might

CHAPTER 5

Adverbs

stand alone. Mark Twain used the conjunctive adverb *whereas* in this line: "War talk by men who have been in a war is always interesting; *whereas,* moon talk by a poet who has not been in the moon is likely to be dull."

Some adverbs, like *clearly, basically, seriously,* and *regrettably,* announce themselves at the beginning of a sentence and are followed by a throat-clearing comma. These words qualify the whole shebang of the sentence and stand in for longer, clumsier collections of words. Telegraphing something along the lines of "let me speak without one iota of delicacy," Rhett Butler was as brutally suave with a sentence adverb as he was with Scarlett: *"Frankly,* my dear, I don't give a damn."

Innocent though they may seem, sentence adverbs can stir wild passions in grammarians. By far the likeliest to raise hackles is *hopefully,* which *can* modify verbs. ("'It's my birthday, you're flush, and I'm hungry,' she hinted hopefully"; *hopefully* tells How she said it, in a hopeful manner.) But everyone seems to prefer *hopefully* as a sentence adverb (*"Hopefully,* you'll get the hint and take me out to dinner"). Some traditionalists disparage the vogue for *hopefully* as a sentence adverb, calling it "one of the ugliest changes in grammar in the twentieth century." Others see in the demise of "I hope that" a thoroughly modern failure to take responsibility, and even worse, a contemporary spiritual *crise,* in which we have ceded even our ability to hope.

Grammarians, get a grip. *Hopefully* as a sentence adverb is here to stay.

Flesh

Adverbs are crashers in the syntax house party. More often than not, they should be deleted when they sneak in the back door. Brilliant raconteurs don't recount in adverbs, and glorious passages tend to pass on them.

Adverbs do manage, though, to steal the show every now and then, as in the title of the film *Truly, Madly, Deeply.* Trust the British—the only people who really know how to turn *actually, absolutely,* and *indubitably* into upper-crust guests—to name a movie with adverbs. The title trio comes from a snippet of dialogue in which the two main characters play a game of adverbial one-upsmanship:

NINA:	I love you.
JAMIE:	I love you.
NINA:	I really love you.
JAMIE:	I really truly love you.
NINA:	I really truly madly love you.
JAMIE:	I really truly madly deeply love you.
NINA:	I really truly madly deeply passionately love you.
JAMIE:	I really truly madly deeply passionately remarkably love you.
NINA:	I really truly madly deeply passionately remarkably deliciously love you.
JAMIE:	I really truly madly passionately remarkably deliciously juicily love you.

(Jamie skipped "deeply" and Nina won the game.)

Occasionally, Americans pull out a good adverb when it counts. A smart ad for Porsche by the agency Goodby, Silverstein & Partners let the adverb *fast* carry as much weight as the noun: "Kills bugs fast." *Fast* is the key word in the phrase, leaving no doubt about what makes this sports car soooo different from a blast of Raid.

Cardinal Sins

You may truly, madly, deeply love adverbs, but don't ever drag one in to prop up a wimpy verb. Why waste time with "He ran very quickly" when you can say "He darted" or "She hightailed it outta there"? Don't use adverbs to bolster shopworn adjectives either; doesn't "She's a knockout" knock you out more than "She's very pretty"? When you're conducting your adverb audit, beware of the most common ways adverbs clutter prose.

CLIP THOSE HEDGES.

Strunk and White said it most concisely: Omit needless words. Watch for adverbs that merely repeat the meaning of the verb:

> **utterly** reject
> screeched **loudly**
> voices **aloud**
> **rudely** insulted
> **gently** caressing
> stumbled **awkwardly**
> meld **together**

All of those verbs are vivid and specific. Set them free.

On the other end of the bad-adverb scale are those that actually contradict the meaning of the verb they are modifying. When President Reagan confessed that he was "not fully informed" about the diversion to the Nicaraguan contras of money made illegally selling arms to Iran, he was using an adverb as an escape route. He wasn't alone: Admiral John M. Poindexter was "not directly involved," and Don Regan was not "thoroughly briefed." Such claims are no less convincing, William Safire pointed out, than the admission of a nonbureaucrat who says she's "a little bit pregnant."

TOO TOO SULLIED PROSE.

Hamlet got away with "this too too sullied flesh," but the rest of us should shun adverbs expressing degree. Knee-jerk attempts to add oomph drain a phrase of whatever energy it might have had. Rather than using an adverb to bolster a weak adjective or verb, search harder for a better word. Say *inexpensive* instead of "pretty reasonably priced," *thrilled* instead of "quite happy," *lethargic* or *wiped out* instead of "very tired," and *touched* instead of "truly moved." *Very unique* and *real unique* should be dropped altogether.

Degree adverbs betray Authorial Laziness—the habit of piling on the first flabby words that come to mind rather than finding one supple, strong one. But something more egregious is also at work here: Authorial Insecurity. Putting words to the page means having the courage of your convictions. "Don't hedge your prose with little timidities," writes William Zinsser in *On Writing Well*. "Good writing is lean and confident. . . . Every little qualifier whittles away some fraction of trust on the part of the reader. Readers want a writer who believes in himself and in what he is saying. Don't diminish that belief. Don't be kind of bold. Be bold."

Certain of these trash adverbs—*really, very, too, pretty*

much, extremely, definitely, totally—reflect the mindless banter of surfers, Valley Girls, and adolescent mall-mouths. Take, for example, these tidbits from the movie *Clueless:*

"I, like, **totally** choked."
"Mr. Hall was **way** harsh."
"Daddy was **way** grateful."
"That's Ren & Stimpy. They are **way** existential."
"Christian is **brutally** hot."
"Oh my god. I'm **totally** buggin'."
"Those shoes are **so** last season."

Even some "grown-ups" stay stuck in linguistic adolescence. Casino kaiser Donald Trump publicly turned on Governor Christine Todd Whitman of New Jersey during her reelection campaign, whining, "I was totally a good friend to her, and she showed totally no loyalty."

Unfortunately, adults who disabuse themselves of adolescent fluff often replace it with pomposity, using adverbs like *arguably, basically, certainly, clearly, eminently, entirely, essentially, highly, fully, rather, quite, virtually, veritably,* and *wholly.* One English rhetorician calls these "adverbial dressing gowns"; Sir Alistair Cooke calls them "tics." Whatever you call 'em, it's *eminently preferable to* stay away from them in prose.

One of today's worst adverbial offenders is *literally*—an adverb most often used when its exact opposite, *figuratively,* is meant: You say, "his eloquence literally swept the audience off its feet," and I'm seeing a hall full of felled bodies. You write "Mario literally exploded during the argument," and I see prose blown to smithereens.

ADVERBS SHOULD ALWAYS BE USED AS ADJECTIVES. NOT.

In the book *English As She Is Taught: Being Genuine Answers to Examination Questions in Our Public Schools,* the nineteenth-century teacher Caroline Bigelow Le Row compiled students' fumbling replies to questions about grammar, among other subjects. One young citizen offered this bizarre twist: "Adverbs should always be used as adjectives and adjectives as adverbs."

Schoolchildren aren't the only ones to conflate adjectives and adverbs, especially the pairs *good/well* and *bad/badly.* But, listen, this isn't rocket science. Use *well* and *badly* when you're modifying verbs: a new truck runs *well* and a jalopy runs *badly.* If you're trying to convey the street, go ahead and write *It runs good.* But know that you ought to be saying *It runs well.*

I f you like that piece of *English As She Is Taught,* you'll love some of the others in what Mark Twain dubbed a "darling literary curiosity." (Twain helped publicize the book and wrote its introductory essay.) Take these:

Every sentence and name of God should begin with a
    caterpillar.
Capital letters begin at breviation.
A quotation is asking a question.
An Exclamation Point is what causes surprise.
Brackets set things off so they wont have anything to do
    with the sentence.

Grammar is how to talk good.

Grammar gives us the languish.

We study Grammar to get the senses.

A common noun is small things.

A proper noun is peoples names.

A pronoun is a word when we cant get a noun.

A pronoun is a word which is just as good as a noun.

The two kinds of Pronouns is I and O.

The plural is formed by turning book into books.

Person in Grammar tells us whether he is a man or a
woman. It is always an animal or something that
isnt alive.

A verb is something to eat.

An intransitiv verb expresses an act not done to another as
James did *not* strike John.

The Moods in English Gram. are the Indicative, Potential,
Subjugated, and Infinitif.

The optative mood is a mood in a verb when any body
knows you have done any thing.

The sign if shows the potative mood.

A dependent sentence is one that hangs from its clause.

All sentences are either simple or confound.

A word governed by another is called its regiment.

Rhythm is a horse trotting on a road.

Rhyme makes two words sound just alike.

A figure means something different from what it says.

Can in poetry is sometimes used for cant.

Prose tells things that are true right along just as they are
and poetry makes it up as you go along.

A preposition is a word that shews the position of one thing
with kind regards to another.

LET'S ONLY HAVE EYES FOR ONLY.

We grant songwriters a lot of license when it comes to grammar, but a prose stylist should understand why "I Only Have Eyes for You" should be "I have eyes only for you." (The first says "my eyes are the only thing I'll give to you"; the second says "my eyes are drawn to you only.")

Adverbs, remember, are modifiers. They need to cozy up to the word they modify. Check out how moving the adverb *only* around in the sentence "she told me that she fantasized about me" changes the meaning:

> **Only** she told me that she fantasized about me.
> (i.e., no one else, so far, has admitted it.)
> She **only** told me that she fantasized about me.
> (i.e., she didn't also write me as much.)
> She told **only** me that she fantasized about me.
> (i.e., I am the sole stud she's said this to.)
> She told me **only** that she fantasized about me.
> (i.e., she didn't betray any other thoughts about me.)
> She told me that **only** she fantasized about me.
> (i.e., she assured me that no one else finds me studly.)
> She told me that she **only** fantasized about me.
> (i.e., she denied doing anything else, like lingering in the hallway hoping to bump into me.)
> She told me that she fantasized about **only** me.
> (I am the sole object of her attentions!)

Just make sure, when you use *only,* that you fantasize about putting it in the right place.

Carnal Pleasures

Finding writers who devote their energies to making mischief with adverbs takes a little scrounging around, but they're out there. Gertrude Stein, ever the linguistic contortionist, subverted the adverb *there* in her famous putdown of Oakland: "There is no there there." The repetition turns the first *there* into a noun. Will Oakland, home of ebonics and other linguistic curiosities, ever forgive her?

Not far from Oakland, the Bonny Doon winery has been doing a little subverting—or perverting—of its own. The label of its Bloody Good Red parodies the overuse of adverbs and the over-the-top, flushed tone they produce:

> ". . . **astonishingly** full-bodied, w/ good, firm backbone yet still **rather** fleshy, **esp**. about the middle . . . great legs and a huge and **utterly** complete nose . . . **excruciatingly** long & dramatic finish . . . all in all, I must admit that it **really** was **bloody** goo. . . ."

Apple Computer's "Think Different" campaign also subverts the adverb, lopping off the final syllable of "Differently." That skimpy tag line should read *Think differently,* since *differently* tells us How we should think. But by swapping in the adjective *different,* Apple creates a double entendre: Not only are we encouraged to think differently, to make our thinking "iconoclastic" and "out of-the-box," we are encouraged to think of an Apple computer as *different* from all the others. The sentence reads as if it contained a colon—Think: Different.

Bones

If you were to compare crafting prose to building a house, the nouns (and pronouns), verbs, adjectives, and adverbs would form the foundation, the framing, *and* the ornamentation. Prepositions might be analogous to closet doors. From the Latin for "to put before," a preposition appears before a noun, called the "object" of the preposition. The objects of prepositions are closets behind the house's doors.

Prepositions are easy to recognize once you get the hang of it, but here's a hunky list to help you out: *about, above, across, after, against, ahead of, along, among, apart from, around, as, as for, as well as, aside from, at, away from, before, behind, below, beside, besides, between, beyond, but, by, by means of, down, during, except, for, from, in, in back of, in front of, inside, instead of, into, like, near, of, off, on, onto, out, out of, outside, over, past, since, through, throughout, till, to, together with, toward, under, until, up, up to, upon, with, within, without, with regard to.*

Now, some people might buy a house for its walk-ins, but the closets could never be called a house's defining feature. Likewise, prepositional phrases exist to modify something more important. Adjectival prepositional phrases modify a noun or pronoun: *Women on the verge of a nervous breakdown* contains two adjectival prepositional phrases—*on the verge* tells us which women we're talking about (the ones on the verge) and *of a nervous breakdown* tells us what they're on the verge of. Adverbial prepositional phrases modify a verb, adjective, or adverb: *In 1964, she wowed the boy next door* contains the adverbial prepositional phrase *in 1964,* which tells us when she wowed the boy next door.

Prepositions often convey spatial relationships, telling us where X is in relation to Y. So inventive school-teachers came up with a useful mnemonic for students struggling with prepositions. To test whether a word is a preposition, try putting it in front of the words "the log." If the phrase makes sense, you've got a preposition:

> *before* the log (Yes)
> *outside* the log (Yes)
> *to* the log (Yes)
> *under* the log (Yes)
> *within* the log (Yes)
> *frog* the log (No)
> *bog* the log (No)
> *clog* the log (No)

Prepositions come solo as well as in clusters, and words that normally act as prepositions might, depending on the context, act instead as adverbs *(inside,* as in "come *inside . . .")* or conjunctions *(". . . but* don't come too close"). Lone prepositions (lacking objects) can attach themselves to verbs, as in some of the favorite phrases of gurus and geeks. Timothy Leary's indelible

"Turn *on,* tune *in,* drop *out"* used such prepositions (often called particles). The prophets of high tech tune in to particles, too: boot *up,* dial *in,* log *on.*

No one, though, knows prepositional ins and outs like poet and professor Morris Bishop, who wrote a ditty in 1947 called "The Naughty Preposition":

> I lately lost a preposition;
> It hid, I thought, **beneath** my chair
> And angrily I cried "Perdition!
> **Up from out of in under** there."

> Correctness is my vade mecum,
> And straggling phrases I abhor.
> And yet I wondered, "What should he come
> **Up from out of in under** for?"

Flesh

A letter dated January 6, 1840, to eight-year-old Charles Dodgson (later known as Lewis Carroll) from his father might be called a lesson in writing with prepositions. It shows how prepositions were in the blood of the author who would start the title of his most famous book, *Through the Looking-Glass,* with one:

> My dearest Charles,
>
> . . . As soon as I get **to** Leeds I shall scream **out in** the middle of the street, *Ironmongers, Ironmongers.* Six hundred men will rush **out of** the street, **in** a moment—fly, fly **in** all directions—ring the bells, call the constables, set the Town **on** fire. I will have a file and a screw driver, and a ring, and if they are not brought directly, **in** forty seconds, I will leave nothing but one

small cat alive **in** the whole town **of** Leeds, and I shall only leave that, because I am afraid I shall not have time to kill it. Then what a bawling and a tearing of hair there will be! Pigs and babies, camels and butterflies, rolling **in** the gutter together—old women rushing **up** the chimneys and cows **after** them—ducks hiding themselves **in** coffee-cups, and fat geese trying to squeeze themselves **into** pencil cases. At last the mayor of Leeds will be found **in** a soup plate covered **up with** custard, and stuck full **of** almonds to make him look **like** sponge cake that he may escape the dreadful destruction **of** the Town. . . . Then comes a man hid **in** a teapot crying and roaring, "Oh, I have dropped my donkey. I put it **up** my nostril, and it has fallen **out of** the spout of the teapot **into** an old woman's thimble and she will squeeze it to death when she puts her thimble **on**.". . .

In the hands of Charles Dodgson, Sr., prepositions create mischief, what with cows rushing up chimneys and mayors in soupplates and men in teapots and donkeys in thimbles. Most writers, though, are content to use prepositions to ground their material, to tie nouns and pronouns logically to other parts of speech. In this regard, prepositions are indispensable. Look how a passage turns into a meaningless meteor shower without prepositions:

The discoveries planets the solar system, stimulating renewed speculation other possible worlds throbbing life, are now drawing closer cosmic terms the world their discoverers.

The latest detection, made this month American astronomers, is a planet twice the mass Jupiter that is orbiting the star Gliese 876, one the Sun's nearest neighbors. . . .

The discovery Gliese 876 adds another element surprise and surmise the continuing quest other planetary systems. The large object is orbiting a red dwarf star one-third the mass the Sun.

Now look at the same passage as it was written for the *New York Times* by John Noble Wilford:

> The discoveries **of** planets **beyond** the solar system, stimulating renewed speculation **of** other possible worlds throbbing **with** life, are now drawing closer **in** cosmic terms **to** the world **of** their discoverers.
>
> The latest detection, made this month **by** American astronomers, is **of** a planet **about** twice the mass **of** Jupiter that is orbiting the star Gliese 876, one **of** the Sun's nearest neighbors. . . .
>
> The discovery **at** Gliese 876 adds another element **of** surprise and surmise **to** the continuing quest **for** other planetary systems. The large object is orbiting a red dwarf star **less than** one-third the mass **of** the Sun.

Prepositional phrases in prose can be grounding, but they can also make passages soar—especially when they are used discriminately and groomed carefully. Ideas expressed through prepositional phrases must be carefully crafted into parallel pieces, as in this clause from the Bible: "Though I speak with the tongues **of** men and **of** angels." Those two prepositional phrases (**of** men and **of** angels) are nice and symmetrical, adding rhythmic value to the sentence.

Parallelism is especially important in lists, where the use of prepositions can get dicey (but not impossibly difficult). In a *New Yorker* profile of Mikhail Baryshnikov, Joan Acocella is able to get away with this complex

sentence only because she carefully tracks her prepositions:

> But what has made him an artist, and a popular artist,
> is the completeness of his performances: the level **of**
> **concentration,** the fullness **of ambition,** the sheer
> amount **of detail,** with the cast **of the shoulder,** the
> angle **of the jaw,** even the play **of the fingers,** all
> deployed in the service of a single, pressing act of
> imagination.

Acocella's complicated sentence contains two embedded sets of prepositional phrases. But the parallel structure of their elements (in the first list, *the* + noun + *of* +
noun; in the second, *the* + noun + *of the* + noun) keeps
everything straight and allows Acocella one *more* string of
prepositional phrases: "**in** the service **of** a single, pressing
act **of** imagination."

The speeches of President John F. Kennedy are also
models of prepositional propriety. Notice the parallelism
in this fragment from his 1961 inaugural address:

> The torch has been passed to a new generation of
> Americans, born **in** this century, tempered **by** war,
> disciplined **by** a hard and bitter peace, proud **of** our
> ancient heritage.

Each phrase contains one adjective followed by one
prepositional phrase. The syntactic symmetry, the even
cadence, is part of what makes the sentence memorable.

Cardinal Sins

Rid your prose of prepositional phrases whenever you can. Lodge your ideas directly in nouns and verbs. The mushiest abstractions and the greatest circumlocutions tend to be expressed as prepositional phrases (or pileups of them).

CLEAR THE CLUTTER.

The most frequent prepositional sin is to replace one good, terse word with a stack of prepositional phrases. The worst prepositional train wrecks crop up in legal writing, with its *hereinbelow*s, *with respect thereto*s, and *therein*s. But lawyers are hardly the only offenders. Have you ever counted the number of ways windy writers and speakers avoid the direct adverb *now*:

> as of now
> at present
> at this point in time
> at this time
> for the time being
> in this day and age
> in the not-too-distant future

Of course, none of these beats Alexander Haig's all-time worst way not to say *now*: "at this juncture of maturization."

Anytime you can replace a cluster of words with one elegant one, do it. Use *before* instead of "prior to" or "in advance of." Use *because of* instead of "due to the fact that" or "in light of the fact that." Use *imagination* rather than "the eye of the mind" and *my thinking* instead of

"I'm inclining in the direction of." Scour your writing for prepositional barnacles worthy only of being scraped away, and replace them with simpler words:

> in regard to → *about*
> with reference to → *about*
> the approximate amount of → *about*
> in the interest of → *for*
> for the purpose of → *for*
> in order to → *to*
> in the event that → *if*
> a lot of → *many*
> a great number of → *many*
> the reason is because → *because*
> according as to whether → *whether*
> neat in appearance → *neat*

Many setups can be replaced by a simpler, shorter word: "He was conveyed to his place of residence in an intoxicated condition" is itself reeling with prepositions; "He was carried home drunk" is better.

Let's see what happens when we lop off a preposition altogether. This headline—"Ferraro's Status as Favored Candidate Is Seen as Jeopardized"—could have been expressed more clearly through nouns and verbs: "Favored Candidate Ferraro Risks Becoming Favorite Has-Been." A common culprit is *as,* which was excised easily from that headline, and is equally cuttable in this sentence: "Now that Apple's back on track, how long will Steven Jobs remain as CEO?" Don't go "visit with chums," just "visit them." Why say "I'll meet up with Fabio" when "I'll see Fabio" is just as exciting?

Beware the parasitic *of,* which sucks blood from the following phrases:

How big of a deal was her departure?
She wasn't that good of an editor.
He gave all of his property.
Outside of the office, he was a real card.
Get down off of that table if you expect me to come
home with you.

Some prepositional phrases are more dungeons than
closets; trapped within are much worthier verbs, yearning to burst out. In *David Copperfield,* Mr. Micawber
corrects his own circumlocution by replacing a prepositional phrase with a simple verb: "It is not an avocation of
a remunerative description—in other words, it does *not*
pay." Unfortunately, not all characters are so astute. Follow the lead of Charles Dickens—get the action front
and center:

to be of the opinion that → *to believe*
to be indicative of → *to indicate*
to put in an appearance → *to appear*
to take into consideration → *to consider*
to raise some doubts about → *to question*
to be in possession of → *to own*
to set out certain of its characteristics → *to expose*
for the purpose of providing → *to provide*
to perform an analysis of → *to analyze*
to study in depth → *to examine*

Lame prepositional phrases can even drain a strong
verb of its energy. In "her dark Dominican eyes brighten
with excitement," excise *with excitement* for a more vivid
description of those wondrous eyes.

PREPOSITIONING SUSPECTS.

Professional obfuscators tend to rely on prepositions to spin out sentences no one can follow or hold them accountable for. But—really—is Linda Tripp's attorney, Anthony Zaccagnini, *proud* of this response to questions about his client's arrest as a nineteen-year-old:

> **Due to** the continuing investigation **into** the unauthorized release **of** information related **to** matters now **under** investigation, what can be said has been said.

It's bad enough that Zaccagnini doubled over in the passive voice ("what can be said has been said"); see how those prepositional phrases make his answer even more wishy-washy? (He could have said, "The continuing investigation of leaks prevents our saying more.")

Senate Judiciary Chairman Orrin Hatch, on NBC's *Meet the Press,* got lost in prepositional hell when discussing another corner of the vast Clinton-Whitewater-Filegate-Lewinsky scandal:

> I don't think the First Lady's going to be indicted, no matter how much her fingerprints are **on** almost everything **from** Whitewater **up to** now **in** the eyes **of** many who are looking **at** this objectively.

Backbenching the prepositions would make Hatch's point clearer: "Any objective observer can see that the First Lady's fingerprints are on almost every White House screwup since Whitewater. But I doubt she'll be indicted."

PREPOSITIONS ARE *NOT* VERBS.

The best headline writers create the journalistic equivalent of haiku—fitting words into tight spaces, breaking their lines just right, and conveying the gist of an entire story in few picas. But boner headlines result when copy editors forget that the best way to state an idea is with a strong subject and a dramatic verb. When they "save space" by relying on teeny prepositions, the ideas shrink to nothingness.

Take this headline that ran in the *New York Times:*

> Killer to Die for Sole Murder
> Of His 10 That Is in Doubt

What's with that headline? Did someone hack up a fish? Rewrite the thing. Since it's a headline, you have to keep within the same amount of space, which is possible with an active verb and fewer prepositional phrases:

> Texas Killer's Execution Hinges
> On His One Unproven Crime

Not only is the new headline clearer, but it adds a bit of information and avoids the horrible phrase "That is in doubt," which, though technically correct, is downright dyspeptic.

Sometimes prepositions are called upon to do the work of verbs, as in "he's into hula." Don't hijack a preposition when a verb would do it better: "He dances the hula every day in the grocery store checkout line."

OBJECTION!

The most common prepositional error is forgetting that the noun in a prepositional phrase is the *object* of the preposition. Remember, pronouns have a subjective and an objective case. The object of the preposition must be expressed in the objective case. During Justice Clarence Thomas's confirmation hearings, Senator Hank Brown goofed in saying "most members are like I." "Like me" would have been more judicious. (Hank, would you say "to they" or "behind she"?) The errors here come mostly when a pair of pronouns follows a preposition:

> Not "just between you and I" → *just between you and me*
> Not "if it's up to Jan and I" → *if it's up to Jan and me*
> Not "the rich are different from you and I" → *the rich are different from you and me*

A footnote on that last example: Did you know that F. Scott Fitzgerald got his grammar *right* in the 1926 story, "All the Sad Young Men"? ("Let me tell you about the very rich. They are different from you and me.") No longer can you misquote him in defense of bonehead grammar!

THE LAST WORD ON PREPOSITIONS.

Can we bury the schoolmarm's rule, "Never end a sentence with a preposition," once and for all?

Preposition, remember, means "to stand before," and, yes, prepositions generally stand before the nouns they govern (their objects). Since we hate to force prepositions apart from their objects, the most graceful sentences don't end with prepositions. But prepositions and their objects should not be unnaturally forced together, either. Winston Churchill made fun of pedants who refuse to allow terminal prepositions. "This is the sort of English up with which I will not put," Winston is said to have written in the margins of a report after a civil servant had convoluted a sentence so as not to end it with a preposition.

When prepositions and verbs are joined at the hip, it is folly to separate them. In "Use *eggnog* as a password when you want to log in," you simply must end on the preposition *in*.

Whatever you do, don't try to have it both ways. One neurologist interviewed on TV decided to cover his bets, using his preposition twice: "the HMOs to which they go to." Similarly, a lawyer at a technology conference in Minneapolis warned an audience nervous about using credit cards on the Internet: "You have to have a reasonable comfort level with whom you're working with." That's one lawyer who needs a reasonable comfort level with prepositions. A San Francisco judge refused to give one convict probation, arguing "It's not the type of crime of which you get a second chance with." That judge doesn't deserve probation, either.

Carnal Pleasures

Online denizens, masters of economy in phrasing (i.e., easy typing), grasped early on that prepositions are a drag. Starting with the belletrists at The Well, keyboard caperers developed a host of initialisms to cut prepositional phrases down to size: BTW replaces *by the way,*

IMHO replaces *in my humble opinion,* IRL replaces *in real life,* and OTOH replaces *on the other hand.*

People who speak pidgin English often do away with prepositions altogether, preferring to take the most direct tack possible. In Sierra Leone, *wait for water small small* means "wait for the water for a little while"; a preposition is also pared in *all dem plenty* ("plenty of them"). Go to Hawaii and listen to the island creole, and you'll hear blunt sentences like "He go school," "She make plenty money," and "Try look da sunset" (in place of "Take a look at the sunset").

While some choose to drop prepositions, certain writers embrace evocative ones that stretch the grammatical frontier. Steve Simpson at Goodby, Silverstein & Partners created an ad for Norwegian Cruise Line that amounted to one long riff on a preposition. Here, *beyond* transcends its syntactic identity, becoming not just a preposition, a doorway, a means to an end, but the end itself.

Beyond the horizon
Beyond heavy woollens
Beyond hurry
Beyond the Nightly News
Beyond snow
Beyond the dayindayout
Beyond the salt spray (and the idea beneath)
Beyond the gossip of seagulls
Beyond your regular stock of adjectives
Beyond work
Beyond the routine spasm . . .
Beyond the need to explain
Beyond the assumptions that keep you warm
Beyond asphalt

Beyond the northern front of cold Canadian air

Beyond the idea you have of a fish and a fish has of you

Beyond the equator

Beyond speech

Beyond the trigonometry of the most meticulous mapmaker

Beyond the grottoes of the sea

Beyond the gull's flight lanes

Beyond the wind

Beyond tomorrow and today and yesterday

Beyond the ideologies of the left

Beyond the ideologies of the right . . .

Beyond the burning pole star

Beyond *the Looking Glass*

Beyond where sleet falls into uncovered souls

Beyond the ordinary everyday vocabulary of 400 words

Beyond talk show hosts who hate you

Beyond *See America First*

Beyond the wave flipping its hair forward to dry

Beyond your property line

Beyond the molecules normally thought to compose you

Beyond any hope you are still reading this

Beyond the one white single-spaced page of your résumé

Beyond all memorized access codes . . .

Beyond *beyond*

Beyond the advertised attractions

Beyond the identity you put on with your good clothes

Beyond the laws of the land

Beyond a decent rate of return in the mutual fund of
    Memory

Beyond ambition

Beyond anything the present 353 words can say

Beyond all that.

It's different out here.

Bones

In our grammatical house, conjunctions are the archways between adjoining rooms, the hallways connecting bedrooms, the staircases leading from floor to floor. Conjunctions, whose name comes from the Latin for "join with," connect words, phrases, and clauses.

Bob Dorough, the Schoolhouse Rocker who unleashed "Conjunction Junction" on kids in 1973, settled on the perfect title for his mnemonic number, since conjunctions place themselves at critical *junctions* in a sentence, where they connect words and link ideas (by "hookin' up words and phrases and clauses").

Different kinds of conjunctions join things in different ways:

- Coordinate conjunctions, or the FANBOYS (*For, And, Nor, But, Or, Yet, So*), coordinate words, phrases, and clauses of equivalent value. A coordinate conjunction might hold together grammatically parallel words (naughty *but* nice) or parts of a list (X, Y, *and* Z). It might also conjoin two phrases playing parallel roles in a sentence ("I'm so broke, I'll have a garage sale *and* hawk all my heirlooms"), or keep distinct thoughts from drifting too far apart ("I'll have the sale soon *so* I won't get too desperate").

Conjunctions

- Correlative conjunctions (*both . . . and, either . . . or, if . . . then, neither . . . nor,* and *not only . . . but also*) create equilibrium too between separate-though-grammatically-equal elements, but they operate differently: they come in pairs, and are separated by the words they bring into relation ("If you buy my stuff, I'm *neither* bound to give change *nor* able to demand it").

- Subordinate conjunctions attach themselves to the beginning of a full-blown clause (a string of words that could stand alone as a sentence) and, by doing so, make that clause dependent on another clause. For example, the clause "I hear snap, crackle, and pop" can stand on its own. But when you add *until* that clause must now attach itself to another independent clause to make sense: *"Until* I hear snap, crackle, and pop, my tears will not stop." Subordinate conjunctions—*after, although, as, as if, as long as, as though, because, before, even though, if, in order that, once, since, so that, though, unless, until, when, whenever, where, whereas, wherever, whether, while*—can come at the beginning of a sentence or smack dab in the middle.

Now we must again pause to pay respects to those strange hybrids, the conjunctive adverbs—*accordingly, afterwards, also, besides, consequently, earlier, finally, first, for example, furthermore, hence, however, indeed, instead, later, likewise, moreover, nevertheless, nonetheless, on the other hand, otherwise, second, similarly, still, then, therefore, thus.*

Conjunctive adverbs have two major roles. First, they help to juxtapose fully formed ideas, linking muscular independent clauses that could just as easily stand alone: "I think; *therefore,* I am." Second, they act as "transitional expressions," momentary bits of commentary that break into the flow of the clause, surrounded by commas: "Quoting Pascal is cool. Subverting him, *however,* is better. Just ask Apple. (I think, therefore iMac.)."

Flesh

In and of themselves, conjunctions offer little in the way of literary flash, but they help to smooth prose, link ideas, and telegraph contradiction. Coordinate conjunctions put ideas in relation to each other: *and* likens them, *or* separates them, and *yet* throws them into opposition.

In *Green Hills of Africa,* Ernest Hemingway describes reading a passage of Tolstoy's *Sevastopol* and being thrown into a reverie about the Boulevard Sébastopol in Paris. His use of *and* turns his sentence into a dreamlike description:

> Riding a bicycle down it in the rain on the way home from Strassburg **and** the slipperiness of the rails of the tram cars **and** the feeling of riding on greasy, slippery asphalt and cobble stones in traffic in the rain, **and** how we had nearly lived on the Boulevard du Temple that time, **and** I remembered the look of that apartment, how it was arranged, **and** the wall paper, **and** instead we had taken the upstairs of the pavilion in Notre Dame des Champs in the courtyard with the sawmill (*and the sudden whine of the saw, the smell of sawdust and the chestnut tree over the roof with a mad woman downstairs*), **and** the year worrying about money (*all of the stories back in the post that came in through a slit in the saw-mill door, with notes of rejection that would never call them stories, but always anecdotes, sketches, contes, etc. They did not*

want them, and we lived on poireaux and drank cahors and water), **and** how fine the fountains were at the Place de L'Observatoire. . . .

In the hands of Hemingway, deceptively simple conjunctions give a passage at once an almost liturgical cadence and a very-twentieth-century stream-of-consciousness aspect.

Correlative conjunctions, too, can bring ideas into a fluid stream, as in this sentence from the Bible, using *neither . . . nor:* "Neither death, nor life, nor angels, nor principalities, nor powers, nor things present, nor things to come, nor height, nor depth, nor any other creature shall be able to separate us from the love of God."

When it comes to building texture and complexity into writing, though, nothing beats subordinate conjunctions and conjunctive adverbs. They set up contradiction—and paradox is, after all, the root of everything deep. They take fully formed, well-spun ideas and make them into macramé.

The opening passage of I Corinthians, 13 (this version is from the 1961 *New English Bible*), uses a series of echoing subordinate clauses to prove that of the three things "that last for ever"—faith, hope, and love—"the greatest of them is love":

I may speak in tongues of men or of angels, **but if** I am without love, I am a sounding gong or a clanging cymbal. I may have the gift of prophecy, and know every hidden truth; I may have faith strong enough to move mountains; **but if** I have no love, I am nothing. I may dole out all I possess, or even give my body to be burnt, **but if** I have no love, I am none the better.

The Brothers Gibb, too, used subordinate conjunctions when *they* riffed on love: "If I can't have you, I don't want nobody baby / If I can't have you, ah, ah, / If I can't have you, I don't want nobody baby / If I can't have you, ah, ah."

The most compelling arguments in academic writing are often expressed via a subordinate conjunction or a conjunctive adverb. In this effective thesis contrasting two Hemingway stories, "The Short Happy Life of Francis Macomber" and "The Snows of Kilimanjaro," the writer telegraphs paradox through the subordinating conjunctions *but* and *while:* "In both stories the hero confronts the African wild, Death, and his unhappy wife, **but** the two men respond oppositely: **while** Francis struggles to live, Harry struggles to die."

The least inspired writers just spit out straightforward sentences without any effort to link ideas and frame the prose; they produce stories that may be precise but lack panache. Great writers, though, find the contradictions in their stories, and then frame them with transitional words. Francis X. Clines, of the *New York Times,* uses subordinate conjunctions to craft leads like this:

> **After** a harrowing week in which President Clinton was sworn in as a defendant in one sex scandal, **then** dragged by the headlines into another, the American public, parsing his language as much as his rectitude, had to wonder about the truth, or at least the passing comfort of the half-truth.

Cardinal Sins

DICK AND JANE.

The principal sins with conjunctions are sins of omission—pasting choppy pieces together without any artful seaming. Hacks unable to weave ideas with conjunctions end up sounding like they ought to go back to grade school.

Speaking of going back to grade school, beware too many simple sentences in a row.

> "See the toys," said Sally.
> "Horses and cows and pigs!
> And a funny red duck!
> I want that funny red duck."

Clearly, it's not enough to just plug in innocent coordinate conjunctions; *and*s and *or*s and *for*s can lead to Dick-and-Jane-and-Sally repetitiveness.

Also, beware too many *but*s, *yet*s, and *however*s. A paragraph can only stand so many changes in tack. Keep your contradictions under control, lest your reader get dizzy: "I want that funny red duck, **but** not if it comes at too high a price. **However,** if Mom and Dad would pay for it, I might change my mind. **Yet,** if Mom and Dad are willing to pay, do you think they might spring for a funny red truck, **however** different it is from a duck?"

LIKE YOU LIKE IT.

Although each part of speech has a distinct function, and although putting the right parts in their right places always makes for more graceful writing and eloquent speech, some errors are so persistent that many grammarians just give up and go descriptive—that is, they stop prescribing "correct" usage and start "describing" common usage. The swapping of *like,* a preposition, for *as* or *as if,* both conjunctions, is one case that only the grittiest grammarians continue to oppose. Believe me, *like* wants to be followed by a good noun; *like* is longing to make a nice, tight prepositional phrase: *He looks like Woody Allen. As* is used correctly when it introduces a clause (a subject and a verb): *Do as I say, not as I do.*

This is not rocket science. It's easy to rephrase a thought through either a subordinate clause or a prepositional phrase. So there's no reason to write "You can learn this little lesson, *like* I have" when these options are available: "You can absorb this little lesson, *as* I have" or "*Like* me, you can learn this little lesson."

But people still use *like* incorrectly all the time: "Looks *like* he'll get the job, lucky sucker." Or "She piled up her hair *like* she was Marie Antoinette." Even Graham Greene wrote about girls who "change their lovers *like* they change their winter clothes."

Greene's compatriot Evelyn Waugh once disparaged this use of *like* as "proletarian grammar." If *you* wanna be a prole, go ahead, use *like* instead of *as.* But if you wanna be a pro, don't act as if you don't know what you're doing.

DON'T BE TONE DEAF.

Conjunctions, though seemingly inconspicuous, can greatly alter the tone of prose. An overabundance of *and*s can make prose so fluid it's downright goopy. On the other hand, too many semicolons in place of *and*s and *for*s can so ratchet up the tension that readers'll need a stiff drink to stay with you. Too many subordinate conjunctions and conjunctive adverbs can make prose more a chore than a pleasure. Keep in command of your tone.

Words like *plus* can seem too breezy and informal; words like *indeed* can make you sound prissy and antiquarian. Unless you *want* to sound like a pontificating professor, stay away from *moreover, nevertheless,* and *thus.* I mean, nobody talks like that.

MAKE MY DAY. START A SENTENCE WITH A CONJUNCTION.

A-student types who memorized everything their English teachers said insist that coordinating conjunctions cannot begin sentences. If editors ever try to feed you such wrongheadedness, throw these gems their way: *And God said, Let there be light; and there was light.* (Courtesy, the Old Testament.) *Man is the only animal that blushes. Or needs to.* (Courtesy, Mark Twain.) *And after all the weather was ideal. They could not have had a more perfect day for a garden-party if they had ordered it.* (Courtesy, Katherine Mansfield).

Carnal Pleasures

The most memorable conjunction scandal happened in the early 1960s when R. J. Reynolds launched an ad campaign with this infamous tag line: "Winston ta: .es good like a cigarette should."

The grammar queens ignited. (And wouldn't you, too, now that you've learned the little lesson of *like?*) They were right: the lowly preposition *like* is just not up to the task of linking the two clauses "Winston tastes good" and "a cigarette should" ("taste good" is implied). What was needed, the pedants proclaimed, was the subordinate conjunction *as.* The tag should have read "Winston tastes good as a cigarette should."

Sure, sure. A preposition is not a conjunction. But guess what? The sentence works. Winston, unbowed, came back with a follow-up series of ads asking, "What do you want—good grammar or good taste?" The exquisite choice is expressed by—what else?—the conjunction *or.*

Bones

To the house constructed of the parts of speech, we must finally add interjections—the banging windows and bursting pipes that add excitement to the story inside. Meaning something "thrown between or among" other things, an interjection is a cry, cluck, or sudden outburst: *wow!, goddammit, oh, jeesh . . . , hey!, tsk! tsk!* Whether single words or short phrases, interjections don't function structurally in sentences. But, boy, are they fun.

You'll most likely find interjections at the beginning of a sentence, followed by a comma or an exclamation point: **Ahem!** *Wake up—this is the last chapter on parts of speech.* Typically, when an interjection pops up in the middle of a sentence, it is surrounded by commas: *I am awake. You're telling me,* **alas,** *that this is the last word on Words?*

You have to look hard to find a philologist who takes this part of speech seriously, but here's what William Mathews, in *Words: Their use and abuse,* had to say back in 1876 about the interjection: "It is heard wherever men interchange thought and feeling, whether on the gravest or the most trivial themes; in tones of the tenderest love and of the deadliest hate; in shouts of joy and ecstasies of rapture, and in the expression of deep anguish, remorse and despair; in

Interjections

short, in the outburst of every human feeling. . . . These little words, so expressive of joy, of hope, of doubt, of fear, which leap from the heart like fiery jets from volcanic isles,—these surviving particles of the ante-Babel tongues, which spring with the flush or blanching of the face to all lips, and are understood by all men,—these 'silver fragments of a broken voice' . . . are emphatically and preëminently language."

Flesh

Interjections sit perhaps most naturally in writing such as Lewis Carroll's *Jabberwocky*—because they carry about as much weight as their nonsense neighbors:

> **One, two! One, two!** And through and through
> The vorpal blade went snicker-snack!
> He left it dead, and with its head
> He went galumphing back.
>
> And hast thou slain the Jabberwock?
> Come to my arms, my beamish boy!
> **Oh** frabjous day! **Callooh, Callay!**

But interjections pop up in serious writing as well. One nineteenth-century critic claimed that the interjection *indeed,* in the following passage from *Othello,* contains "the gist of the chief action of the play, and it implies all that the plot develops":

> IAGO: I did not think he had been acquainted
>   with her.
> OTHELLO: O yes, and went between us very oft.

> IAGO: INDEED!
> OTHELLO: Indeed? ay. Indeed. discern'st thou aught
>   in that? Is he not honest?
> IAGO: Honest, my lord?
> OTHELLO: Honest! ay, honest!

In the dialogue of plays or novels, interjections convey colloquial verve, as in this example from Tennessee Williams's *The Glass Menagerie:*

> Knowledge—**Zzzzzp!** Money—**Zzzzzp!** Power! that's
> the cycle democracy is built on!

Zzzzzp is hardly Standard Written English, but it's the kind of word we throw into speech all the time. It fits perfectly in Williams's script.

Since speech tics reveal as much individuality as proper syntax, interjections can help impart character. While editors and copy editors may strike any interjection they see, reporters who care about conveying the salt of the people they've interviewed should fight to keep them in. That's what David Kline did for his 1994 interview with John Malone, the head of cable TV giant TCI. Known as telecom's Darth Vader, the bad boy of the cable industry, Malone peppers his speech with expletives and earthy metaphors. Kline left his interjections in, as they reflected the personality of the "Infobahn Warrior":

> **Look,** if you could really get the RBOCs to tell the truth,
> they'd tell you that the plain old telephone business is
> huge—**I mean,** look at their revenues—and that's what
> they're primarily going after. And the interactive video
> business is a lucky strike extra, **OK?** US West's attitude,
> when we started seeing the penetrations we were getting

in the UK . . . **I mean,** they just said, "**Geez,** if you project these numbers to the US—**wow!** This is a terrific business!"

Leaving in so many interjections is not typical in profiles of corporate CEOs. But then, Malone is no typical CEO.

Finally, consider interjections in your own narratives. Injected—er, interjected—strategically, these clumps of consonants make phrasing less formal. Use 'em when you're ready to loosen the old rhetorical tie, when you want to sound like *you,* talking. In his facetious treatment of portals (those commercial Web sites that serve as gateways to the Internet), *Wired's* Randall Rothenberg throws in a few interjections to contribute a sense of off-the-cuff comedy:

> **So,** I've decided to become a portal.
>
> The reason is simple. My friends and family believe I've been drifting, resting on the boy-wonder thing long after both my hair and my career prospects have thinned. "What are you up to?" they ask, with obvious concern. . . . I can't tell them the truth: In my field, communications, everything reeks of familiarity. Newspapers, magazines, books? Been there. Speechwriting, annual reports, graffiti? Done that.
>
> But to be a portal! There's something to wake the senses. People love portals. On the Net, everybody's got to pass through them. Companies are desperate to associate with them. Wall Street is valuing them at something like 27 times 1999 revenues—present earnings being a bit difficult to come by. At those ratios, I (who, like portals, also don't have much in the way of earnings) can go from making . . . **well,** very little, to a net worth of . . . **boy,** a whole lot.

Cardinal Sins

Some would argue that every interjection is a sin. "Brutish and inarticulate," critics have called them. "Beautiful and gaudy," say others, and "the miserable refuge of the speechless." Interjections aren't evil, but it's good to watch for certain bad habits.

NOW HEAR THIS.

In fact-based journalism, copy editors often airbrush out all interjections. But listen to jittery broadcast reporters, and you'll hear them filling their patter with a relentless series of *uh*s and *yeah*s and *well*s. One TV reporter in the San Francisco Bay Area begins almost every sentence with the interjection *now*: "Now, you may be wondering. . . . Now, officials say. . . . Now, the parade starts at. . . ."

Don't let your writing be as thoughtless as breathless broadcast. Don't do impromptu prose. If you want to use interjections, don't merely repeat them ad infinitum. Make sure they add something.

THERE WAS, LIKE, THIS INTERJECTION. . . .

As you know from reading chapter 7, the preposition *like* often gets hijacked and carried off into conjunctionland. Even worse, sometimes it gets enslaved as an interjection. In speech, *like* as an interjection buys you a little time when your mind can't keep up with your mouth. But in prose it has the effect of whittling your words down to whimpering, simpering sissyspeak.

Cobweblike

The folksinger Loudon Wainwright III vents his spleen about the misuse of *like* in a song called "Cobwebs" on his 1995 recording, *Grown Man.* "I prefer *ah* or *er.*" Wainwright sings, dissing *like* as "just an ugly little four-letter word." Mark *his* avoidance of the little sucker:

> *Well it stumbles and it falls off of almost every tonque*
> *Give a listen and you will hear*
> *It's lurkin' like a land mine*
> *In almost every sentence*
> *It's an assault to my mind's ear*
>
> *Used to be a preposition*
> *Then it was a conjunction*
> *Now it's used as an audible pause.*
> *Oh I hate it when I hear it. . . .*
> *There oughta be some laws.*

Wainwright wonders aloud whether using *like* instead of *as if* started "back with Jack Kerouac." But whenever it started, he notes, "the meaning's covered in cobwebs."

Carnal Pleasures

Political impersonators hang entire caricatures of Ronald Reagan on the Great Communicator's predilection for the interjection *Well—*. Rich Little said a presidential aide's advice to start everything with *Well* gave him the hook he needed to mimic Reagan. Comedians couldn't get enough of Reagan's put-down of Jimmy Carter ("Well, there you go again"), and *Saturday Night Live*'s

Jim Morris was still doing the Reagan *Well* in 1998: "Well, am I still president? No? Well, I'll have you know. . . ."

Segueing from comedy to comics, we can find the true home of interjections. In comics, these "throwaways" hold their own against nouns and verbs and are styled bold for extra intonation and emphasis. *Beetlejuice #1,* by Harvey Comics, is packed with 'em:

Smek!
Thoom!
Skathrak!
Bwaaaah!
Puff! Gasp! Wheeze!
Thump! Thump! Thump!
Eeyew! Glub! Gasp!
Umm . . . Thank you!
Gaaah!

The comic book *Hate,* drawn by Peter Bagge and Jim Blanchard, gives us slacker twentysomethings in all their rhetorical glory. As two characters, Buddy and Sherrill, go on a date at an Italian restaurant, the balloons hovering above their heads deliver Sherrill's interjection-studded style, with "Ya," "uh," " 'cuz," "eww," "ugh," and "ya know." The look on Buddy's face betrays his feigned interest in his date's conversation; his reply is understated ("hmmm . . ."). Until, that is, Sherrill invites him home. Buddy out loud utters "Errr . . . sure! That sounds good . . . ," but, oh, the interjections bubbling in his head: "Oh Boy! Oh Boy!"

Some interjections—"?!?," for example, or "#@%*!"— go completely off the deep end. Leaving letters in the dust, they let us depart the world of words altogether.

PART 2

A sentence brings words together into a stream of thought. It lets fragments flow together and become complete ideas. It has direction, a current, momentum.

Much more than "everything between the capital letter and the period," it tells who did what to whom. Consider the sentence a story, a mini-narrative, a yarn, with a beginning and an ending and a dramatic arc.

These principles will help to give your sentences energy:

RELISH EVERY WORD.

Sentences should be as varied as our objects of desire—sometimes we want them brawny, sometimes we want them brainy, sometimes silken, sometimes brutal. We *don't* want them to stay the same, day after day.

Yet we're so used to sound bites, to narrowcasting and net surfing, to teenagers bypassing whole paragraphs with "duh" or "whatever," that we are tempted, in sentences, to the short and quick. But, remember, the imagination courses in unpredictable waves. As writers we must become intimate with the ferocity of simple sentences, as well as the gentle tumbling of phrases and clauses.

BE SIMPLE, BUT GO DEEP.

In high school, many of us were assigned term papers that seemed impossibly long. *(How do*

Sentences

I fill fifteen pages?!?) We learned to stretch them out, to write windy, to "state, restate, and summarize." We must unlearn such tricks as we refine our writing skills. The best sentences are models of economy, getting to the point (well, the period) quickly. Sentences derive energy from strong structure and packed phrasing.

Mangia! cries the Italian *mamma,* and her single-word sentence speaks worlds. You'd be surprised how little *you* need to get your points across. Strip sentences down to the essentials. Clear out the clutter.

Henry David Thoreau worked tirelessly in this vein, peeling off unnecessary phrases until he reached the pith. In a first draft of *Walden,* he crafted this sentence:

> Over the south shore of the pond which was a low hill covered with shrub oaks & scattered pines which seemed to rise to an illimitable tableland—I seemed to look toward the country of a new ideal race of Tartars, where tribes of men dwelt in tents.

By the sixth version, Thoreau was able to make the same sentence much more elemental:

> The low shrub oak plateau to which the opposite shore arose stretched away toward the prairies of the West & the steppes of Tartary, affording ample room for all the roving families of men.

Thoreau simplified his sentence structure, keeping to one main clause and restricting himself to one *which.*

Sentences can meander—but they should have reason to do so. Virginia Woolf used wordathons to explore the labyrinthine interiors of her characters. Jamaica Kincaid created one breathless outpouring as a fitting response to a lifetime of commandments forced on a girl by her mother. William Faulkner spun out vast Southern sagas in sentences that include a 1,300-word doozy beginning "They both bore it as though in deliberate flagellant exaltation of physical misery transmogrified into the spirits' travail of the two young men during that time fifty years ago. . . ."

Before *you* go spinning out a 1,300-word opus, heed Hugh Blair, a very emeritus Edinburgh professor whose advice has stood the test of two centuries: "Remember . . . every Audience is ready to tire; and the moment they begin to tire, all our Eloquence goes for nothing. A loose and verbose manner never fails to create disgust . . . better [to say] too little, than too much."

TAKE RISKS.

Tame savage sentences, combing through them until every hair is in place. Then muss them up and see how you like the look.

Experiment. Be dangerous. Play with words, mixing the curt with the lofty. Play with chains of words. Play with phrases and clauses and dashes and full stops. Mix short and long, neat and nasty.

Notice how Cormac McCarthy, in *All the Pretty Horses,* ever so carefully calibrates his sentences. Like the pace of the mounts they're describing, the sentences in the following passage start at a controlled clip before stretching out into a graceful canter as horses and riders reach the Texas high prairie:

> They rode out along the fenceline and across the open pastureland. The leather creaked in the morning cold. They pushed the horses into a lope. The lights fell away behind them. They rode out on the high prairie where they slowed the horses to a walk and the stars swarmed around them out of the blackness. They heard somewhere in that tenantless night a bell that tolled and ceased where no bell was and they rode out on the round dais of the earth which alone was dark and no light to it and which carried their figures and bore them up into the swarming stars so that they rode not under but among them

and they rode at once jaunty and circumspect, like thieves newly
loosed in that dark electric, like young thieves in a glowing orchard,
loosely jacketed against the cold and ten thousand worlds for the
choosing.

McCarthy's paragraph starts with simple sentences. But the final
sentence, with its infinite phrases and clauses, is as wide and arcing
as the night sky.

Entire sentences can play off one another just as solo words do.
Consider the patterns. Which best suits your story: lots of staccato? a powerful crescendo? a long, slow diminuendo? pure cacophony?

SEEK BEAUTY.

T. S. Eliot, in *Little Gidding,* defined the "right" sentence this way:

> . . . Every word is at home,
> Taking its place to support the others,
> The word neither diffident nor ostentatious,
> An easy commerce of the old and the new,
> The common word exact without vulgarity,
> The formal word precise but not pedantic,
> The complete consort dancing together.

Whether minuet, foxtrot, or samba, "the complete consort
dancing together" needs energy and grace. If you don't pay attention to your every step, sentences will flatten out and grow listless.

How do you keep them lively and lovely? Listen to the way the
words combine—the cadences, the blending of vowels, the balances
and imbalances. The nineteenth-century critic George Saintsbury
once noted how "shrift ought to be sooth" was identical in meaning
to "confession ought to be truthful" but very different in music.

Saintsbury's descendants, Strunk and White, mused similarly about Thomas Paine's "These are the times that try men's souls." They noted how changes in phrasing muck up Paine's elegant pentameter:

> Times like these try men's souls.
> How trying it is to live in these times!
> These are trying times for men's souls.
> Soulwise, these are trying times.

All the alternatives lack the original's spirit.

Whether you call it "turning a phrase" or "line editing," the simple reordering of words can add ineffable beauty to a sentence. Can you hear the subtle difference between these two sentences:

> Many of the veterans knew more about the soldiers he was describing than the president *did*.
> Many of the veterans knew more about the soldiers he was describing than *did* the president.

The ever-so-slight change makes the second more elegant and memorable.

In *What I Saw at the Revolution,* speechwriter Peggy Noonan recalls a line she wrote for Ronald Reagan about the Democrats:

> They've gone so far left, they left America behind.

Fearing that the sentence gave Democrats credit for moving forward while the rest of the country was stuck in place, Noonan's White House boss, Richard Darman, changed two beats and transformed the sentence:

> They're so far left, they've left America.

FIND THE RIGHT PITCH.

Why do so many of us, when we sit down to write, sound like word processors rather than wordsmiths? Why do we spew the slogans of the consumer culture we work for, rather than sounding like the bards we want to be?

Let's face it, we're surrounded by chatter, clatter, clutter, and cloudiness. We read less and watch more, which leaves us swimming in unrefined language, unedited sentences, ill-considered commentary. New media offer a world of content providers and off-the-cuff "chat," but little creative inspiration. Our litigious times lead us to words full of ominous legality but empty of soaring humanity.

Our sense of language is also blunted by the bureaucratese around us. We try to follow politicians like George Bush ("I am less interested in what the definition is. You might argue technically, are we in a recession or not. But when there's this kind of sluggishness and concern—definitions, heck with it.") and lose our way in the mangled syntax of bureaucrats like Alexander Haig ("We must push this to a lower decibel of public fixation. I don't think there's much of a learning curve to be achieved in this area of content.").

Not all bureaucrats resort to Bushspeak or to Haigiography. Some manage to craft simple, clear, and deep sentences that are also human, humble, and real. Take, for example, the strong words delivered to Lieutenant Colonel Oliver North by senators George Mitchell and Warren Rudman at the end of the Iran-contra hearings in 1987. Rudman's crisp sentences convey all the blunt rhythms of his New Hampshire roots:

> People in this country oppose aid to the contras. . . . And that is why this Congress has been fickle and vacillates. . . . I want to point out to you, Colonel North, that the Constitution starts with the words, "We the people." There is no way to carry out

a consistent policy if we the people disagree with it. Because this Congress represents the people. The President of the United States, the greatest communicator probably we've seen in the White House in years, has tried for eight years, and he's failed. . . . The last thing I want to say to you, Colonel, is [that] the American people have the constitutional right to be wrong.

Rudman's short sentences, his strong cadences, are perfect foils for the lofty democratic ideals he is espousing.

In language as conversational as Rudman's, George Mitchell uses softer words and grander sentences; his cadences reflect his own judicious temperament:

Now, you've addressed several pleas to this committee—very eloquently. . . . You asked that Congress not cut off aid to the contras "For the love of God and for the love of country." I now address a plea to you. Of all the qualities which the American people find compelling about you, none is more impressive than your obvious deep devotion to this country. Please remember that others share that devotion, and recognize that it is possible for an American to disagree with you on aid to the contras and still love God and still love this country just as much as you do. Although he's regularly asked to do so, God does not take sides in American politics. And in America, disagreement with the policies of the government is not evidence of lack of patriotism.

Fired by the passion of his own patriotism, Mitchell matches the eloquence he applauds in North.

Crafting sentences that are *true* may be a struggle for politicians, professionals, and pure prose stylists, but it can also be an opportunity. Writing affords us a luxury we lack in conversation: we can go back to recast our sentences, paying attention to syntax and sensuality in a way that's impossible when we're expounding extemporaneously—in speaking or in writing. And, paradoxically, when rewriting works, the prose sounds natural. It echoes our true voices.

Bones

"I came. I saw. I conquered." In each sentencette, Julius Caesar showed unity of thought and expressed himself in the most direct way possible. Like Caesar, you should put your faith in the sentence's bare bones: subject and predicate.

The subject of a sentence is *who* or *what* the thing is about. In Caesar's statements, the subject is the pronoun *I*. In other sentences, the subject might be a noun (*"The masseuse* makes me melt") or a noun phrase (*"Anyone with the Shiatsu touch* makes me melt").

The predicate, at its core, is a verb that tells what the subject *does* or *is*. In Caesar's statements, the predicates are the single verbs *came, saw,* and *conquered.* In our sentences, the predicate is the entire statement about the subjects: *makes me melt.* The predicate, in short, is everything that is not the subject. In addition to the verb, it can contain direct objects, indirect objects, and various kinds of phrases—all of which we'll come to in later chapters.

"The verb is the heartthrob of a sentence," writes Karen Elizabeth Gordon in *The Transitive Vampire.* "Without a verb, a group of words can never hope to be anything more than a fragment, a hopelessly incomplete sentence, a eunuch or dummy of a grammatical expression."

Indeed, no sentence is complete until you know what the subject *did*. The verb must be explicit, although the subject can be implied, almost embedded in the verb. One of the strongest opening lines in American literature—"Call me Ishmael"—seems to possess no subject. But Herman Melville merely exploits the imperative voice, in which the subject—*you*— is implied.

Readme.

The imperative mood can be used to convey immediacy, by co-opting the reader, or it can be used as a command, to convey authority: *Be there or be square,* for example, or *Readme.* First-person pronouns can also make implied subjects: *Been there. Done that.* (*I* is the subject.) *Let's go!* (*We* is the subject.)

For more, go to Appendix 2, which dwells on the imperative and other moods.

A sentence must have a subject and a predicate, but it can have more than one of each. In a sentence with a compound subject, nouns gang up on a verb: *"The Easter Bunny* and *his personal assistant* put the eggs in a basket." In a compound predicate a subject does more than one thing: *"Put* all your eggs in one basket and—*WATCH* THAT BASKET."

DOES ANYONE REMEMBER how to diagram a sentence? I know, I know, memories of grammar school make you groan, but diagramming sentences really puts things into perspective. Why? Because diagramming casts the sentence as a stream, as a straight line, with a start (the subject) and a finish (the predicate):

$$\rightarrow \text{Subject} \mid \text{Predicate} \rightarrow$$

Caesar's "I came," for example, would be diagrammed:

$$\rightarrow \text{I} \mid \text{came} \rightarrow$$

Diagramming shows that every sentence, no matter how complicated, derives energy, clear direction, and momentum from the subject and the predicate.

Here's the diagram of a less simple sentence—"The waterway flowed sombre under an overcast sky"—which is a fragment from the opening of *Heart of Darkness:*

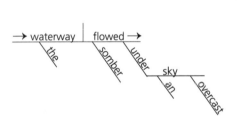

Diagramming sentences also exposes a brutal truth about pileups of modifiers and phrases: they do not advance the message; they dangle off the hull of a sentence like tow lines. The more a sentence drags extraneous words and phrases, the more it slows from schooner to barge.

Here's a less elegant sentence, courtesy of the Bulwer-Lytton Fiction Contest, which invites authors to craft the opening sentence to the worst of all possible novels: "Like an overripe beefsteak tomato rimmed with cottage cheese, the corpulent remains of Santa Claus lay dead on the hotel floor." The sentence diagram shows why that sentence is such a brilliant boner:

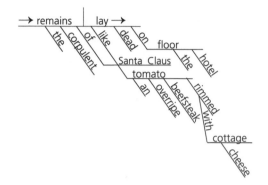

As you can see, the stuff of this sentence does not follow the throughline, but rather drags it down.

Flesh

To tell a story in few words, think strong subject, strong predicate. No one knows this better than the headline writers of the world, who, when they pull it out, manage to convey the news and the blues with a minimum of words and a maximum of wit.

The winner in the subject-predicate category would have to be this headline from the *New York Post,* announcing that Elizabeth Taylor tied the knot in 1991 for the eighth (count 'em) time:

I do . . . I do . . . I do . . . I do . . . I do, I do . . . I do . . . I DO!

(That double "I do, I do" in the middle stands for the two separate weddings of Liz and Richard Burton.)

Like headline writers, the best reporters stand back,

squint like painters taking in landscapes, and sketch out the bold outlines of their stories through strong subjects and predicates. Their stories distill the drama into a few select sentences.

The classic news lead is Subject-Predicate City, collapsing a story into a thirty-five-words-or-fewer sentence that tells Who, What, When, Where, and maybe even Why. When an American caused a royal stir in London, Jason Bennetto, of the *London Independent*, nailed all five *W*s in the opening of his story:

> Buckingham Palace came under aerial assault Saturday for the first time since World War II, when a half-naked American paraglider landed on the roof.

In case you missed 'em all, here are the five *W*s: Who—a half-naked American. What—landed on the palace roof. When—Saturday. Where—er, London. Why—Don't you want to read on to find out?

Even when reporters at the best metropolitan dailies defy the five-*W* formula with abandon, they hardly abandon simple subjects and predicates. Take Beth Hughes's opener for a story on the California tofu business that ran in the *San Francisco Examiner*:

> It's white. It's weird. It wiggles on a plate.

DIRECT, DECLARATIVE SENTENCES are also staples of the staccato dialogues of David Mamet. With an infallible ear for the rhythms of American speech, Mamet puts the basic sentence on display in his plays and in prose like this snippet from *Make-Believe Town*:

For years I played cards every day. The game was held in an old junk store on the North Side of Chicago. The junk store was a front for a fence, and the fence ran a game every day of the year from noon till eight P.M., and I was there every day.

One morning, before the game, I'd gone downtown on some errand, and thought to stop in and visit my dad and say hello. We drank coffee in his office. As noon approached, I said I had to go. He asked where I was going. "Poker," I said. "You still using cards?" he said.

Now, at the time, and for some time thereafter, I found his remark recherché, quite overmuch the comment a wise, tough man—and he was both—would enjoy making to his son. "Are you still using cards?" That is, "Do you still require the artificial constrictions of a self-delimiting game? Do you still need a circumscribed arena, and can you not see that the Game goes on around you all the time?"

Mamet's subjects and predicates have *oomph*. His crisp sentences are deliberate. The parody of what his father *might* have said ("Do you still require the artificial constrictions . . .") reveals how thoroughly Mamet appreciates the wise and tough stuff of simple sentences like "Are you still using cards?"

Whether you write short, punchy sentences or long, flowing ones, keeping track of your subjects and predicates can prevent your prose from shifting and drifting.

Memorable stories are a collection of taut sentences whose focus never wanders. In a *New Yorker* profile of North Carolina IRS agent Garland Bunting, Alec Wilkinson tracks his subject without ever losing him. Almost every sentence features as its subject *Garland, Garland Bunting,* or *he*:

For more than thirty years, **Garland Bunting** has been engaged in capturing and prosecuting men and women in North Carolina who make and sell liquor illegally. To do this, **he** has driven taxis, delivered sermons, peddled fish, buckdanced, worked carnivals as a barker, operated bulldozers, loaded carriages and hauled logs at sawmills, feigned drunkenness, and pretended to be an idiot. In the mind of many people, **he** is the most successful revenue agent in the history of a state that has always been enormously productive of moonshine.

Garland is fifty-nine. **He** is of medium height and portly. **He** has a small mouth, thin lips, a nose that is slightly hooked, and eyes that are clear and close-set and steel blue. What hair he has is bristly and gray. A billed cap bearing the emblem of a fertilizer company or a trucking concern or an outfit that makes farm equipment customarily adorns his head. **He** has a splayfooted walk and a paunch like a feed sack. **He** possesses what he calls "that sweet-potato shape—small at both ends and big in the middle," and he says, "It's hard to keep pants up on a thing like that." A few years ago, **he** walked into a clothing store to buy a suit, spread his jacket wide for a salesman, and said, "I'd like to see something to fit this," and the salesman said, "I would, too."

To trail a man by car, **Garland** will sometimes wear a disguise—usually a mustache or a woman's blond wig. Truck drivers occasionally flirt with their horns at the sight of him wearing his wig. "I put on my wig and some glasses," **he** says, "and those drivers think I'm Sweet Mama Tree-Top Tall."

In only a couple of sentences of those first fifteen does Wilkinson let his subject stray: "A billed cap . . . customarily adorns his head" and "Truck drivers occasionally flirt. . . ." What's more, Wilkinson is disciplined and avoids the classic cliché of the novice narrative writer, gunking up the profile with sentences like "I met Garland Bunting on my first day in North Carolina. . . ." Instead, Wilkinson lets his presence recede, throwing Garland Bunting into relief.

Cardinal Sins

Remember, every sentence is a mini-narrative. Stop for a second and think before you write. What is your subject? Does every sentence pertain to your subject? Can you reframe sentences so they don't wander off on tangents? Here are some sins to watch out for:

LOTSA PAP, LITTLE PITH.

Subjects and predicates—especially if they're not strong—can get lost in a mass of fluffy words. This line from a *Times of London* editorial on July 25, 1815, announced that the defeated Napoleon had arrived in England—well, sort of: "He is, therefore, what we may call, here." That sentence, in all its softness, equivocation, and absence of action, worked to describe a broken and imprisoned ex-emperor. But that doesn't mean *you* should wimp out on subjects and predicates in our un-Napoleonic times.

Mushy-mouthedness can come from a refusal to commit. Attorney General Elliot Richardson once said, "And yet, on balance, affirmative action has, I think, been a qualified success." Why couldn't the man dig his subject and predicate out of that rubble and say "Affirmative action usually works"?

MISSING IN ACTION.

Sentence fragments may start with a capital letter and end with a period, but these globs of words lack either a subject or, more often, a verb. They are shards of thought, shadows of ideas, shams in the prose department. Granted, every now and then sentence fragments work rhetorically. (We'll get to those gems later.) But fragments usually make prose halting and choppy, and come off as phony—gratuitous attempts at edgy informality.

A letter offering a credit card from Chase Manhattan Bank starts off with a bona fide sentence, but then veers into bonehead fragments:

> As someone with a good credit history, you know the importance of having a flexible financial tool. <u>One that enables you to pay for all your major expenses, yet still allows you to make low monthly payments. A credit option that gives you greater cash flow, without stretching the limits of your credit cards or using your home as collateral. A flexible tool like Chase Advantage Credit</u> ®. It's the line of credit you access simply by writing a check.

Despite the periods, none of the underlined statements is a complete sentence ("that" makes two of them dependent clauses). That last line qualifies as a sentence, but—really—*access* as a verb?

It's one thing to see fragments in the compressed lines of advertising copy. But when magazine editors start using the gimmick, they should go back to J-school. The headline above the editor's note in the début issue of *Business 2.0* promised "Not Business as Usual." Did the editor really mean he was planning to forsake the good old sentence?

> Some magazines are for coffee tables. Others for the trash. *Business 2.0* targets a nobler destination: your mind. Because everything that was comfortable and familiar about business is changing.
>
> We're at the beginning of an age that will see the relentless act of connecting everything to everything else. This networked economy—decentralized and antihierarchical—will be the most important force shaping the next decade. . . .
>
> The brightest minds of our day are working hard on these issues, and that's where we join in. We'll explore the people, companies, and ideas that are making the New Economy happen. Figure out what makes them tick. Discover their flaws. Illuminate their victories.

A magazine that sends verbs to the trash is sure to end up there itself. Remember: sentence fragments are not fully fleshed thoughts. Use them at your peril.

DON'T TRY YOUR READER'S PATIENCE.

If subjects and predicates drift too far apart in sentences, separated by endless intervening clauses, the reader may give up. The second sentence in this paragraph from the *San Francisco Chronicle* needed a copy editor:

> The baby was delivered Tuesday by Caesarean section. With the approval of the infant's family, the respirator that had kept the mother's heart and lungs functioning for 64 days so the baby could live in her womb was turned off.

Here's how that sentence might have been tamed:

> The baby was delivered Tuesday by Caesarean section. With the approval of the infant's family, the doctors then turned off the respirator that had kept the mother's heart and lungs functioning for 64 days so the baby could mature in her womb.

Sometimes the opposite occurs: statements get so condensed, so squished together, that subjects and predicates become indistinguishable. Can you figure out what story this headline in the *Toronto Star* is trying to tell?

> Fire put woman in coma highrise inquest told

Maybe some punctuation would have helped ("Fire put woman in coma, highrise inquest told"), but that headline writer was thinking comas, not commas.

Richard Lederer, in *Anguished English,* has collected what he calls "two-headed headlines," in which the blurring of subject and predicate makes for syntactical mayhem:

WILLIAM KELLY, 87, WAS FED SECRETARY

How did she taste?

CARTER PLANS SWELL DEFICIT

Was the budget planning really going to be that much fun?

HERSHEY BARS PROTEST

Are candy bars going on strike?

STUD TIRES OUT

Did the hunk lose his edge? Or were the tires just not cool anymore?

BRITISH LEFT WAFFLES ON FALKLAND ISLANDS

And the Argentineans ask, *Donde están los* waffles?

TEACHER STRIKES IDLE KIDS

Ouch!

THE SUBJECT-VERB TANGO.

Some sentences do contain a clear subject and a clear predicate, but the poor things aren't dancing in unison. Just as pronouns must agree with their antecedents, verbs must agree with their subjects. A singular subject requires a singular verb; a plural subject requires—guess what?—a plural verb.

Here's a description of a nineteenth-century lady whose subject and verb are improper, despite her very proper kid gloves:

> A horse car. Enter an elaborately dressed lady, diamond solitaires, eight-button kids, etc. Car crowded. At first no one moves. Soon a gentleman offers his seat. "Thank you; you are the only gentleman here. The rest is hogs."

Since the "lady" is referring to all the other men on the car, her sentence should have been "The rest *are* hogs."

Get these or get thee to a mummery.

Here's a simplified, slimmed-down list of tricky subject-verb agreements:

- When two nouns are joined by *and,* that compound subject is plural and needs a plural verb: "**The green eggs and the yellow eggs** are in the Easter basket; the blue egg is still hidden in the yard."
- When two nouns are joined by *and* but act as one entity, the verb must agree with the single subject: "**Green eggs and ham** is not my favorite breakfast (much as I love Dr. Seuss)."
- When two nouns are linked by prepositions like *with, in addition to,* and *as well as,* beware—the verb must agree with the first noun, the true subject: "*Green Eggs and Ham*, together with *The Cat in the Hat*, keeps the kids from horsing around."
- When an indefinite pronoun is the subject, take special care. Pronouns like *anybody, each, everyone, much,* and *nobody*

take singular verbs: "**Everyone** remembers that cold, cold wet day." But other indefinite pronouns, like *both, few, most,* and *some,* take plural verbs: "**Few**, though, ever face Thing One and Thing Two."

- Collective nouns *(government, corporation, band, group)* are singular, and so take the singular verb: "**The company** decides whether or not its chef can serve green eggs and ham."
- Some nouns that might seem plural—partly because they end in *s*, like *the United States* or *mathematics*—are actually singular: "**Mathematics** always makes me want to seek refuge in green eggs and ham."
- Certain plural quantities act as singular entities when they are the subject of a sentence: "**Twelve months** is a long time to wait for a change of menu."
- Certain words *(alumnus/alumni, criterion/criteria, datum/ data, medium/media, memorandum/memoranda)* live in a weird limbo between Latin and English. Latin telegraphs a word's number via its ending: *-us, -ion,* and *-um* are *singularis.* So if you want to sound hypercorrect, observe the Latin: "This new **medium**, this World Wide Web, is no place for Dr. Seuss." If you want to sound hyperhip, forget the Latin: "This **data** on green eggs and ham is taxing my hard drive."

FALSE STARTS.

Beware of sentences that get off on the wrong foot by starting with "I think," "There was," or "It is." Strike those beginnings and start right in with your true subject:

~~I think that~~ this book will set you straight.

~~There are~~ writers out there ~~who~~ are desperate for pithy advice.

~~It is my opinion that~~ everyone needs grammar.

If you are a reporter taking care to get down, verbatim, everything a source says, you're on the right track. But you don't have to report every "I think" a subject utters. Make the cut in quotes like this:

> "~~I think~~ the biggest problem in American schools has been the search for one right way," says Chris Whittle, founder of the Edison Project.

Part of rewriting and editing is taking the slack out of sentences, eliminating the false starts and fitfulnesses. Here, for example, is how *Wired* writer Po Bronson tightened a graf in a story on Silicon Valley headhunters:

> If I show up at 3Com with a knockout candidate, you think they're going to slam the door in my face? Every time a startup backs off from an IPO, ~~there's~~ disappointed employees there ~~who~~ will take my call. Every time a new manager takes over an ongoing project, ~~there are~~ employees who are supposed to work under him ~~who~~ won't get along with the new boss, and they'll take my call.

Carnal Pleasures

In the hands of skillful writers, sentence fragments can perk up prose, making it less stiff and formal. They can also help punctuate long sentences. Call it pause and effect, the fragment brightening the narrative with a dash of staccato.

In *The God of Small Things,* Arundhati Roy uses sentence fragments, often to comic effect. In the following paragraphs, she mixes long and lyrical sentences with some pipsqueaks. In doing so, she adds punch to the pathos of a family's failed enterprises:

From the dining-room window where she stood, with
the wind in her hair, Rahel could see the rain drum
down on the rusted tin roof of what used to be their
grandmother's pickle factory.

Paradise Pickles & Preserves.

It lay between the house and the river.

They used to make pickles, squashes, jams, curry
powders and canned pineapples. And banana jam
(illegally) after the FPO (Food Products Organization)
banned it because according to their specification it was
neither jam nor jelly. Too thin for jelly and too thick for
jam. An ambiguous, unclassifiable consistency, they said.

As per their books.

Sentence fragments can also be poetic. Heather Millar
wrote a piece for *Wired* magazine about monks and nuns
forgoing the traditional industries of brandy-making and
fruitcake-baking in favor of typing digital documents and
designing Web pages. To underscore the central theme,
Millar used some strategically placed sentence fragments:

Humble work lies at the center of the monastic vocation,
but their choice of lifestyle doesn't mean that they are a
different strain of humanity. Many monastics devote
much time to the human condition: teaching and working
in hospitals and homeless shelters. But isn't the decision
to withdraw from the world that lies at the center of the
monastic vocation at odds with working on the Internet,
with its pockets of humanity at its wildest and woolliest?

Negotiating a balance between separation and
connection has always been one of the central
challenges for monks and nuns. As the Rule of Life for
the Monks of Jerusalem puts it, "Give up theaters and
cinemas once and for all. This is part of the necessary

break. But be well-informed, open to others, attentive to the city's cries for help."

Separation. Connection. Separation. Connection.

These men and women are happy to walk the line.

CARNAL PLEASURES ARE EVEN MORE common when we get out of the monastery. This headline from the *New York Post* proves you don't always need a subject and a verb to hook readers onto a story:

Headless Body in Topless Bar

The fragments known as email subject headers—the words you see when you check your daily torrent of messages—must do the same double duty as newspaper headlines. The good subject headers pack a terse sentence into the subject field, as in this one from an editor to her lover:

>Subject: go ahead and call—coast is clear. m

That got two sentences and a signature into a few bits.

Sometimes, though, the subject and predicate are artfully embedded in a few keystrokes. In the following subject header, the mini-narrative lurks not in a subject and predicate but in the punctuation itself:

>Subject: dinner?

A one-word narrative. In the crook of the question mark is the crux of the sentence ("Would you like to join me for . . .").

Sometimes headers are flat-out teases, catching your interest by keeping the subject and predicate a mystery:

>Subject: airsex

Is *airsex* the subject? Is *airsex* the verb? You can bet a lot of Dilberts opened this email, which contained a news-wire story on "a trend toward more brazen consensual sex" on all commercial flights:

> Formerly rare seat and lavatory couplings are now
> reported as commonplace by flight crews worldwide.
> Flight attendant consultants' advice on how to deal with
> in-seat trysters: address passengers by name, crouch
> down to eye-to-eye level with them, and don't threaten.

Whether or not they technically contain a subject and a predicate, the best headers convey everything a sentence conveys. Doesn't each of these headers make you want to open the email and hear the story?

>Subject: i have just one word for you
>Subject: my mother
>Subject: Oh, Mexico . . .
>Subject: woe
>Subject: RSVP to Soiree 98 by 1/18!!
>Subject: Part Two, Wherein Lies the Joke. . . .
>Subject: the official word
>Subject: point blank pie
>Subject: Prepare to Be Overwhelmed
>Subject: last chance
>Subject: SOS
>Subject: writer threatening suicide
>Subject: peep

That last one is enigmatic. Is *peep* the plaintive cry of someone badly in need of attention? Is it the promise of a risqué glimpse? Or is it an imperative (Look here or you will forever face regret. . . .)? That *peep* works because it could be all three.

Bones

Now that you've got the notion of subject and predicate, let's dive deeper into the waters of the simple sentence. A few definitions before we leap. (You do want to outswim the grammar divas, right?)

We said in the last chapter that a sentence's main verb is "the simple predicate." The rest of the predicate might include other words, phrases, or clauses. A sentence comprising one and only one subject-predicate pair is a simple sentence.

In *Animals swerve,* the subject is *animals;* the verb is *swerve.* Those two words make a simple sentence. (*Animals swerve and flutter through dense walls of green* has a compound predicate—*swerve and flutter through dense walls of green*—but only one subject, so it's still a simple sentence.)

The simple sentence comes in four basic patterns. (The sentences that illustrate those patterns, like the one in the preceding paragraph, come from Diane Ackerman's description of the Brazilian rain forest in *The Rarest of the Rare.*)

s + v.

In the first pattern, the subject is paired with an intransitive verb, as in *Cicadas buzz* or *Mosquitoes whine.* Intransitive verbs, remember, do not need objects to complete an action, so the minimum requirement for a S + V sentence is merely a subject and verb. Of course, any number of adjectives and adverbs or prepositional phrases may join the fray. In *Gemlike hummingbirds swoop among bird-of-paradise flowers,* the single subject-predicate pair *(hummingbirds swoop)* keeps it a simple sentence:

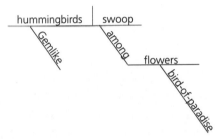

S + V + DO.

In the second pattern, the subject is paired with a transitive verb. Transitive verbs require direct objects—the noun or pronoun that receives the action—so the complete sentence pattern includes the subject, the transitive verb, and the direct object: *The meek inherit nothing.*

S + V + IO + O.

In the third pattern, the subject is paired with a ditransitive verb, which may take an indirect object as well as a direct object. Ditransitives include *give, send, cook, make, prepare,* and *tell.* Indirect objects identify the person or thing to whom or for whom something is being done. So here the complete sentence pattern includes the subject, the verb, the indirect object, and the direct object, usually in that order: *The scientists give the monkeys bananas and crickets.*

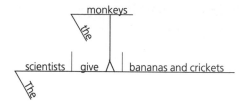

(This sentence pattern, common though it is, can befuddle grammar novices. Perhaps the best mnemonic example is Patrick Henry's "Give me liberty or give me death.")

Objects of our attention.

One way to think of the direct object is as the answer to the question *Who?* or *What?* With *The meek inherit nothing,* when you ask the question "The meek inherit *what?*" The answer, the direct object, is "nothing." With *Slime-coated vines may send golden lion tamarins skidding,* the question becomes "The slime-coated vines may send *whom* skidding?" The answer, the direct object, is "golden lion tamarins." (For our purposes, *who* and *whom* extend to the animal kingdom.)

The indirect object answers the question *To (or For) whom* is the action committed? or *To (For) what?* In *The scientists give the monkeys bananas and crickets,* when you ask the question "*To whom* do the scientists give bananas and crickets?" the answer, the indirect object, is "the monkeys."

S + LV + C .

In the fourth simple sentence pattern, the subject is paired with a linking verb, which is followed by a noun or an adjective called a complement. (Complements are also called predicate nouns and predicate adjectives.) The linking verb sets up a kind of "relationship of equals" between the subject and the complement. The complement may re-identify the subject if it is a noun: in "Jungle plants have become incredible tricksters and manipulators, conning others into performing sex acts with them," *plants* are re-identified as *tricksters* and *manipulators*.

```
  plants  |  have become  \  tricksters and manipulators
 Jungle
```

Complements, with my compliments.

This complement stuff gets complicated. In addition to the subjective complement—which is what the predicate nouns and predicate adjectives following a linking verb really are—there is a part of the sentence known as an "objective complement." This is a noun or adjective that follows a complex transitive verb and a direct object and modifies the direct object. Here are some sample objective complements from *The Deluxe Transitive Vampire* to clue you in:

NOUNS:

The robot designated the dentist **his partner.**

Sir Gallimauf appointed Carmilla **ambassador.**

ADJECTIVES:

Those furtive tidings made Gwendolyn **gruff.**

All this friction makes Alyosha's hands **rough.**

These teethmarks render our marriage **null** and **void.**

The complement can also do the usual modifier thing and describe the subject: in "Plants are promiscuous," *promiscuous* is a straight-up adjective:

$$\underline{\text{Plants} \mid \text{are} \setminus \text{promiscuous}}$$

Remember, linking verbs include state-of-being verbs like *to be* or *to become;* the "senses" verbs *to look, to sound, to feel, to smell,* and *to taste;* and that group of verbs including *to appear, to prove, to remain,* and *to seem.* Occasionally the complement is an adverbial prepositional phrase: Suzy's graduation bash will be *at the Mokuleia beachhouse.*

Flesh

In a journalistic rite of passage, new beat reporters with Faulknerian delusions are hauled into the city editor's office for an upbraiding. "Remember, kid," begins the salty veteran. "You get paid by the period."

For power and punch, nothing beats the simple sentence. The best journalists know it cold, and nowhere do they use the simple sentence better than in opening paragraphs, known in newspaper parlance as "ledes."

Crime reporter Gene Miller, now an editor at the *Miami Herald,* got so good at launching stories with a couple of longish sentences followed by one short one that his brand of news lede earned its own name: the Miller Chop. *Miami Herald* crime-beat veteran Edna Buchanan, one of his disciples, crafted this lede with Miller for a story on the murder of a high-living Miami lawyer:

. . . He had his golf clubs in the trunk of his Cadillac. Wednesday looked like an easy day. He figured he might pick up a game later with Eddie Arcaro, the jockey. He didn't.

Buchanan, author of *The Corpse Had a Familiar Face,* has improvised on the Miller Chop, crafting what Calvin Trillin calls, in a profile of her, "the simple, matter-of-fact statement that registers with a jolt." On the killing of a rowdy ex-con who lurched into a Church's outlet, demanded fried chicken, and started a fatal brawl when offered chicken nuggets instead, Buchanan led with this simple sentence:

Gary Robinson died hungry.

Then there's her lede in a story about a lovers' spat:

The man she loved slapped her face. Furious, she says she told him never, ever to do that again. "What are you going to do, kill me?" he asked, and handed her a gun. "Here, kill me," he challenged. She did.

IF YOU THINK THE SIMPLE sentence is solely the province of the Fourth Estate, think again. Charlotte Brontë made music out of the S + V + DO sentence (punctuated with semicolons rather than periods) in the following passage from *Villette,* in which the narrator awaits reunion with her beloved:

The sun passes the equinox; the days shorten; the leaves grow sere; but—he is coming.

Frosts appear at night. November has sent his fogs in advance; the wind takes its autumn moan; but—he is coming.

The skies hang full and dark; a rack sails from the west; the clouds case themselves into strange forms— arches and broad radiations; there rise resplendent mornings—glorious, royal, purple as monarch in his state; the heavens are one flame; so wild are they, they rival battle at its thickest—so bloody, they shame victory in her pride. I know some signs of the sky, I have noted them ever since childhood. God watch that sail! Oh, guard it!

Muhammad Ali makes a wholly different kind of poetry out of the simple sentence. While in Zaire in 1974 preparing for his "Rumble in the Jungle" against heavyweight champion George Foreman, Ali forged this unforgettable S + V + DO rap:

Only last week, I murdered a rock. Injured a stone. Hospitalized a brick. I'm so mean, I make *medicine* sick.

Cardinal Sins

PURPLE PROSE.

By one account, Samuel Johnson suffered when he picked up a revised version of the New Testament at the country house of a friend. There, in the eleventh chapter of John, he found the simple, touching words "Jesus wept" unceremoniously replaced with "Jesus, the Saviour of the world, overcome with grief, burst into a flood of tears." Dr. Sam blew a gasket.

So should you when you find purple prose ruining a good read. But what, exactly, is purple prose? For some famously atrocious sentences, let's turn again to winners of the Bulwer-Lytton Fiction Contest for the worst opening lines of (hypothetical) lousy novels. You may not recognize Edward George Bulwer-Lytton's name, but you know his words (from the opening of *Paul Clifford*): "It was a dark and stormy night." The litterateurs who ranked high in the competition created doozies like these:

> The sun oozed over the horizon, shoved aside darkness, crept along the greensward, and, with sickly fingers, pushed through the castle window, revealing the pillaged princess, hand at throat, crown asunder, gaping in frenzied horror at the sated, sodden amphibian lying beside her, disbelieving the magnitude of the frog's deception, screaming madly, "You lied!"

> With a curvaceous figure that Venus would have envied, a tanned, unblemished oval face framed with lustrous thick brown hair, deep azure-blue eyes fringed with long black lashes, perfect teeth that vied for competition, and a small straight nose, Marilee had a beauty that defied description.

Marilee's beauty may have defied description, but it inspired purple prose. Unless you're competing in spoof writing contests, tame sentences like these. Break 'em up. And while you're at it, could ya trim a few adjectives?

PLAIN BORING.

Every now and then, the Plain English movement—a loose network of government and business types crusading to get rid of gobbledygook—reappears in the news. Jimmy Carter heeded its calls for deflating prose through short sentences, everyday words, and an avoidance of jargon, and Bill Clinton signed an executive order demanding that government agencies use Plain English. Those are noble goals. But if bureaucrats banish lively sentences in the name of Plain English, have we won the battle but lost the war? How many recipients of this insipid letter from the U.S. Postal Service read to the end?

DEAR POSTAL CUSTOMER

We sincerely regret the damage to your mail that occurred during handling in the post service.

We realize how important your mail is and you have every right to expect it to be delivered intact and in good condition. We are very concerned with incidents such as this and do everything possible to reduce mail damage to the lowest possible level.

Due to the fact that the post office handles millions of pieces daily, it is imperative that mechanical methods be used. Heavy volume and modern production methods do not permit personal attention to individual pieces of mail.

Most problems occur when contents become separated from poorly prepared envelopes or containers. This causes damage to that piece as well as any properly prepared mail that may follow it. No matter how careful we are, mail will occasionally be damaged.

Whatever the circumstances, please accept our apologies for this most unfortunate incident.

PLANT MANAGER
BULK MAIL CENTER

That letter *should* have been signed "The Bulk Writing Center." Sure, it follows the rules of Plain English—"use short sentences, plain words, active voice, and friendly pronouns"—but it also uses mealy-mouthed modifiers *(sincerely, very, important)*; relies on redundancies *(intact and in good condition* and *reduce to the lowest possible level)*; and gives airtime to *due to the fact that*. As for that "Most problems occur when . . ."—please, spare us the details! And don't blame the sender.

Perhaps recipients still wouldn't read a more succinct letter, but wouldn't you rather save federal ink? Try this:

We apologize for damaging your mail.

Because the post office handles millions of items daily, we must rely on mechanical processing rather than personally handling each piece. We do take great care to minimize damage, which is often caused when one envelope gums up the works.

We realize how much you value letters and packages and do our best to deliver them in good condition. Again, our sincere apologies.

WHO KNOWS GRAMMAR BETTER THAN WHOM?

There is only one good answer to the question "Whom shall I say is calling?" That answer is: "Someone who knows grammar better than you do." (The correct question would be "Who shall I say is calling?")

Sentence syntax makes the distinction between *who* and *whom* so easy you're gonna cry. Think *subjects* and *objects*. *Who* is the subject of a sentence or of a clause: **Who** is calling? *Whom* the object of a verb or of a preposition: **You** are calling whom? or **To whom** shall I direct your call? If you're ever in any doubt about whether to use *who* or *whom,* substitute *he* and *him* in the same sentence. If *he* (a pronoun in the subjective case) sounds right, stick to *who* (another pronoun in the subjective case). If *him* sounds right (a pronoun in the objective case), go with *whom* (another pronoun in the objective case).

Sometimes, especially in sentences containing an internal clause, it takes a bit of parsing to figure out whether a pronoun is a subject or an object: With "Who/Whom shall I say is calling?" you must evaporate out the internal clause; you're left with either the grammatically gorgeous "Who is calling?" or the boner "Whom is calling?"

And finally, since we've done away with the shibboleth about not ending sentences with prepositions, go ahead and use *who* at the beginning of a question if *whom* seems unbearably British: "**Who** did you go to the nightclub with?" (Asking "**Whom** did you go to the nightclub with?"—or, worse, "**With whom** did you go to the nightclub?"—will brand you as terminally unhip.)

In spoken English, *whom* anywhere in the sentence is often considered stiff, pretentious. Use what fits best. But err knowingly, and take pleasure in the company of those before you who have done so: Shakespeare allowed King Lear to ask "To who, my lord?" (shoulda been "to whom"), and the translators of the King James Bible allowed "Whom say men that I am?" (shoulda been *who,* as in "Men say that I am who?").

LAY THIS ERROR TO REST.

When Sing and Snore Ernie débuted on toy store shelves, the talking Muppet committed a cardinal sin: He uttered, "It feels good to lay down." Sing and Snore

Ernie joined the august company of Byron ("there let him lay") and Bob Dylan ("Lay lady lay") in confusing *lay,* the transitive verb, with *lie,* the intransitive verb. Granted, Bob Dylan was talking about some serious sinning, but not of the grammatical sort. You should keep in mind that *lay* needs a direct object; *lie* needs no object. Sing and Snore Ernie meant "It feels good to lie down." After lying down, though, he could have said "Now I lay me down to sleep," and he would have been correct, thanks to the direct object "myself."

A copywriter for the watchmaker Tourneau must have liked lying down, too, or was just half asleep when penning this ad: "If you are fortunate enough to have an old watch or two laying around. . . ." The poor professional was busted by William Safire, who scolded: "The present participle should be the intransitive *lying,* not the transitive *laying,* which requires an object like a Fabergé egg."

"IT'S ME" IS OK, BUT "THIS IS HER" IS UNFORGIVABLE.

"Hello," you say, answering the phone. "May I speak to the head of the household?" the telemarketer asks. It may sound stuffy to reply "This is she," but it is correct. (Who wants to cozy up to a goddam telemarketer anyway?) Remember, a S + LV + C sentence puts the subject and the predicate on an equal footing, so a noun complement should be in the subjective, not the objective case. Do not utter "This is her" or "This is him."

A concession to the linguistically loose is, however, in order here. The technically "incorrect" *It's me* and *That's me* have become part of our DNA. Maybe we just crave a simple English equivalent of the French *C'est moi.* There's something nice and humble about *It's me* and

That's me, and it would be crazy to insist on "It is I" and "That is I." ("If somebody knocked at my door and called 'It's I,' " a New York schoolteacher once told the *New York Times,* "I'd faint.") So go ahead, be ungrammatical if it feels right.

Carnal Pleasures

What would advertising be without the short and declarative? If a tag line sticks in your mind, it's probably because it's a simple sentence. Of course, admen and -women spice up their copy with slang and muss up punctuation so as not to seem too straight and narrow.

Brylcreem's "A little dab'll do ya," from 1966, is straight S + V + DO. So's "Flick Your Bic," with which the ad agency Wells Rich Greene turned the brand known for indestructible pens (*stylos* that withstood flames) into a brand known for fire itself. In one oh-so-seventies spot for the disposable lighter, a woman declares, "Myron and I have a liberated marriage. I flick his Bic as often as he flicks mine." Mmmmm. Direct object as object of desire.

Speaking of objects of desire: Goodby Silverstein's "got milk?" campaign shrinks the phrase "Do you have" down to "got" and gives "milk" equal billing in the sentence. (Why, the sentence isn't even capitalized!) Result: the direct object *milk* gets all the attention.

SALON, THE ONLINE MAGAZINE where the digerati meet the literati, held a contest in early 1998 to poke fun at the soullessness of on-screen language. *Salon* challenged readers to consider the error message, written by coders to inform you that you must reboot and start all over. The programmed missive usually brings bad news in worse prose: "abort/retry/fail?" and "404—file not found." (Translation: you have just lost all your work and you are wasting your time.)

Inviting readers to submit error messages, *Salon* required that they be written in 5/7/5 haiku (three-liners in which the first line contains five syllables, the second line seven, and the third line five). The best entries were—you guessed it—simple sentences:

Printer not ready.
Could be a fatal error.
Have a pen handy?
—*Pat Davis*

Everything is gone;
Your life's work has been destroyed.
Squeeze trigger (yes/no)?
—*David Carlson*

Three things are certain:
Death, taxes, and lost data.
Guess which has occurred.
—*David Dixon*

This site has been moved.
We'd tell you where, but then we'd
have to delete you.
—*Charles Matthews*

Chaos reigns within.
Reflect, repent, and reboot.
Order shall return.
—*Suzie Wagner*

Windows NT crashed.
I am the Blue Screen of Death.
No one hears your screams.
—*Peter Rothman*

First snow, then silence.
This thousand dollar screen dies
so beautifully.
—*Simon Firth*

Yesterday it worked
Today it is not working
Windows is like that
—*Margaret Segall*

Serious error.
All shortcuts have disappeared.
Screen. Mind. Both are blank.
—*Ian Hughes*

Hal, open the file
Hal, open the damn file, Hal
open the, please Hal
—*Jennifer Jo Lane*

Bones

If sentences are streams of thought, phrases and clauses are the creeks and underground springs that feed them. Like sentences, phrases and clauses have beginnings and endings, and they flow in a clear direction.

Phrases are simple word groupings—bits of organized thought that are part of the complete idea behind a sentence. "A phrase can't do much of anything alone," Karen Elizabeth Gordon writes in *The Deluxe Transitive Vampire,* "but it's positively a virtuoso when it comes to embellishing, showing relationships, and giving you many different ways to arrange the rest of the sentence, which *it* *needs* to fulfill its promise."

So, who are these virtuosi?

- The noun phrase. This cluster of words, such as *that obscure object of desire,* acts as the subject or direct object of a sentence.
- The verb phrase. Working in concert, the main verb and its helpers constitute the verb phrase, as in *had been chattering.*
- The appositive phrase. This phrase clarifies a nearby noun by renaming it in different words. "Miss Goldenfingers, *my typing teacher,* was fond of tongue-twisters." (These identi-

fiers are especially prevalent in news articles, offering a quick way to identify a source: "Sammy Sosa, *the home-run wonder,* grew up using a cut-open milk carton as a baseball glove.") Appositives are usually, though not always, enclosed in commas.

• The prepositional phrase. Comprising a preposition and its object, the phrase *over the lazy dog,* gives us the preposition *(over),* the object *(dog),* and the object's own modifier *(lazy).* Some phrases do the usual adverbial foxtrot: in "The quick brown fox jumps over the lazy dog," the phrase *over the lazy dog* tells Where the fox jumps. Adjectival prepositional phrases modify a noun; in "Time is a river without banks," the phrase *without banks* tells us what kind of river Time resembles. When a prepositional phrase kicks off a sentence, it is usually followed by a comma: "Over the lazy dog, the fox pirouetted."

• The verbals—infinitive, participial, and gerund phrases. These are fun, if dangerous, devices. (For the dangerous part, see Cardinal Sins.) Infinitive phrases behave as nouns, adjectives, and adverbs: In the sentence "To err is human, to forgive divine," the infinitive phrases *to err* and *to forgive* are nouns; in "the lonesome whippoorwill sounds too blue to fly," the phrase *to fly* acts as an adverb (How blue?). Participial phrases are marked by either the present or the past participle of a verb, but in sentences they behave as adjectives: in "Swearing he'd rather fight than switch, the hunk lit up," everything before the comma modifies the noun *hunk.* Gerund phrases also end in -*ing,* but they always behave as nouns: the *weeping of the robin* and the *crawling of time* made Hank Williams so lonesome he could cry.

Participling the waters. . . .

Participles are limber little suckers. Most often, when they're not part of the verb phrase itself, they're acting as adjectives. They can modify single words ("the *finger-picking* guitarist") or they can be parts of adjectival phrases *("Finger-picking* his way through 'Honeysuckle Rose,' Led Kaapana thrilled the crowd"). But sometimes participles contort themselves into prepositions *(according to, concerning, regarding, speaking of)* and even conjunctions *(supposing, provided that, granted that).*

• Absolute phrase. These are actually full sentences from which the verb has gone AWOL—either morphing into a verbal phrase or disappearing into the mist. In the sentence "The bottle of Zin having been drained, we grabbed the Cab," the absolute phrase suggests a full sentence: *The bottle of Zin has been drained.* The absolute phrase functions as an adjective, but it modifies the entire sentence or clause rather than a single noun within it. Because of this, absolute phrases cannot dangle. Like participial phrases, absolute phrases are set apart from the rest of the sentence by commas.

WIDER AND DEEPER THAN A PHRASE is the clause. It contains a subject and a predicate, but, like a phrase, a clause flows into a larger sentence.

An independent clause *could* stand alone as a sentence, but finds other clauses clinging to it. Independent clauses might be coupled—linked by a conjunction, a relative pronoun, or a hearty piece of punctuation (a semicolon, say): in "Marriage has many pains, but celibacy has no pleasures," the two independent clauses are joined with the conjunction *but.*

A dependent clause *cannot* stand alone; it acts as a noun, adjective, or adverb within the sentence. One kind of dependent clause starts with a subordinate conjunction: in "Marriage, if one will face the truth, is an evil, but a necessary evil," *if one will face the truth* is a dependent clause introduced by the subordinate conjunction *if.* Another kind of dependent clause starts with a relative pronoun, such as *who, whom, whose, that, which, whoever,* and *whomever:* In "Never say that marriage has more of joy than pain," the relative clause *that marriage has more of joy than pain* acts as a direct object of the verb *say.*

That brings us to one troublesome fork in the clause delta: *that* or *which*? When dependent clauses are adjectival—that is, when they describe or define a noun or pronoun—they begin either with *that* or with *which.* Grammarians have probably devoted as much ink to *that* and *which* as they have to anything, but confusion remains—in profusion!

Here's what you need to know: First of all, forget those notions of *which* being more proper. The Brits favor *which,* but *that* predominates in the more relaxed American letters. Use *that* whenever a clause is necessary to understand the meaning of the sentence. In "Elizabeth Taylor could address the questions *that you have about marriage,*" the clause is necessary: "Elizabeth Taylor could address the questions" is too vague—we are left wondering what questions she could address. (No offense, Liz.) Use *which* whenever the clause adds information, but could just as easily be left out of the sentence: "All these questions, *which concern the merits and demerits of independence and dependence,* could be asked of Liz, you know."

While *that* clauses tend to follow straight after the word they modify and need no punctuation, *which* clauses provide extraneous info and are usually enclosed in commas.

The wedding cake or the icing?

If you're a real grammar masochist—in other words, your eyes have *not* glazed over, and you are twitching for more—this box is for you.

Some grammarians wax on about "restrictive" and "nonrestrictive" clauses, or "essential" and "nonessential" clauses, or "defining" and "nondefining" clauses. No matter the nomenclature, all these names attempt to explain when to use *that* and when to use *which*. Just to reiterate: The information in a *that* clause is restrictive/essential/defining—it is necessary to bake the cake that is the sentence. The information in a *which* clause is nonrestrictive/nonessential/nondefining—it just ices the cake.

If that seems straight to you, here's a little more refinement. Every now and then *which* is used when *that* is called for grammatically. Clarity trumps grammar. In the proverb "All that glitters is not gold," *that* introduces the restrictive clause. But we swap *that* with *which* when the clause appears in a sentence like "He said that that which glitters is not gold." Three *that*s in a row would only confuse.

A couple other random points: in restrictive/essential/defining clauses, the relative pronoun *that* can stand in for people or things; the relative pronoun *who* can also stand in for people and, for those of the Garbo persuasion, pets.

Flesh

The cognitive scientist Steven Pinker, in *The Language Instinct,* writes that phrases and clauses offer "one solution to the engineering problem of taking an interconnected web of thoughts in the mind and encoding them as a string of words that must be uttered, one at a time, by the mouth." The more complex the idea, the more complexity is required in the form of the sentence. But words, phrases, and clauses all work together toward the same end: to keep sentences as simple and clear as possible.

Phrases and clauses affect style as well as substance. Phrases can unstarch sentences and give them grace. Notice, for example, the beautiful fluidity imparted by participial phrases in John F. Kennedy's 1961 inaugural address:

> Let the word go forth from this time and place, to friend and foe alike, that the torch has been passed to a new generation of Americans, **born in this century, tempered by war, disciplined by a hard and bitter peace, proud of our ancient heritage,** and **unwilling to witness or permit the slow undoing** of those human rights to which this nation has always been committed, and to which we are committed today at home and around the world.

Kennedy's string of participial phrases works so well because the phrases are so symmetrical—semantically and rhythmically. Kennedy keeps his parts parallel: in each phrase, the adjective (*born, tempered, disciplined, proud, unwilling*) is followed by a prepositional phrase; the rhythm crescendos as each phrase stretches a little longer than the previous one.

Like Kennedy, Thomas Jefferson kept his parts paral-

lel, turning to the relative clause when he was crafting
the rich sentences that begin the Declaration of Independence:

> We hold these truths to be self-evident: That all men are
> created equal; that they are endowed by their Creator
> with certain inalienable rights; that among these are life,
> liberty, and the pursuit of happiness. That, to secure
> these rights, governments are instituted among men,
> deriving their just powers from the consent of the
> governed; that, whenever any form of government
> becomes destructive of these ends, it is the right of the
> people to alter or to abolish it, and to institute a new
> government, laying its foundation on such principles,
> and organizing its powers in such form, as to them shall
> seem most likely to effect their safety and happiness.

Each relative clause begins with *that;* all the clauses are
parallel, and all hold together in exquisite tension—allowing Jefferson to fluidly and memorably bind his ideas.

SO WHAT IF YOU'RE NOT trying to write soaring national
appeals? What if you're just looking for a way to lessen
the staccato of successive simple sentences? Try down-
grading some declarative sentences to independent
clauses tied together with coordinate conjunctions like
and or *but.* Or let a single subject have multiple predicates. News stories often get their fluidity out of such
linking, as in this lead from an Associated Press story:

> Colin Powell ruled out a 1996 bid for the White House
> Wednesday **and** said he wouldn't be a candidate for vice
> president either. He declared himself a Republican, **but**

wouldn't commit himself to vote for the GOP nominee next year.

There are other ways to pack a lede with information while keeping the sentences limber. Notice how Francis X. Clines, of the *New York Times*, finesses the same problem (and the same story):

> **Resisting** an enormous popular drumbeat for his candidacy, Gen. Colin L. Powell, the hero of the Gulf War, declined today to compete in the 1996 Presidential election **because**, he admitted, he lacked "a passion and commitment that, **despite** my every effort, I do not have for political life."

Clines uses every arrow in his quiver: he starts with the softening participial phrase (*Resisting an enormous popular drumbeat for his candidacy*), drops in the subject, adds an appositive (*the hero of the Gulf War*) and Powell's relative clauses (*that . . . I do not have for political life*), and uses subordinate conjunctions (*because* and *despite*) for everything they're worth.

Cardinal Sins

Some of the most hilarious errors in English result from phrases that aren't properly tracked. If you don't know what you're doing, phrases will deliver you straight to The Danger Zone.

DANGLING DOOZIES.

The most common and comical sin is called the Dangling Participle. Remember, participles exist so that verbs can modify nouns. Dangling participles are adjectival phrases that have come unmoored from the nouns they are supposed to modify and instead modify the nearest noun they can find. Here's a dangling participle reprinted in the *New Yorker* as a space filler:

> In San Diego, the "in" place for years has been McDini's for corned beef. Thinly sliced and heaped on rye, corned beef lovers won't be disappointed.

When was the last time *you* were thinly sliced and heaped on rye?

Here's one lifted from Constance Schrader in *Our Town*:

> For over a half-century Rumpelmayer's has been one of New York's most popular ice-cream parlors. Decorated with cuddly stuffed animals and trimmed with large pink velvet bows, you feel like you're sitting inside a present.

It's hard to say which is worse, being thinly sliced and heaped on rye, or being decorated with cuddly stuffed animals and trimmed with large pink velvet bows.

Classified newspaper ads are a great source of dangling-participle howlers, like this one from a shopper in San Mateo, California:

> Redwood City Trailer Rancho: single-wide, 1-bedroom, 1-bath, queen-size bed, pets, children OK if neutered or spayed.

The things they do to their kids in Redwood City!

There's nothing new about dangling participles. Here's one from a notice fixed on a Hertfordshire door in nineteenth-century England:

> This is to give notice that no person is to be buried in this churchyard but those living in the parish; and those who wish to be buried are desired to apply to me. Ephraim Grubb, Parish Clerk.

Surely Ephraim meant well, but *living in the parish* modifies *those who wish to be buried*. Doesn't burying people alive seem a little, well, pagan?

MORE MAYHEM.

Participials aren't the only phrases known to dangle. If prepositional phrases are not placed next to the word they modify, Mayday! Here's a dangler from a collection of "genuine, authentic, and unretouched student bloopers" collected by Richard Lederer in *Anguished English*:

> Abraham Lincoln wrote the Gettysburg address while traveling from Washington to Gettysburg on the back of an envelope.

Some people have magic carpets, some people have magic envelopes.

And some people have magic piano cases. Here's another real ad from the classifieds:

> FOR SALE: an Erard grand piano, the property of a lady about to travel in a walnut-wood case with carved legs.

Then there's the lady with, er, magic legs:

FOR SALE: Mahogany table by a lady with Chippendale legs.

The offending preposition in that first ad is *in*. In the second, it's *with*.

This prepositional dangler appeared in the *Los Angeles Times:*

Pop star Whitney Houston will make her first Southern California concert appearance since the birth of her daughter at the Hollywood Bowl on August 22.

That bit of bad phrasing was snagged by the *New Yorker* (again!), which wryly commented that Whitney Houston has "probably been trying to figure out how to top her last show."

Finally, here's someone on intimate terms with the comedy lurking in dangling things. Groucho Marx made *his* prepositional slips intentionally, like this one from *Animal Crackers:*

I once shot an elephant in my pajamas. How he got into my pajamas I'll never know.

MISCELLANEOUS MISFIRES.

Writers careless with phrases can create havoc in all kinds of ways. Sometimes their phrases dangle, sometimes they just hopelessly tangle. The Brooklyn Church Music Committee received the following (unintentional?) gender-bending reply to a job it advertised back in the 1800s:

Gentleman, I noticed your advertisement for organist and music teacher, either lady or gentleman. Having been both for several years, I offer you my services.

The Church Music Committee was lucky to get an applicant. You can't help but wonder if the following contemporaneous classified ad was ever answered:

WANTED: A woman to wash, iron and milk two cows.

Ironing cows is, after all, a rare skill.

How 'bout this book dedication by a writer who abandoned the serial comma (i.e., the comma preceding *and* in a list) and in doing so created a delusional appositive:

This book is dedicated to my parents, Ayn Rand and God.

Carnal Pleasures

Because we think in chunks, not just words, phrases and clauses in pidgins and dialects can make for some wacko linguistic odysseys. In that breezy language tango called Spanglish, words, phrases, and entire sentences swing back and forth between English and Spanish. A handy Spanish word might stand in for an English one, or an English word might be hijacked into Spanish—"chilling out" becomes *chileando,* and "e-mail" becomes *e-mailiar.* Notice the switch-hitting in the lyrics of a Los Lobos song:

"Let's go *bailando, noche's* looking fine, jump into the *carro*, drink a bunch of wine."

Cristina Saralegui, a celebrity on the Univision Network, claims that even her miniature dachshund, Cosa, speaks Spanglish. When Cristina tells her dog, *"Bajate de la cama!"* (Get off the bed!) Cosa ignores her. Only when she insists, *"Cosa, por favor,* get down," does the dog obey. Whether you're a person or a *perro*, the key to Spanglish is fluency not just with single words, but with *groups* of words—phrases—like *Que no?* or *Yo se,* or *Oye, chica.*

In the Hawaiian creole known as Pidgin English, syntax is scrambled and words from different languages—Hawaiian, Japanese, Chinese, Filipino—are folded into English sentences. The popular song "Manuela Boy" includes this refrain:

> Manuela Boy, my dear boy
> You no more *hilahila*
> No more five cents, no more house
> Go A'ala Paka *hiamoe.*

Hilahila is Hawaiian for "shame"; the phrases in the last line jump from language to language: *Go* is obviously an English imperative ("you go"); *A'ala Paka* is a hybrid, a transliteration of A'ala Park; *hiamoe* is Hawaiian for the infinitive phrase "to fall asleep."

The Hawaiian writer Lois-Ann Yamanaka plays with Pidgin English in her novels of life in the fiftieth state. *Wild Meat and the Bully Burgers* tells the story of Lovey Nariyoshi, a young girl growing up in Hilo, with its patois of Polynesian words *(luna, lanai)*, Japanese phrases *(kendo sensei),* and Hawaiian-English hybrids *(haolified, haole-ish)*:

My other neighbor Katy and me sit on her porch across the street from my house. It's really Katy's mother's house with the big jacaranda tree in the front yard and a white wicker swing like the plantation lunas have on their lanais.

I put Katy's big, swollen legs on an old apple crate. She says, "Eh, Lovey, try press my legs. So swollen going have one white dot where you wen' press your finger. Try."

I do and the white dot on one of her swollen red legs stays for a second, then fades back to brown. I make four dots with all fingers at once and Katy laughs. We drink Kool-Aid with lots of ice cubes.

Katy says she likes the name Charlene if she has a girl and Charles if she has a boy. Named after her ji-chan who was a kendo sensei at a dojo near the pancake house by the airport.

I give her my suggestions since lately I've been Katy's main visitor. "Autumn, Summer, or Heather for a girl. . . ."

Katy says, "When the baby comes, I let you bathe him and change his diaper like that. But no name him—you too haolified with your names, Lovey. Who you think you? Sometimes you act too haole-ish to me. You crazy—you like be haole or what?" I don't say anything. Katy goes on. "I know I got one boy in here. But I gotta name um."

Bones

The best sentences unify their elements—clear subjects and predicates, elegant phrases, clauses that twist and turn and surprise—into a strong, coursing stream. Structurally, they may be simple sentences—containing one subject or predicate along with any number of adjectives, adverbs, or phrases. But if a sentence contains more than one subject-predicate pair, more than one clause, it qualifies as one of the following:

• A compound sentence. When two independent clauses, each detailing a complete action, are hitched by a coordinate conjunction, the two parts balance each other in weight and importance. At the same time, hitching them together brings separate ideas into juxtaposition, as in Mark Twain's "Tell the truth or trump—but get the trick."

Pay attention to punctuation: independent clauses in a compound sentence require a coordinate conjunction (*for, and, nor, but, or, yet, so*) and a comma or a dash. When you want to bolt the clauses together without the softening influence of a conjunction, use a bracing piece of punctuation like Mark Twain's semicolon in the following: "Training is

everything. The peach was once a bitter almond; cauli-
flower is nothing but a cabbage with a college education."

- A complex sentence. Here, one or more "dependent"
clauses lean on an independent clause. What dooms a
clause to dependency? Subordinate conjunctions (like
if, since, or *while*) and relative pronouns (*who,
whomever, that*). Take Mark Twain's maxim about the
principal difference between a dog and a man: "If you
pick up a starving dog and make him prosperous, he will
not bite you." The sentence begins with a subordinate
clause, *If you pick up a starving dog and make him prosperous,* followed by an independent clause, *he will not
bite you.* A complex sentence has an internal dynamic:
the clauses have a distinct relationship to each other
and allow us to emphasize the relationship of ideas.

   If a subordinate clause begins a complex sentence,
it must be separated from the independent clause by a
comma.

- A compound-complex sentence. This contains one or
more dependent clauses and at least two independent
clauses. Mark Twain did these sentences, too: "When
angry, count to four; when very angry, swear." *When
angry* is a dependent clause leaning on the independent *count to four,* and *when very angry* is a dependent
clause leaning on *swear.* This short but intense sentence holds several different ideas, operating on different levels, in place.

Flesh

Mark Twain, who was a master of memorable sentences,
favored the short and pithy. To the writer itching to in-

Balancing acts.

Punctuation gets dicey once you leave the world of simple sentences. Keep in mind that whole thoughts—entire clauses—need to be marked off by either punctuation or a conjunction. Here are the five basic ways to punctuate two complete thoughts, with independent clauses indicated by underlining:

- Let the two clauses stand on their own, separated by a period (and thank you, Leo Tolstoy):
  <u>All happy families resemble each other. Each unhappy family is unhappy in its own way.</u>
- Link the two clauses ever so slightly, by using a semicolon instead of a period:
  <u>All happy families resemble each other; each unhappy family is unhappy in its own way.</u>
- Strengthen the linkage by using a coordinate conjunction and a comma between the two clauses:
  <u>All happy families resemble each other, but each unhappy family is unhappy in its own way.</u>
- Subordinate one clause to the other, by starting it with a subordinate conjunction:
  <u>Although all happy families resemble each other, each unhappy family is unhappy in its own way.</u>
- Emphasize the paradox by separating the two clauses with a conjunctive adverb:
  <u>All happy families resemble each other; however, each unhappy family is unhappy in its own way.</u>

dulge in a long sentence, he counseled: "Make sure that there are no folds in it, no vaguenesses, no parenthetical interruptions of its view as a whole; when [you have] done with it, it won't be a sea-serpent with half of its arches under the water, it will be a torch-light procession."

Simple sentences offer the most straightforward way to get to the point quickly and clearly. But when you want your writing to have the stately grace of a torchlight procession, you can play with syntax and style—with the contrast of short and long, with rhythm and repetition, with pauses and parentheticals, with endings that bang and endings that whimper.

Even in a story that demands a quiet tone and humble language, sentence variety prevents the narrative from becoming choppy. Simplicity and spareness, for example, are perfectly appropriate in a memoir, published in the *Honolulu Advertiser,* of Antone Correa, a Portuguese immigrant who toiled forty-four years as a laborer on a Hawaiian sugar plantation, and thirty more years in his own backyard. The words are simple, but the sentence structure has all the variety of Papa's potted plants:

> Clearly, Papa had once been handsome. His face, in repose, was still remarkable: eyes sunk deep between prominent cheekbones, a set of enormously bushy gray-black eyebrows, both high forehead and arched nose noble in bearing, skin brown and leathery and stretched taut over his jaw.
>
> But by the time we knew Papa, his body was hinged at the waist and starting to wither. He always wore baggy plantation khakis, and a white cotton shirt. I never saw him in a pair of shoes. Instead, he wore leather thongs that crossed over his toes, which bunched together like overgrown tree roots. His legs had weakened: he used a walker to move around the house and the yard. The walker kept his upper body strong. He was barrel-chested, with thick hairy arms and stubby fingers. One of his fingers was a stump, as a result of an accident with a saw. Stump or no, he had a gentle touch.

Despite his difficulty walking, Papa was a tremendous gardener. Beds of flowers and ferns surrounded the house, but Papa spent even more time caring for countless potted plants, on several raised wooden platforms in the backyard. There—in old coffee tins—he sprouted trees and raised vegetables. He was forever sending us home with avocados and bananas.

That description of a simple man mixes simple sentences, a variety of phrases, compound sentences, and one complex sentence.

WHEN WINSTON CHURCHILL ADDRESSED the House of Commons in 1940, after the defeat at Dunkirk, he exploited the straightforward sentence for all its determined power:

We shall not flag or fail. We shall go on to the end. We shall fight in France, we shall fight on the seas and oceans, we shall fight with growing confidence and strength in the air, we shall defend our island, whatever the cost may be, we shall fight on the beaches, we shall fight on the landing grounds, we shall fight in the fields and in the streets, we shall fight in the hills; we shall never surrender.

Churchill knew the value of parallelism. His speech comprises a succession of S + V sentences and clauses (only "we shall defend our island" stands apart structurally as a S + V + DO). In the compelling, swelling compound sentence, Churchill keeps his subject and verb (*we shall fight*) steady and creates a powerful crescendo. When Churchill breaks his incantation with *we shall never surrender,* the structural change emphasizes his resolve.

You don't always have to be so tidy. Look at what Gabriel García Márquez unleashes in the opening of *Autumn of the Patriarch*:

> Over the weekend the vultures got into the presidential palace by pecking through the screens on the balcony windows and the flapping of their wings stirred up the stagnant time inside, and at dawn on Monday the city awoke out of its lethargy of centuries with the warm, soft breeze of a great man dead and rotting grandeur.

García Marquez's winding masterpiece comprises three main clauses (*the vultures got, the flapping of their wings stirred up,* and *the city awoke*) and innumerable phrases, all befitting his magical-realist style. The sentence arcs slowly, like the vultures it describes.

THE ART OF SENTENCE-MAKING comes down to variety. Just because you can do the three-and-a-half somersault tuck off the high board doesn't mean you must ditch the gorgeous swan dive. Good sentences can be short and muscular and they can be long and graceful. Like the imagination, they shift and surprise. You, the writer, must play with them. Try a sentence one way, then another. The English critic George Saintsbury once compared the secret of sentence-making—the letting out and pulling in of clauses—to the letting out and pulling in of the slides of a trombone or the "draws" of a telescope.

The contrast of a lone short sentence amid long ones can add emphasis. A one-word sentence or fragment can stop readers in their tracks—and can mirror the action of the narrative. Former *Washington Post* editor Ben Bradlee effectively contrasted long sentences and fragments in his memoir, *A Good Life:*

> Some stories are hard to see, generally because the clues are hidden or disguised. By accident, or on purpose. Other stories hit you in the face. Like Watergate, for instance.

Had Bradlee deleted that "for instance," he would have had a *killer* fragment.

The *New Yorker*'s Roger Angell uses every play in the sentence book when writing about running into Willie Mays at the Giants' Scottsdale Stadium in Arizona. Angell notes that Mays's psychological defenses often discourage conversation with fans and followers. Consequently, interviewers have a hard time lighting up what Angell calls Mays's "Proustian hot stove." But then "a visiting senior writer from back East" (i.e., Angell) brings up the Billy Cox play, and the sentences take on the unpredictability of hits, runs, and outs:

"Damn!" Mays cried excitedly. "You saw that? You were there?"

Yes, the writer had been there—as a fan at the Polo Grounds. "August, 1951," he said. "Cox was the base runner at third. You caught the ball running full tilt toward right, turned in midair, and threw him out at the plate. You threw before you could get turned around—let the ball go with your back to the plate. The throw went to the catcher on the fly—it must have been Westrum—and he tagged Cox out, sliding."

"You got it!" Mays said. "I've been sayin' this for a long time, and nobody here believes me." He was kidding, of course, but his voice had come up at last: almost the old, high Willie piping. "Now tell 'em how it was."

I told it again—it was easy because I'd never seen such a play, before or since—and, as I did, it seemed to me that Willie Mays and I could still see the long, curving flight of the white ball through the afternoon light, bang into the big mitt, and the slide and the amazing out, and together remember the expanding moment when the staring players on the field and those just emerging from the dugouts, and the shouting fans, and maybe even the startled twenty-year-old rookie center fielder himself, now retrieving his fallen cap from the grass, understood that something new and electric had just begun to happen to baseball.

Angell's final sentence is as risky, as borderline out-of-control, as savagely confident, as was that throw to home by Willie Mays, with his back to the plate.

Cardinal Sins

SKEW LINES.

To string together phrases and clauses for rhetorical effect, remember that Churchillian rhetoric works because of parallel structure. Parallelism—internal syntactical balance—requires that you use similar phrasing for each element of the list. If you can't keep track of your phrases and clauses, you will end up with linguistic rats' nests instead of elegant parallels.

William Safire caught this infelicity in an ad for Harvard Business School: "What's innovative, time-tested, diverse, intense, global and develops leaders?" The problem with Harvard's list is that the first five elements are adjectives, and the last is a clause. Not parallel. Not good.

One media critic tried to get away with this paragraph on Elvis:

> The symbol of rock and roll rebellion returned a mutant, a maker of dumb Hawaiian beach movies, a troubled superstar stuffing himself with drugs, passing out Cadillac cars like candy bars, with a retinue living in a tacky mansion and, eventually, a Vegas act whose jeweled jumpsuits now come more readily to mind than the quiet, oblivious, oddball kid.

A sharp copy editor tamed that sentence, whose various parts career from appositives to participials to prepositionals. Here's the parallel version; each modifying phrase is anchored by a clear noun phrase:

> The symbol of rock-and-roll rebellion returned to the States a mutant: **a pretty face** gracing dumb Hawaiian beach movies, **a troubled superstar** stuffing himself with drugs, **an aging freak** passing out Cadillac cars like candy bars, **a patriarch** lording over a retinue living in a tacky mansion, and, eventually, **a Vegas act** whose jeweled jumpsuits now come more readily to mind than the quiet, oblivious, oddball kid.

RUNAWAYS.

Playing with long sentences does *not* mean ignoring basic rules. There is still no excuse for muddy thinking, ill-formed ideas, or flooding streams of consciousness. That's why we just went through all this sentence stuff.

If you don't get the structural underpinnings of every sentence you craft, go back to simple subjects and predicates.

A run-on sentence from the front page of the *New York Times* on May 26, 1998 (months before Monicagate nixed everyone's best-laid plans), desperately needed an editor with a Day-Glo pen:

> Representative Robert L. Livingston supports Speaker Newt Gingrich as long as he wants to stay in the job, but when he leaves, Mr. Livingston knows who should be his replacement and that is the person Mr. Livingston faces in the mirror.

That paragraph begins what's known in the newsroom as "a teaser": it synopsizes a story appearing on an inside page. The problem is, the editor who summed up the story lacked the reporter's sentence know-how. Here's how the teaser should have been written:

> Representative Robert L. Livingston supports Newt Gingrich in the job of Speaker of the House. But when Mr. Gingrich leaves, the Louisiana congressman knows who should replace him: Robert L. Livingston.

The president of the run-on must be George Bush, whose syntax slips were so bad that political correspondents tagged his weak rhetoric as "Goofy mode" (as in the Walt Disney character). Bush got Goofy one night in a Milwaukee suburb during the 1988 campaign. Telling the crowd how he had brought his two grandchildren to a Halloween rally the night before, Bush headed blithely down the slippery slope:

We had last night, last night we had a couple of our grandchildren with us in Kansas City—6-year-old twins, one of them went as a package of Juicy Fruit, arms sticking out of the pack, the other was Dracula. A big rally there.

And Dracula's wig fell off in the middle of my speech and I got to thinking, watching those kids, and I said if I could look back and I had been president for four years: What would you like to do? Those young kids here. And I'd love to be able to say that working with our allies, working with the Soviets, I'd found a way to ban chemical and biological weapons from the face of the earth.

Maybe it seems unfair to poke fun at Bush for his off-the-cuff syntax, but his scripted speeches were often no better.

TOWERS OF BABBLE.

As if it weren't bad enough that the Ivory Tower gives us lugubrious nouns, ludicrous adjectives, and pompous prepositional pileups, think of the *sentences* churned out by academics. *Philosophy and Literature,* a journal published by the Johns Hopkins University Press, runs an annual contest for the ugliest, most stylistically awful sentence to come out of scholarly books and articles. Winners include untameable sentences like this one, by Stephen T. Tyman in *The Philosophy of Paul Ricoeur:*

With the last gasp of Romanticism, the quelling of its florid uprising against the vapid formalism of one strain of the Enlightenment, the dimming of its yearning for the imagined grandeur of the archaic, and the dashing of

its too sanguine hopes for a revitalised, fulfilled
humanity, the horror of its more lasting, more Gothic
legacy has settled in, distributed and diffused enough, to
be sure, that lugubriousness is recognisable only as
languor, or as a certain sardonic laconicism disguising
itself in a new sanctification of the destructive instincts,
a new genius for displacing cultural reifications in the
interminable shell game of the analysis of the human
psyche, where nothing remains sacred.

That's not a stream of thought; it's a bunch of big words
thrown into an Osterizer.

Carnal Pleasures

It takes great writers to carry off sentences that seem to
have no end. The chief wordsmith at Bonny Doon Vineyards, Randall Grahm, wrote a whopper for the label of a
wine named Old Telegram:

> BROODING DEPTH YES MOUTHFUL LEGS YES
> DAZZLING BREADTH STAGGERING LENGTH
> YES SUBLIME ROBUST VIRILE UNCTUOUS
> HARMONIOUS COMPLETE YES POWERFUL
> FINISH GOES ON FOREVER YES DON'T STOP.

The Bonny Doon run-on is not a Bush-league goof, but
rather a spoof: the description parodies the stream-of-
consciousness ending of *Ulysses*.

Speaking of *Ulysses*, James Joyce's punctuationless
paragraphs and endless sentences worked because of his
superior command of cadence. Phrases and clauses did
their work—even without commas—and words them-

selves ("and," "O," "yes") became Joyce's punctuation. The Irish novelist's ear was impeccable; it's far easier to spoof him than to best him. So we'll let Joyce, in the ending of *Ulysses,* give us the last word on sentences:

. . . and the night we missed the boat at Algeciras the watchman going about serene with his lamp and O that awful deepdown torrent O and the sea the sea crimson sometimes like fire and the glorious sunsets and the figtrees in the Alameda gardens yes and all the queer little streets and pink and blue and yellow houses and the rosegardens and the jessamine and geraniums and cactuses and Gibraltar as a girl where I was a Flower of the mountain yes when I put the rose in my hair like the Andalusian girls used or shall I wear a red yes and how he kissed me under the Moorish wall and I thought well as well him as another and then I asked him with my eyes to ask again yes and then he asked me would I yes to say yes my mountain flower and first I put my arms around him yes and drew him down to me so he could feel my breasts all perfume yes and his heart was going like mad and yes I said yes I will Yes.

PART 3

Whed you get your grammar down, when you simplify your syntax, you are halfway to mastering the craft of writing. You have achieved what the critic Walter Pater called the "radical merits" of prose thought: "order, precision, directness."

But prose can be more than just ordered output. It can also be art, possessing all the qualities we associate with its more highfalutin cousin, poetry. Prose can have voice, lyricism, melody, and rhythm.

But how do you get there?

RELISH EVERY WORD.

Appreciate music in prose, and develop your ear for it. Devour novels. Cue up recordings of famous speeches. Fall in love with poetry. Go to the video store and check out all those Shakespeare movies. Read your writing aloud.

To paraphrase Ezra Pound slightly, don't imagine that the art of prose is any simpler than the art of music; spend as much time developing your craft as a pianist spends practicing scales. "Let the neophyte know assonance and alliteration, rhyme immediate and delayed, simple and polyphonic, as a musician would expect to know harmony and counterpoint," Pound argued in his 1913 essay, "A Few Don'ts."

Also, cultivate catholic tastes. Expand your literary horizons. If you are a lawyer, loll about

Music

in the laconic images of Chinese poetry. If you are a novelist prone to the prolix, study the staccato sentences of David Mamet. If you are a lit teacher, take up Tom Clancy. If you write a newsletter for an accounting firm, read *Salon*. If you are an advertising copy-writer, go for Gabriel García Márquez. Shake up your sensibilities. Discover the rut you're in, and climb out.

Learn to love other tongues. "Let the candidate fill his mind with the finest cadences he can discover, preferably in a foreign language," commanded Pound. "Saxon charms, He-bridean Folk Songs, the verse of Dante, and the lyrics of Shake-speare. . . . Dissociate the vocabulary from the cadence. . . . Dissect the lyrics of Goethe coldly into their component sound values, syllables long and short, stressed and unstressed, into vowels and consonants."

Sound a little highbrow? OK, then, listen to the nightly news on Univision, especially if *no hablas español.*

BE SIMPLE, BUT GO DEEP.

Every now and then, politicians become infatuated with "Plain English." Granted, using simple words, short sentences, and a user-friendly conversational style has its merits. Plain English beats the tufts of fuzz many bureaucrats let loose. But, much as we de-serve clarity from our public servants, we should hold our hired rhetoricians to a higher plane than "plain."

In his remarks closing the U.S. Senate's public hearings on the Iran-contra affair in 1987, Senator Daniel K. Inouye ventured be-yond Plain English. His oratory wasn't merely simple, it was deep:

> In describing their motives for riding roughshod over the constitu-
> tional restraints built into our form of government, Admiral
> Poindexter and Lt. Col. North use almost the identical words.
> "This is a dangerous world," they said. That, my fellow citizens, is
> an excuse for autocracy, not policy. Because no times were more
> dangerous than when our country was born, when revolution

was our midwife. Our system of government has withstood the tests and tensions of civil conflict, the depression and two world wars, times hardly less challenging than our own present. Indeed, as our greatest military leaders, such as Washington, Marshall, and Eisenhower, have recognized, our form of government is what gives us strength. It must be safeguarded, particularly when times are dangerous and the temptation to arrogant power is the greatest. Vigilance abroad does not require us to abandon our ideas of rule of law at home. On the contrary, without our principles and without our ideals we have little that is special or worthy to defend.

With an eloquence to suit the occasion, Inouye did not shrink from polysyllables *(restraints, autocracy, safeguarded, temptation, arrogant, vigilance)*, nor did he keep his sentences short. (He did, however, stick to straight syntax.) But what elevates Inouye's speech is its music: the sounds of the words ("autocracy, not policy," "tests and tensions"), the imagery ("revolution was our midwife"), and the cadences ("Vigilance abroad does not require us to abandon our ideas of rule of law at home").

When occasions call for eloquence, you need poetry, not Plain English.

TAKE RISKS.

Language offers us a surprising, savage terrain full of pockets and peaks. Despite this, English teachers still hew to Standard Written English as some vague paragon of virtue. Don't hew, too.

Eschew the standard. Americans have always inclined, wrote H. L. Mencken, "toward a directness of statement which, at its greatest, lacks restraint and urbanity altogether, and toward a hospitality which often admits novelties for the mere sake of their novelty, and is quite uncritical of the difference between a genuine improvement in succinctness and clarity, and mere extravagant raciness." Maybe being "quite uncritical" is a little too lax, but what's wrong with appreciating "extravagant raciness"?

Extravagant raciness isn't only the province of American English. David Dabydeen, a prize-winning British poet, writes verse in what he calls the "angry, crude, energetic" creole of his native West Indies. In an essay titled "On Not Being Milton: Nigger Talk in England Today," Dabydeen argues that contemporary English poetry is afflicted with "the disease of gentility." Dabydeen champions the work of poets like John Agard, whose "Listen Mr. Oxford Don" thumbs its nose at the very notion of "correct" English:

> Dem accuse me of assault
> on de Oxford dictionary/ . . .
> I slashing suffix in self-defense
> I bashing future with present tense
> and if necessary
>
> I making de Queen's English accessory / to my offence

The patois of British blacks, Dabydeen writes, is like Caliban "tearing up the pages of Prospero's magic book and repasting it in his own order, by his own method, and for his own purpose." And what a purpose it is.

Whether West Indian creole, the idioms of the Deep South, or Lake Wobegonics, nonstandard English remembers the strong link between the spoken and the written, a link getting even stronger in this age of email. Slang, vernacular, the colloquial—all have a place in literary writing. Without abandoning prose with a capital *P,* we can build the musicality of our writing by listening to the street.

Don't settle for the safe. Find language that conjures up fresh images and lets its cadences rise and fall and refuse to go flat.

SEEK BEAUTY.

Some language types mistakenly diss our mother tongue, calling it less musical than those exotic languages—Italian, perhaps, or Tahitian—that drip with mellifluous vowels. But English, rooted in an Anglo-Saxon full of crisp consonants and punchy words, makes its own kind of music.

The Spanish-born, Paris- and Oxford-educated writer Salvador de Madariaga waxed ecstatic about the beauty and "fidelity" of English words in 1928: "They are marvellous, those English mono-syllables. Their fidelity is so perfect that one is tempted to think English words are the right and proper names which acts are meant to have, and all other words are pitiable failures. How could one improve upon *splash, smash, ooze, shriek, slush, glide, squeak, coo?* Is not the word *sweet* a kiss in itself, and what could suggest a more peremptory obstacle than *stop?*"

If you want to wallow, like de Madariaga, in the simple beauty of English, pick up the book of Psalms and read them out loud. Memorize the Gettysburg Address and linger on the speeches in the anthology *Lend Me Your Ears.* Refresh yourself with some Walt Whitman, some Zora Neale Hurston, some William Carlos Williams. Or listen to the lyrics of Cole Porter.

FIND THE RIGHT PITCH.

There is a story of a super-respectful official of the Raj who found his British superior laboriously correcting a letter he had written to a fellow Indian: "Your honour puts yourself to much trouble cor-recting my English and doubtless the final letter will be much better literature," the corrected one commented. "But it will go from me Mukherji to him Bannerji, and he Bannerji will understand it a great deal better as I Mukherji write it than as your honour corrects it."

He, Mukherji, got it—better than his boss: Voice gives writing validity.

And voice is especially valuable in an era when information trumps insight, where the flow of data exceeds our capacity to distill—to make it ours and to make it matter. The word processor, the copier, the optical scanner, the fax—all these machines make it easy to spew and propagate words without choosing them carefully.

In a world of TV anchors who deliver the news in banal and accentless bursts, at a time when "branding" beats originality and when you can't escape mindless—and endless—"Just Do It" commercials, we urgently long for writing that is original, passionate, and personal. We search for writers whose voices are distinct and recognizable. We celebrate prose that is musical.

Bones

Voice is the *je ne sais quoi* of spirited writing. It separates brochures and brilliance, memo and memoir, a ship's log and *The Old Man and the Sea*. The best writers stamp prose with their own distinctive personality; their timbre and tone are as recognizable as their voices on the phone. To cultivate voice, you must listen for the music of language—the vernacular, the syntactic tics, the cadences.

Strong voice is conversational: The writer leaves us with a sense that we are *listening* to a skilled raconteur rather than *passing our eyes* over ink on paper. This involves more than just following the simplistic command "Write the way you talk": voice involves more than accurate transcription. The true zing of conversation comes from attentive listening and painstaking revision.

Conversation was *the* critical element in Robert Frost's poetry, and it formed the basis of a theory of language he applied to both poetry and prose. Frost scholar Peter J. Stanlis remarks that for the New England poet, good writing was synonymous with good conversation. "I was after poetry that talked," Frost once said. An essay by Stanlis in *Modern Age* quarterly describes the evolution of Frost's effort to convert colloquial speech into art and the poet's belief that language allows a "correspondence" between writer and reader. Stanlis quotes Frost:

> If my poems were talking poems—if to read them you heard a voice—that would be to my liking! . . . Whenever I write a line it is because that line has already been spoken clearly by a voice within my mind, an audible voice.
>
>   I have unconsciously tried to do just what Chaucer did when the language was young and untried and virile. I have sought only those words I had met up with as a boy in New Hampshire, working on farms during the summer vacations. I listened to the men with whom I worked. . . . When I started to carry their conversation over into poetry, I could hear their voices, and the sound posture differentiated between one and the other.

Prose stylists need to listen for that "audible voice" within. It gives prose strength, the sense of a person speaking naturally. But a real person, not a type or stereotype. Strong voice comes when contemporary writers play with the full palette available to them: literary English (formally correct, rich in vocabulary, complex in sentence structure, and, at its best, flowing with stately grace); conversational English (ranging from high-minded palaver to lowbrow banter); jargon (the professional patois of doctors, lawyers, and corporate chiefs); and colloquial, idiomatic English (the language of the street, whether Spanglish, Pidgin English, or Valley Girl chat).

Prose with a strong voice might reflect a narrator or central characters who are colorful. The voice of Limerick-born Frank McCourt comes to mind. His memoir, *Angela's Ashes,* brims with Irish authenticity:

There may be a lack of tea or bread in the house but Mam and Dad always manage to get the fags, the Wild Woodbines. They have to have the Woodbines in the morning and anytime they drink tea. They tell us every day we should never smoke, it's bad for your lungs, it's bad for your chest, it stunts your growth, and they sit by the fire puffing away. Mam says, If 'tis a thing I ever see you with a fag in your gob I'll break your face. They tell us the cigarettes rot your teeth and you can see they're not lying. The teeth turn brown and black in their heads and fall out one by one. Dad says he has holes in his teeth big enough for a sparrow to raise a family.

Frank McCourt's strong voice is rooted in vocabulary true to his characters (*fags, 'tis, gob*) and in his ability to recapture the metaphors that spring from his father's lips as easily as songs about dying for Ireland.

At its most risky, voice swings, it swears, it swivels at the hip. But it can't be co-opted cavalierly. It must be true, *appropriate*. Every time you write, you are having a conversation with a silent partner, your reader. Respect this reader. You want to entice your audience into conversations, rather than shutting them out.

Flesh

"The pen must at length comply with the tongue," Samuel Johnson wrote in the preface to his dictionary, and among the writers of his time who mastered the art of unaffected conversation were the poet John Dryden and the parodist Jonathan Swift. Across the Atlantic and into the next century, the literary evangelist Walt Whitman was bent on developing a truly *American* voice, reflecting "the liberties and the brawn of These States." But it took Mark Twain to really limn the rhythms and vocabulary of American English, to write prose that was at once literary *and* colloquial. (T. S. Eliot ranked Twain with Dryden and Swift as "one of those rare writers who have brought their language up to date, and in so doing, 'purified the dialect of the tribe.' ")

In *Huckleberry Finn,* Twain zestily explored the new American vernacular, using what he called "the Missouri Negro dialect, the extremist form of the backwoods Southwestern dialect, the ordinary 'Pike County' dialect, and four modified varieties of this last." Elsewhere, Twain dabbled in "Injun-English," the slang of prospectors in California and Nevada, as well as "the vigorous new vernacular of the occidental plains and mountains." Here's a sample, from "The Celebrated Jumping Frog of Calaveras County":

> Well, thish-yer Smiley had rat-tarriers, and chicken cocks, and tomcats, and all them kind of things, till you

couldn't rest, and you couldn't fetch nothing for him to bet on but he'd match you. He ketched a frog one day, and took him home, and said he cal'lated to educate him; and so he never done nothing for three months but set in his back yard and learn that frog to jump. And you bet you he *did* learn him, too. He'd give him a little punch behind, and the next minute you'd see that frog whirling in the air like a doughnut—see him turn one summerset, or maybe a couple, if he got a good start, and come down flat-footed and all right, like a cat. He got him up so in the matter of ketching flies, and kep' him in practice so constant, that he'd nail a fly every time as fur as he could see him. Smiley said all a frog wanted was education, and he could do 'most anything—and I believe him.

Writing does not have to be fiction to be full of voice. Nor does the writer have to be as flamboyant as Mark Twain. In fact, some of the strongest prose stylists of this century—E. B. White, James Thurber, Lewis Thomas— write in such understated voices that their work seems downright uncrafted. Now *that's* illusion of the highest order. Writing in a natural conversational voice takes some serious work.

EMAIL—THAT NEW LITERARY FORM—brims with voice. A cross between speaking and writing, it involves informal, conversational communication spiced by immediacy and urgency. Partly because it's *not* face to face, partly because we use it in a spontaneous way, email is closer to phone conversations than to sober memos and magazine articles. It is chatty, colloquial, intimate. It is composed not in long hours of reflection and revision but in blunt bursts and on-the-fly fragments. Since the "rules" of writing never took hold in cyberspace, email tends to the raw, the typo-laden, the impassioned, and the unpolished.

The best online prose, like the best email, is unpretentious, personal, and full of voice. When Phil Agre, the publisher of Red Rock Eater, asked members of his mailing list to describe their immediate physical surroundings, he elicited a series of vignettes that were published online under the heading "Where I Sit." The following two posts, from John Farrell—co-author of *Managers as Facilitators* <www.facilitator.org>—and Sara Miles, a writer living in San Francisco, convey a clear sense of the person before the screen.

Date: Mon, 12 Aug 1996 05:21:47 -0500
From: iq@usinternet.com (John Farrell)

I lease office space in a beautiful old building in downtown Minneapolis. I can see Nicollet Mall from my second-story office window. Pictures of my family are scattered throughout my office. My little girl's artwork covers part of two walls. My computer sits on the skinny part of the "L" on my desk. There are two large "flip-chart" papers covered with the outline of a course (in black, blue, green and red marker) I and a colleague are teaching later this week. My desk is covered with papers and my "project box" is stuffed full of work to be done for various clients.

I have four unopened "TRY AMERICA ONLINE FREE!" diskette packages sitting on my little computer speakers. I think I'll throw them away.

There, that feels better.

Date: Mon, 12 Aug 1996 12:00:17 -0700 (PDT)

From: Sara Miles <smiles@igc.apc.org>

I work in a big, sunlit room the color of roses. On the walls
are pressed flowers my great-great-grandfather, a Transcendentalist, picked a hundred years ago and labelled in his spi-
dery hand: "Convovolus Sepium, Hedge Bindweed, June 19,
'86." On my desk are piles of paper from current projects:
the manuscript of an anthology I'm editing on gay and les-
bian sexual cultures for NYU Press; a piece I'm writing for
HotWired on interactive gaming; an essay on electronic
cash, and a manuscript about the prophetic tradition in law.
There's an old White House press pass on a metal chain that
my daughter's been playing with, a story I clipped from the
business section of the New York Times, a gorgeous photo
of my girlfriend laughing, six pens, two pencils, a pair of scis-
sors, and a PowerBook165 with the slowest modem in the
world. My windows look out on the Cesar Chavez Elemen-
tary School, a bright blue building covered in murals; there's
a sign in Spanish taped to the front door directing!! parents
to the Wednesday night computer class. I can see the drug
dealer from down the block walking his Rottweiler, Mrs.
Mayzyk sweeping her stairs, and the guys on the corner fix-
ing their car. It's not that I don't care about the future, but
the tangle of many pasts and the gravity and beauty of the
undeniable present tend to focus my attention at this desk.

John Farrell's description is straightforward and simple, but it is far from static. When he thinks out loud—or,
rather, online—"I'll think I'll throw them away," and then
in the next beat says "There, that feels better," we feel as

though we are sitting next to him, in real time. That's voice! Our strong sense of Miles comes partly through the detail she gives us, about her Transcendentalist grandfather, her girlfriend laughing, and Mrs. Mayzyk sweeping her stairs. But it also comes through the immediacy of *I*, the rhythm of the telling, the inclusion of the double ! !s.

FICTION WRITERS — AND A FEW skillful journalists—go beyond just "writing as they talk," peppering their prose with the voices of their characters. Among the young contemporary prose stylists who play with the poetry of nonstandard English is Junot Díaz, who shifts from the barrios of the Caribbean to the New Jersey 'hood. Díaz, born in the Dominican Republic, plies his own brand of language in short stories like "The Sun, the Moon, the Stars":

> I don't even want to tell you where we're at. We're in Casa de Campo. The Resort That Shame Forgot. The average asshole would love this place. It's the largest, wealthiest resort on the Island, which means it's a goddam fortress, walled away from everybody else. *Guachimanes* and peacocks and ambitious topiaries everywhere. Advertises itself in the States as its own country, and it might as well be. Has its own airport, thirty-six holes of golf, beaches so white they ache to be trampled, and the only Island Dominicans you're guaranteed to see are either caked up or changing your sheets. Let's just say my *abuelo* has never been here, and neither has yours. This is where the Garcías and the Colóns come to relax after a long month of oppressing the masses, where the *tutumpotes* can trade tips with their colleagues from abroad. Chill here too long and you'll be sure to have your ghetto pass revoked, no questions asked. . . .

The sun is blazing and the blue of the ocean is an over-load on the brain. Casa de Campo has got beaches the way the rest of the island has problems. These, though, have no merengue, no little kids, nobody trying to sell you *chicharrones,* and there's a massive melanin deficit in evidence. Every fifty feet there's at least one Eurofuck beached out on a towel like some scary pale monster that the sea's vomited up. They look like philosophy professors, like budget Foucaults, and too many of them are in the company of a dark-assed Dominican girl. I mean it, these girls can't be no more than sixteen, look *puro ingenio* to me. You can tell by their inability to communicate that these two didn't meet back in their Left Bank days.

Díaz's startling narrative voice emerges first out of vocabulary that embraces Spanish words *(tutumpotes)* and slang *(caked up* and *Chill here)* and profane inventions *(Eurofuck)*. It also plays with sentence fragments ("The Resort That Shame Forgot") and sorry syntax ("these girls can't be no more than sixteen") to reflect the way characters really talk. Díaz also adopts an informal point of view ("Let's just say my *abuelo* has never been here, and neither has yours") and gets in some highbrow-lowbrow disses ("beaches so white they ache to be trampled" and "They look like philosophy professors, like budget Foucaults"). Sum total: distinctive voice.

Cardinal Sins

WRITING OFF KEY.

Using the wrong voice and tone for the occasion and the audience is a cardinal sin. "Choosing a tone requires *tact,"* write the poet Donald Hall and the critic Sven Birkerts in *Writing Well.* "Audience determines tone; tone is the writer's choice of a connection with the reader. The doctor delivering a paper to his colleagues writes a formal and scientifically exact prose; the same person, contributing to an alumni newsletter, writes a relaxed and conversational prose."

Formal, though, does not have to mean stiff. A formal tone—often created by too much puffed-up vocabulary—can be off-putting. Watch for too many nouns ending in *-tion,* too many verbs ending in *-ize,* too many adjectives ending in *-wide.* (Go back to chapters 1–8 for a refresher on which words to avoid.) Stay away from nonsense pileups of nouns ("interactive facilitated sessions with direct feedback and reinforcement materials") or cadences that, instead of rolling along, bump and grind like an avalanche of concrete blocks ("we have nonviolent and nonage-identified behavior issues").

Stiff, overly formal, voiceless prose is so endemic in academia that some professors make a sport out of lampooning each other's excesses. The judges of an academics' "Bad Writing" contest sponsored by the journal *Philosophy and Literature* declared Fredric Jameson a "winner": they said reading the comp lit professor's own lit was like "swimming through cold porridge." The Duke University doc does have a respectable academic following, the judges noted, but check out the voiceless mouthful that opens his *Signatures of the Visible:*

> The visual is *essentially* pornographic, which is to say
> that it has its end in rapt, mindless fascination; thinking
> about its attributes becomes an adjunct to that, if it is
> unwilling to betray its object; while the most austere
> films necessarily draw their energy from the attempt to

repress their own excess (rather than from the more
thankless effort to discipline the viewer).

Unfortunately, too many students adopt the style of
their professors. Even when formality is appropriate,
don't drone like a robot. In a cover letter for a job, be po-
lite, but remember it's *you* an employer wants to know
about, not a boilerplate applicant. Be yourself. Whether
you're crafting résumés or reportage, try mixing formal
and informal diction. Go for an occasional surprise.

THE FALSE FIRST PERSON.

Some novice writers mistake the first-person pronoun *I*
for voice. While personal narrative does usually rely on
strong voice for success, not all narratives need be personal, and many become muddied by the ill-considered
use of the first person. Some writing is way too up-close-
and-personal for its own good.

In "Africa Rising," a report on that continent that ran
in *Wired* magazine, the word *I* appears 235 times, the
word *Africa* a mere 78. John Perry Barlow's "report" is too
too solipsistic—it is more about him than about Africa:

> I am not ready. Indeed, I am afraid, and fear is not a
> common affliction of mine. I'm not afraid of being killed,
> nor of any of the projected African perils that have my loved
> ones so spooked. I figure their horrific images are mostly
> mediamagoria. I think I'm afraid of becoming someone
> else, which is, I suppose, a sort of death. I feel as if I am
> setting out on quest for the next version of myself, much as
> I did nine years ago when I closed down my first life and
> went venturing off to Silicon Valley. Now I'm due for a new
> mission, but it's an odyssey I don't know how to prepare for.

The line between self-expression and self-indulgence can be hard to discern. Test every temptation to use *I*, and try other devices if you care about voice.

PHONEY TONES.

In *Simple and Direct,* Jacques Barzun describes what he calls the "pseudo-Hemingway" tone: writing that creates an impression of headlong speed punctuated by frequent shocks, full of fragments and crime-story clichés. One student of Barzun's nailed the "pseudo-Hemingway" tone in this parody:

> I saw her first. She was tall, blond. She looked good. She smiled. I stepped back. She came up close. She smelled good. She put her arms around me. I kissed her. She raised an eyebrow. I nodded. We were engaged.

Remember, "being earnest" does *not* mean mimicking Hemingway.

Carnal Pleasures

If the writer is skilled enough, voice captures the syntax and spirit of the subject. Whether in fiction or nonfiction, the narrator can take on the personality of the characters. Such play-acting was one of the major innovations of the New Journalism. Tom Wolfe, in his 1973 essay on that movement, wrote about writers picking up voice as a defense against "a century-old British tradition in which it was understood that the narrator shall assume a calm, cultivated and, in fact, genteel voice. The idea was that the narrator's own voice should be like the off-white or putty-colored walls that Syrie Maugham popularized in interior decoration . . . a 'neutral background' against which bits of color would stand out. . . . By the early 1960s understatement had become an absolute pall." Continuing, Wolfe wrote that that pale beige tone became a signal to readers "that a well-known bore was here again, 'the journalist,' a pedestrian mind, a phlegmatic spirit, a faded personality, and there was no way to get rid of the pallid little troll, short of ceasing to read."

So Wolfe et alia ditched Standard Written English. In a story about Junior Johnson, a stock-car racer from Ingle Hollow, North Carolina, who learned to drive by running moonshine whiskey, Wolfe adopts Johnson's Ingle Hollow lingo:

> Working mash wouldn't wait for a man. It started coming to a head when it got ready to and a man had to be there to take it off, out there in the woods, in the brush, in the brambles, in the muck, in the snow. Wouldn't it have been something if you could have just set it all up inside a good old shed with a corrugated metal roof and order those parts like you want them and not have to smuggle all that copper and all that sugar and all that everything out here in the woods and be a coppersmith and a plumber and a cooper and a carpenter and a pack horse and every other goddamned thing God ever saw in the world, all at once. And live decent hours. . . .

It's not just literary journalists who want to be hip to voice. Bonny Doon Vineyards elevates PR to pure wit by parodying the voice of academia. For a wine called "Critique of Pure Riesling," the copy on the wine label reflects the pompous, inflated style of philosophical drivel:

Kant? Or won't? The philosophical imbiber asks himself, "What ought I to consume with Asian cuisine, with charcuterie or while simply enjoying a moment of repose and reflection?" One might argue categorically the imperative of experiencing this potation directly, as a wein-an-sich, eschewing any a priori conception of the wine's wineness whilst remaining particularly vigilant of the dominant and pernicious, transcendental chardo-centric paradigm. Harvested omnino from the vintage MCMXCVI, this dry Riesling represents the *summun bonum* of impeccable vineyards in the great state of Washington.

Bones

The lyre—the small harp of the ancient Greeks—haunts the term *lyricism,* harking back to the days when narratives were accompanied by strings. And today, the ultimate "lyrical" writing still happens when poets put words to song.

The best Country Western lyricists, like Hank Williams, use words to mainline emotions like lust, love, and lonesomeness:

> Hear that lonesome whippoorwill
> He sounds too blue to fly
> The midnight train is whining low
> I'm so lonesome I could cry
>
> Did you ever see the night so long
> When time goes crawling by
> The moon just went behind a cloud
> To hide her face and cry

Williams's lyricism springs mostly from vivid descriptions that work on our reservoir of feelings and associations. In the first stanza, he does it through adjectives and imagery: the lonesome whippoorwill, the midnight train. In the second he relies on metaphor, turning Time into a crawling animal. He endows the whippoorwill and the moon with human feelings, just in case we don't make the connections.

Prose can be as lyrical as Country

Lyricism

Western croons, if you work your words so that they convey deep emotions and direct thoughts. Let your imagination leap and your words sing. Lyricism springs from connotation, imagery, and metaphor:

- Connotation seeks felicitous words with layers of meaning and resonances beyond the concrete. One reason many Christians cling sentimentally to the King James Bible is the poetry in its words. In phrases like "Neither cast ye your pearls before swine" the words have connotations that were lost in the New English Bible of 1961, with its "Do not feed your pearls to pigs." "Feed" in the modern version cannot even imagine the nuances of "cast," and "pig" trades the suggestion of evil and moral depravity of "swine" for the generic term for the barnyard animal.
- Imagery taps deep feelings through visual descriptions. Images are our link to memory, to the imagination, to the collective unconscious. Hank Williams's moon slipping behind a cloud is an image every listener recognizes. When M. F. K. Fisher describes a person as a "trembling daffodil," she uses imagery to convey psychology.
- Metaphor—the comparison of disparate things—surprises us, revealing deeper truths and providing unexpected insights. (We are using metaphor as a catchall term including simile, symbol, and analogy.)

When William Finnegan describes the February surf at Ocean Beach, he uses metaphor: "The first wall of sandy, grumbling white water felt like a barrel of gritty ice cubes poured down my back."

Metaphor might also be expressed more implicitly. Finnegan calls offshore winds, those that blow from land to sea, "the wonder drug of surfing" and compares them to a "sculptor's blade":

Because they cross so little water before they reach the waves, they create no troublesome chop, and because they strike the waves from the front they don't force the waves to topple prematurely and haphazardly, the way onshores do, letting the power of a wave rise, gather, and concentrate in the crest before it can overcome the wind's resistance. . . . The sum effect of offshore winds is greater than any of its parts. On a good day, their sculptor's blade, meticulous and invisible, seems to drench whole coastlines in grace.

Finnegan doesn't need metaphor to precisely describe the effect of offshore winds; he needs it to put us there, on the beach. To give us a visceral response—the rush of seeing the whole coastline drenched in grace.

More on metaphor.

Imagery relies upon the re-creation in words of a concrete visual image. An image means only what it literally is: a marigold, an Appaloosa, a black Underwood typewriter.

Metaphor and **simile** involve comparisons between unlike things. In simile the comparison is expressed through words such as *like, as, than, similar to*, and *resembles* ("louder than a bomb"). In metaphor the comparison is expressed when a figurative term is substituted for a literal term. When a man's buddies refer to his Marla Maples–lookalike spouse as a "trophy wife" they're not just jealous, they are masters of metaphor. When a too-busy trial lawyer tells her hubby she doesn't "have the bandwidth" to plan dinner, her metaphor says: "I am *not* a trophy wife."

Symbol refers to the use of one thing to mean much more than what it is. A light bulb is a trite symbol for an idea. "The Road Not Taken" is a poetic symbol for the consequences of choice.

Analogy is a whole web of metaphors in which a likeness is drawn though parallel structure, like explaining a complicated war in terms of a simple football game.

Flesh

In prose, a single word is often enough to kick imagery and metaphor into gear. When a reporter slips an image into a lede, he or she takes the story beyond the Who What When Where, into the How and the Why. In 1989, J. Michael Kennedy and Bob Baker conveyed the drama and horror of a plane crash near Sioux City through vivid imagery:

> A crippled United Airlines DC-10 crashed a half-mile short of a runway while trying to make an emergency landing Wednesday afternoon, bursting into a cart-wheeling fireball that broke into what one eyewitness described as "15,000 pieces."

That "cartwheeling fireball," together with the snapshot of "15,000 pieces," made the *L.A. Times* opening stand out from the hundreds of ledes printed across the country about the disaster in an Iowa cornfield.

Metaphor might also be a swift phrase or a deft stroke that zeroes in on a character or a subject. Novelist James Salter used "the silence of a folded flag" to describe the quiet of an afternoon in provincial France. *Newsweek*'s Jack Kroll, in praising the film *1984,* added that the director "found a new color spectrum, the bleached-out rainbow of hopelessness." Henry Louis Gates, Jr., used a knot of comparisons to convey basketball legend Michael Jordan as an archetype: "The man is both hulking and suave, and it's easy to see why he has become a totem of black masculinity; he makes Bill Cosby look like Uncle Ben." Later in the same *New Yorker* profile, Gates gives an account of Jordan's contentious contract negotiations with Chicago Bulls general manager Jerry

Reinsdorf: "Jordan, considered strictly as an athlete, is the Second Coming, and Reinsdorf, considered strictly as a mogul, is a second-rater. It's as if Pat Robertson were making Jesus punch a time card."

LYRICAL WRITING, LIKE ALL WRITING, still depends on concrete images and strong detail. But the occasional metaphor makes descriptive passages sail, as in this opening of a spring essay by Ian Frazier called "Stuck in Trees":

> This is the season of plastic bags stuck in trees. Stray shopping bags—many of them white, with handles, perhaps from a deli or a fruit-and-vegetable store originally—roll along the streets, fill with air, levitate like disembodied undershirts, fly, snag by their handles in the branches. Trees wave them in the breeze. They luff and whirr like spinnakers and twist into knots. Daniel, a guy who works at the Brooklyn Botanic Garden, was removing a plastic bag from a Japanese flowering cherry tree at the Eastern Parkway entrance with a leaf rake as I walked by. He held the rake above him at arm's length and snatched at the bag with the tines. It took him a while; finally, he pulled the bag down and squashed it into a ball in his hand. I asked if I could see it. Its blue logo read, "MARTIN PAINT . . . 'It Ain't Just Paint.' "

Frazier turns litter into kites and spinnakers and spectres. And he does his metaphor just right: he keeps his similes simple and ties them to concrete images and literal language. Don't overdo it.

Virginia Woolf casts an exquisite metaphor in her

essay "A Room of One's Own." Based upon two papers that Woolf read to the Arts Society at Newnham and the Odtaa at Girton, the 1928 essay addressed the complicated issue of "women and fiction." Woolf writes that she "sat down on the banks of a river and began to wonder what the words meant":

> Here I was then . . . sitting on the banks of a river a week or two ago in fine October weather, lost in thought. . . . To the right and left bushes of some sort, golden and crimson, glowed with the colour, even it seemed burnt with the heat, of fire. On the further bank the willows wept in perpetual lamentation, their hair about their shoulders. The river reflected whatever it chose of sky and bridge and burning tree, and when the undergraduate had oared his boat through the reflections they closed again, completely, as if he had never been. There one might have sat the clock round lost in thought. Thought—to call it by a prouder name than it deserved—had let its line down into the stream. It swayed minute after minute, hither and thither among the reflections and the weeds, letting the water lift it and sink it, until—you know the little tug—the sudden conglomeration of an idea at the end of one's line: and then the cautious hauling of it in, and the careful laying of it out. Alas, laid on the grass how small, how insignificant this thought of mine looked; the sort of fish that a good fisherman puts back into the water so that it may grow fatter and be one day worth cooking and eating.

Woolf extends her metaphor: an idea begins as a fish gently tugging at the end of the line, then becomes prey—something with which the thinker toys—then shifts yet again—to a disappointment, or perhaps a promise of fatter fish to come.

Vladimir Nabokov, too, was a master of applying poetic devices in prose. In *Pnin*, he lets loose a brilliant metaphor in a paragraph in which a middle-aged professor returns from the dentist, contemplating the psychological effect of a new set of dentures:

> A warm flow of pain was gradually replacing the ice and wood of the anesthetic in his thawing, still half-dead, abominably martyred mouth. After that, during a few days he was in mourning for an intimate part of himself. It surprised him to realize how fond he had been of his teeth. His tongue, a fat sleek seal, used to flop and slide so happily among the familiar rocks, checking the contours of a battered but still secure kingdom, plunging from cave to cove, climbing this jag, puzzling that notch, finding a shred of sweet seaweed in the same old cleft; but now not a landmark remained, and all there existed was a great dark wound, a terra incognita of gums which dread and disgust forbade one to investigate. And when the plates were thrust in, it was like a poor fossil skull being fitted with the grinning jaws of a perfect stranger.

It takes true imagination to turn a tongue into a fat sleek seal on the familiar rocks.

Cardinal Sins

TIN-EAR-ICAL.

Sometimes writers stretching for the lyrical founder on infelicities. They may come up with combinations that just don't jibe, like a description of a cybergang member whose eyes were "black as blueberries." (Since when are blueberries black?) When it comes to bad metaphors, the eyes have it. David Mamet in *Make Believe Town*, mocks screenwriters who gush, "she has a pair of eyes that makes you think of olives in a plate of milk." Bet you wouldn't want to *taste* a combo of olives and milk. Who would want to behold it?

Sometimes writers paste adjectives onto metaphors without thinking through the concomitant image. Stop and use some brain cells before resorting to a phrase like "the biggest bottleneck." How can a bottleneck be gaping? "Most troublesome," maybe. A media critic once described Microsoft's excitable chief technology officer Nathan Myhrvold as "speaking at the hypertext speed of the information revolution." Hypertext speed? Since when is hypertext—a system of coding text that links electronic documents with each other—*speedy*? A music critic for the *Wilmington News Journal* once heralded "the synergistic combination of the European style with the Russian melodic fertilizer which Tchaikovsky managed to spread across the orchestral field."

Now that's a tin ear.

DEAD METAPHORS.

Metaphors must be original, invented by the writer for the story at hand. A metaphor has the shelf life of a fresh vegetable. Too many of the metaphors in print are worn out, used up, hackneyed, empty. (Sorry for the redundancy, but, *really.*) George Orwell railed against dead metaphors like *toe the line, ride roughshod over, the hammer and the anvil,* and *no axe to grind,* pointing out that these are used unthinkingly by writers ignorant of the original vivid meaning. Such ignorance leads to common editing errors like "tow the line," which appears as often in print as the correct metaphor, refering to the athlete's practice of standing at the starting line before a race. Similarly, writers often imply that the anvil gets the worst of it, while, as Orwell scolds, "in real life it is always the anvil that breaks the hammer." A Silicon Valley venture capitalist once bragged about a partnership with a Parisian bank that "provides us with a European beachfront to help our US companies establish overseas partners." That guy needs a trip out of Silicon Valley—to Normandy?—to learn the difference between *beachfront* and *beachhead.*

Related to dead metaphors are clichés, combinations of words repeated so often in the same shape as to lose their force. Don't use combinations you have heard before. *Leave no stone unturned* was probably once a vivid way to describe painstaking effort, but now it seems limp and unimaginative. Beware of combos you can complete without thinking: *loud and clear, hue and cry, gild the lily, at the end of the day.*

And don't forget that buried in many a cliché is a metaphor. When a woman in Ireland came to President Clinton's defense in 1998, she argued: "If everybody's washing were hung out, there would be skeletons in all their closets." Think about that one.

MIXED METAPHORS.

Sometimes, in an attempt to be "creative" or to make prose more "exciting," writers confuse metaphors, as did the Irishwoman just quoted. The result is no more intelligible than scrambled radio signals.

When Boyle Roche, a member of the British Parliament in the nineteenth century, said, "Mr. Speaker, I smell a rat; I see him floating in the air; I hear him rustling in the breeze, but I shall nip him in the bud," he turned a rat into a bird into a broad leaf into a rose. Mixed Metaphor City.

A century later, Donald Nixon mangled an attempt to spin his brother's Watergate troubles: "It is unfortunate that it happened, but people are using it as a political football to bury my brother." How can a football dig a grave?

Ever on the lookout, the *New Yorker* collects slips of the pen from reputable newspapers all over the country, reprinting them under the heading "Block That Metaphor." Here are some picks:

It was an irresistible example of how public money and engineering genius could bring water to fire the engine of growth.

Like a giant sheet of carbon paper, South Florida spreads its familiar arms from baseball camp to baseball camp, catching time in a bottle and wrapping the Boys of Springtime in a velvet glove of comfortable déjà vu.

It was a battle to wrestle control of our classrooms away from the stranglehold of our current discipline system that allows students to fall into the ravine of failure by the thousands and knock over their peers along the way, like an endless, winding game of dominoes.

Don't let mixed metaphors get a stranglehold on you.

Carnal Pleasures

Lyricism doesn't have to be lofty: it can also be lowbrow. And funny. Politics has given us some metaphorical howls: Teddy Roosevelt accused his predecessor, William McKinley, of showing "all the backbone of a chocolate eclair," while Harold Ickes, Franklin Roosevelt's secretary of the interior, declared that Louisiana's Huey Long was "suffering from halitosis of the intellect." Then there was Secretary of State John Milton Hay's put-down of William Jennings Bryan as "a half-baked, glib little briefless jack leg lawyer."

Some writers cleverly subvert clichés, giving them a second life. When Diane Ackerman says of the rain forest, "the meek inherit nothing," she plays off the established phrase (the meek shall inherit the earth), making her own more striking. When *Washington Post* columnist Mark Shields, a regular metaphor machine, refers not to "smoking guns" in trumped-up investigations, but to "smoking water pistols," he creates a fresh metaphor out of a stale one. (If you still need convincing of Shields's rhetorical genius, try this metaphor, from April 1998: "We don't know if Ken Starr's going to come in with something that looks like double parking outside an orphanage on Christmas Eve, or like Lizzie Borden in drag." Or this one: "Everybody in Washington is an ethical eunuch and a moral leper who would steal a hot stove and go back for the smoke.")

Businesses often tweak clichés into clever names; think of all those hair salons: The Mane Attraction, About Faces, A Head of Our Times, and Shear Delight.

In Black English, invective riffs called "doing the dozens" kid others about intellectual deficiencies, physical shortcomings, or, especially, "your mamma." The rhythmic, often rhyming ripostes—also called "signifying" or "sounding"—demand an ability to ad lib in metaphor:

> Your mamma's so old she used to drive chariots to
>   high school.
> Your mamma's so mean you have to take two trains
>   and a bus to get on her good side.
> Your hair is so short it's like blowing dust off a jug.
> Your teeth are so yellow you put the sun out of business.
> You're so ugly you look like you been hit by a ugly stick.

The comedian Moms Mabley created a comic pile-on of metaphors in a sketch about the man her father forced her to marry when she was a teenager, the metaphor in each sentence topping the previous one:

> This O-L-D . . . puny . . . moanin' man. I mean an
> O-L-D man. Santa Claus looked like his son. He was
> older than his mother. . . . The nearest thing to death
> you've ever seen in your life. His shadow weighed more
> than he did. He got out of breath threading a needle.
> And U-G-L-Y! He was so ugly he hurt my feelings.

Bones

We think of melody as the collection of stirring notes that give a tune sweetness. In prose, melody translates into "euphony"—the acoustic effect of words combined to be pleasing and harmonious. Sweet words, euphonious phrasing, sensuous sentences—they affect us as much as meaning does.

Our earliest memories of storytelling—listening to nursery rhymes and fairy tales intoned in the familiar voices of a parent or grandparent—are sense memories. But our love of the sound of words may go further back; it may be our legacy from the days when all narrative was set to song.

The poetic devices available to the sound-conscious prose stylist include assonance, consonance, rhyme, alliteration, and onomatopoeia:

- Assonance repeats vowel sounds within words for effect (clean ... neat). Consonance lets the initial consonants of words echo with internal consonants (Sala-ma-sond). Dr. Seuss used both devices in this bit from *Yertle the Turtle and Other Stories*: "On the far-away Island of Sala-ma-Sond,/ Yertle the Turtle was king of the pond./ A nice little pond. It was clean. It was neat./ The water was warm. There was plenty to eat."

Melody

- Rhyme sets up an exact correspondence between the final syllable or syllables of words. Dr. Seuss loved rhyming names like Yertle the Turtle, and he loved rhyming titles—*Fox in Socks, The Cat in the Hat, Hop on Pop,* and *One Fish Two Fish Red Fish Blue Fish.*
- Alliteration refers to the repetition of the initial sound—one or more letters—of words in a phrase or sentence. Dr. Seuss's *Hooray for Diffendorfer Day* combines alliteration (and rhyme) in the title as well as in the text: "Miss Twining teaches tying knots/In neckerchiefs and noodles,/And how to tell chrysanthemums / From miniature poodles. / Miss Vining teaches all the ways/A pigeon may be peppered,/ And how to put a saddle / On a lizard or a leopard."
- Onomatopoeia may be Greek to you and me, but those twelve letters just mean "name-making." Pronounced "onna-matta-pee-ah," the term carries the idea that we can name a thing (or action) by imitating the sounds associated with it. With onomatopoeia, the sound of the word defines it. In *The Lorax,* "Grickle grass" is the name given by Dr. Seuss to the town's unruly tufts. Seuss characters like the Grinch and the Sneetches owe their names to onomatopoeia.

    Zap, zowie, bam, socko, wow, oof, wham, bing, and *grrr*—comics rely as heavily on onomatopoeia as does the kid-book doc. But words used in more serious contexts also rely on sound to convey sense. What could be a better word for a chattering, flighty, silly person than *flibbertigibbet?*

Onomato-meaning.

Some sounds have acquired a kind of meaning of their own. Consider these:

A short *i* often suggests smallness, as *little, slim, kid, chit, thin, skinny, imp, shrimp, piddling.*

An *fl-* at the start of a word can convey awkward or jerky movement, as in *flounder, flitter, flail, flutter, flipflop, flurry, fling.*

The hard consonants *b, d, c, k, q, p,* and *t*—especially when followed by *-ash*—represent explosive action, as in *bash, blast, crash, dash, gash, gnash, trash,* or suggest sudden noise: *pop, tap, quack, crackle.*

A closing *-sh* often suggests soft, rustling sounds or the flow of water: *swish, hush, flush, gush, rush, slush.*

The nasal *sn-* sound begins many words concerning the nose—or facial contortions: *sneeze, snort, sniff, sniffle, snuff, snarl, snivel, snout, sneer, snicker.*

Finally, *-in, -ing,* and *-ong* are used to convey a bell-like chime, as in *ring, ding, ding-dong, bong, gong, ping,* and Edgar Allan Poe's *tintinnabulation* ("The tintinnabulation that so musically wells / From the bells, bells, bells, bells. . . .").

Flesh

Dr. Seuss isn't the only children's writer to play to our love of sound. Think of the Lewis Carroll characters Tweedledee and Tweedledum. Then there's Rudyard Kipling's *Rikki-tikki-tavi,* whose title is all onomatopoeia, and whose opening lines make a medley of exotic sounds:

> This is the story of the great war that Rikki-tikki-tavi fought single-handed, through the bathroom of the big bungalow in Segowlee cantonment. Darzee, the tailor-bird, helped him, and Chuchundra, the musk-rat, who never comes out into the middle of the floor, but always creeps round by the wall, gave him advice, but Rikki-tikki-tavi did the real fighting.
>
> He was a mongoose, rather like a little cat in his fur and his tail, but quite like a weasel in his head and his habits. His eyes and the end of his restless nose were pink; he could scratch himself anywhere he pleased, with any leg, front or back, that he chose to use. He could fluff up his tail till it looked like a bottle-brush, and his war cry, as he scuttled through the long grass, was *"Rikk-tikk-tikki-tikki-tchk!"*

Like onomatopoeia, assonance and consonance are hardly children's play—even adults delight in word combos like *wishy-washy, mishmash, flimflam, riffraff,* and *chitchat.* The novelist Zora Neale Hurston opens *Their Eyes Were Watching God* with a sentence made memorable by assonance:

> Ships at a distance have every man's wish on board. For some they come in with the tide. For others they sail forever on the horizon, never out of sight, never landing until the Watcher turns his eyes away in resignation, his dreams mocked to death by Time. That is the life of men.

Much of Hurston's story, about an African-American woman's struggles to live free and fulfilled, is written in the dialect of her native Florida. An entire culture, a way of life, a worldview are packed into the simple song of Hurston's sentences:

> Course, talkin' don't amount tuh uh hill uh beans when yuh can't do nothin' else. And listenin' tuh dat kind uh talk is jus' lak openin' yo' mouth and lettin' de moon shine down yo' throat. It's uh known fact, Phoeby, you got tuh *go* there tuh *know* there. Yo' papa and yo' mama and nobody else can't tell yuh and show yuh. Two things everybody's got tuh do fuh theyselves. They got tuh go tuh God, and they got tuh find out about living fuh theyselves.

In the dialect, in the assonance in her heroine's speech, Hurston finds echoes in *to, a, you,* and *for.* In phrases like *yo papa and yo mama* she makes English as musical as Italian. And *got tuh go tuh God* uses assonance, consonance, and rhythm to make a phrase more musical than its "correct" equivalent, *must go to God.*

THE GREAT VERBAL IMPROVISATIONALIST Muhammad Ali sparred with assonance and consonance as much as he sparred with other heavyweights: assonance and consonance made his "Rumble in the Jungle" catch on as the descriptor for his fight with George Foreman in Zaire. Ali even worked rhyme into his riffs, as in this one, comparing his condition in that fall of 1974 to his condition in 1964 when, as an upstart in professional boxing, he fought Sonny Liston for the first time:

> I'm experienced now. Professional. Jaw's been broke. Been knocked down a couple times. I'm bad! I been

chopping trees. I done something new for this fight: I done rassled with a alligator. I done tussled with a whale. I done handcuffed lightning, throwed thunder in jail. That's bad!

In the consonance corner, Ali gives us *rassled* and *tussled*. As far as rhyme, who would have expected *whale* and *jail*?

We think of rhyme as the province of rappers (Ali's descendants), and find it infrequently in prose. Alliteration, on the other hand, is a more common device in all kinds of writing.

When Francis X. Clines of the *New York Times* called Matt Drudge the Internet's "Walter Winchell wannabe," he finds euphony in alliteration. And when Elaine Sciolino, also at the *Times,* profiled Richard Holbrooke after he was nominated as chief U.S. representative to the United Nations, sound repetition enlivened her lede about a very lively man:

> He is the energizer envoy, a nonstop negotiator who can outflank and outflatter, outbluff and outbully all the other players in the room.

Sciolino's "energizer envoy" is a nice word play as well as nice euphony.

THE MEMOIRIST HAS A LITTLE more linguistic berth than the journalist, especially if the family he is remembering is the Irish clan of Frank McCourt. In *Angela's Ashes,* McCourt captures the colloquial poetry of his father, and indeed of Ireland itself. McCourt, Sr., is driven to distraction by the questions of his son, raised in New

York and abruptly plopped down in the Irish countryside ("What are cows, Dad?"—"Cows are cows, son"—and "What are sheep, Dad?"). The elder McCourt finally erupts in sonorous harmony with the surrounding landscape:

Is there any end to your questions? Sheep are sheep, cows are cows, and that over there is a goat. A goat is a goat. The goat gives milk, the sheep gives wool, the cow gives everything. What else in God's name do you want to know?

And Malachy yelped with fright because Dad never talked like that, never spoke sharply to us. He might get us up in the middle of the night and make us promise to die for Ireland but he never barked like this. Malachy ran to Mam and she said, There, there, love, don't cry. Your father is just worn out carrying the twins and 'tis hard answering all those questions when you're carting twins through the world.

Dad set the twins on the road and held out his arms to Malachy. Now the twins started to cry and Malachy clung to Mam, sobbing. The cows mooed, the sheep maaed, the goats ehehed, the birds twittered in the trees, and the beep beep of a motor car cut through everything.

Cardinal Sins

We can twist poet Alexander Pope's diktat—"the sound must seem an echo of the sense"—into a caveat for the novice writer: When sound *doesn't* echo sense, the writing misfires.

HEAVYHANDEDNESS.

Techniques like rhyme and alliteration only work when they sound natural. They must be used like salt: sparingly. When Spiro Agnew denounced the Eastern liberal establishment as "nattering nabobs of negativism," he may have uttered a quotable phrase, but the alliteration seemed forced: No one talks that way, not even William Safire, who as White House speechwriter actually coined the phrase.

Of course, politicos easily fall prey to such follies. Perhaps the worst was Warren Harding's "not nostrums but normalcy, not revolution but restoration, not agitation but adjustment, not surgery but serenity, not the dramatic but the dispassionate, not experiment but equipoise."

Jesse Jackson defends his own rhyming phrases, saying that "Down with dope, up with hope" gets the point across more powerfully than "Off with narcotics, up with sobriety." He's got a point. But rhyme is best when it's surprising, not canned. You almost don't need Jackson around to complete his pat and predictable rhymes:

> If my mind can conceive it and my heart can believe it, then I can achieve it.

> I've not decided to run the race for 2000, but I'm going to set the pace for 2000.

Johnny Cochran's unforgettable phrase about the glove—"If it doesn't fit, you must acquit"—may have worked magic on the O.J. jury, but such rhetoric loses its fizz over time. Cochran's too-facile rhyme even inspired a *Seinfeld* parody—in the character of Kramer's lawyer, Jackie Chiles.

Carnal Pleasures

In *The God of Small Things,* the central character, an Indian girl named Rahel, negotiates between English and Malayalam, the native language that the adults in her family use to camouflage talk they don't want children to hear. The author, Arundhati Roy, plays with the *sounds* of English to comic and sometimes ominous effect, as in the moment when bad behavior during an airport meeting with a cousin earns Rahel and her twin brother, Estappen, the wrath of their mother, Ammu.

"Estappen!" Ammu said. And an angry feeling rose in her and stopped around her heart. A Far More Angry Than Necessary feeling. She felt somehow humiliated by this public revolt in her area of jurisdiction. She had wanted a smooth performance. A prize for her children in the Indo-British Behavior Competition.

Chacko said to Ammu in Malayalam, "Please. Later. Not now."

And Ammu's angry eyes on Estha said *All right. Later.*

And Later became a horrible, menacing, goose-bumpy word.

Lay. Ter.

Like a deep-sounding bell in a mossy well. Shivery, and furred. Like moth's feet.

The Play had gone bad. Like pickle in the monsoon.

Roy repeats "Lay. Ter."—as well as other sound improvisations ("A Wake A Live A Lert")—as her novel wends its way to a horrible, menacing, goose-bumpy end.

IF SOUNDS GIVE SENSUALITY TO PROSE, few have mastered their charms quite like Vladimir Nabokov. He was one novelist who knew how to turn sensuality into carnality. What could be more lascivious than these lines, which capture perfectly Humbert Humbert's obsession with the twelve-year-old Dolores Haze:

> Lolita, light of my life, fire of my loins. My sin, my soul. Lo-lee-ta: the tip of the tongue taking a trip of three steps down the palate to tap, at three, on the teeth. Lo. Lee. Ta.
>
> She was Lo, plain Lo, in the morning, standing four feet ten in one sock. She was Lola in slacks. She was Dolly at school. She was Dolores on the dotted line. But in my arms she was always Lolita.

Bones

We all know what rhythm means to poetry: it's those dear little dactyls, it's sure-footed Shakespeare, it's Wordsworth, "wándering lónely ás a clóud." But what does rhythm mean to prose? Do we just trade the "da-dah da-dah da-dah da-dah da-dah" of iambic pentameter for the banal "yaddah yaddah yaddah" of *Seinfeld*?

Whatever the genre, rhythm remains, essentially, *beat*—whether the 4/4 time of rhapsodies or the urgent tempos of rap. Rhythm is repetition, incantation, timing—perhaps comedic, perhaps dramatic. Rhythm is that deep-down sense of music that is as inborn as a heartbeat.

In most poetry, rhythm is reliable and identifiable. It's meter: the arrangement of sounds into set patterns of stressed and unstressed syllables, into longs and shorts. The basic metrical units are called "feet" and consist of at least two syllables; the most familiar feet are the iamb (◡╱), the trochee(╱◡), the anapest (◡◡╱), and the dactyl (╱◡◡).

As a prose stylist, you don't really need to memorize the names of metric feet, but you *do* need to appreciate their effect. Many believe that iambic pentameter—the five-foot lines of, say, Shakespearean sonnets—reflects the natural rhythm of English. "It fits with-

Put your best foot forward.

Metric feet can have up to five syllables (as does the dochmiac), but the most common have two or three:

Two-fers
iamb ⏑ /
trochee / ⏑
spondee / /
pyrrhic ⏑ ⏑

Three-fers
anapest ⏑ ⏑ /
dactyl / ⏑ ⏑
amphibrach ⏑ / ⏑
tribrach ⏑ ⏑ ⏑
bacchic / / ⏑
anti-bacchic ⏑ / /
cretic / ⏑ /
molossus / / /

Here's a little ditty, cited in Richard Lederer's *The Miracle of Language,* to help you get a handle on meter. Read it out loud:

The íambs gó from shórt to lóng.
Tróchees síng a márching sóng.
Dáctyls go dáncing as líght as a féather.
But the ánapest's dífferent, you sée, altogéther.

out stress, makes a full phrase, and leaves little breath at the end," writes the poet Mary Oliver. "It is, one might say, the norm."

But if meter is regular and recognizable in poetry, it's unpredictable in prose, varying from line to line with the flow of the words and the undercurrents of meaning. In prose—conversation, oration, and narration—rhythm is a matter of more subtle patterns, of longs and shorts, ins and outs, ups and downs.

Flesh

When we listen carefully to our writing and reshape its rhythms to our liking, prose can become music. "If we were more studious to write prose that could be read aloud with pleasure to the ear," wrote Sir Arthur Quiller-Couch in 1916, "we should be opening the pores to the ancient sap."

Speaking of the ancient sap, many of the most memorable phrases of the Bible, and especially the King James Bible of 1611, are so easily received, remembered, and recited *because* of their rhythms.

Many of those lines unfold in classic iambic and anapestic combinations, like this line from the King James Bible: "Render therefore unto Caesar the things which be Caesar's, and unto God the things which be God's." Even when that line was revised for the New English Bible the rhythms remained: "Pay Caesar what is due to Caesar, and pay God what is due to God."

Today's jargon-jamming Antipoet—deaf to the musical tradition of meter—might wreck such Biblical cadences with words like "Appropriate to Caesar the things that appertain to that chief executive." But don't go thinking metrical schemes are obsolete in our post-Biblical times. Check out this passage from *Make-Believe Town,* in which the playwright David Mamet recounts the cleansing poker player David "Chip" Brown took in a round of seven-card stud:

> Chip was in a game with a drunk. He held a pair of aces, and the drunk, after his fourth card, held four diamonds. Chip was an eleven-to-ten favorite to win the hand, but the drunk wouldn't go home. They raised each other thirty-six times, and the drunk caught his fifth diamond, and Chip retired broke.

There it is: the good old iamb ("he héld a páir of áces"; "Chíp retíred bróke").

Mamet insists that his characters prefer iambic pentameter and that he indulges them, if loosely: "None of us think about it, but we tend to speak that way," Mamet said in an interview on WHYY radio's *Fresh Air*. "I mean, most of the blues is written that way, too: 'I hate to see that evening sun go down.' That's iambic pentameter." Mamet further explained: "Look here, you know, I could sit and talk to you all day, but finally at the end, what would we say? That you and I had sat and that we spoke, but what we'd spoken of—what would that be? The tíme, the pláce, the rádio, the dáy—OK, so you see here I'm on my way to a sonnet that's all iambic pentameter."

RHYTHM IS NOT SIMPLY a matter of metrics. Winston Churchill's stirring rhetoric depended less on meter, per se, than on the rhythms of individual words. In his first statement to the House of Commons as prime minister, Churchill declared: "I have nothing to offer but blood, toil, tears, and sweat." His tough, muscular words announce his courage and resolve with the authority of a kettle drum.

Two decades later, John F. Kennedy charmed the press and the public with a speaking style of neat staccato bursts. When asked how he became a hero, Kennedy replied iambically, "It was involuntary. They sank my boat." With the help of speechwriters like Theodore Sorenson, Kennedy's sentences stretched out, his crisp diction complemented by lyrical cadences. President Kennedy's inaugural address in 1961 set up repeating rhythmic patterns that let words and phrases play off each other. Rhythms helped his phrases settle easily into our national consciousness:

If a free society cannot help the many who are poor, it cannot save the few who are rich.

Let us never negotiate out of fear, but let us never fear to negotiate.

And so, my fellow Americans, ask not what your country can do for you; ask what you can do for your country.

SPEECHES INTENDED TO MOVE audiences need to be ringing, strong, visceral. And they often achieve these effects—as Kennedy proved—through rhythmic repetition. But repetition in prose is not always so neat, especially in more subtle, less strident passages.

Ernest Hemingway often used seemingly simple word repetition. Sometimes it underscored his theme and verged on incantation (check out the use of *nada* in "A Clean Well-Lighted Place"). At other times, Hemingway built his repetitions into a distinctive pulse. Take, for example, the following description in *For Whom the Bell Tolls*. Robert Jordan, the American hero fighting in a guerrilla band against the Fascists in the Spanish Civil War, makes love with Maria:

> Then there was the smell of heather crushed and the
> roughness of the bent stalks under her head and the sun
> bright on her closed eyes . . . and for her everything was
> red, orange, god-red from the sun on the closed eyes. . . .
> For him it was a dark passage which led to nowhere,
> then to nowhere, then again to nowhere, once again to
> nowhere, always and forever to nowhere, heavy on the
> elbows in the earth to nowhere . . . now beyond all
> bearing up, up, up and into nowhere, suddenly,
> scaldingly, holdingly all nowhere gone and time

absolutely still and they were both there, time having stopped and he felt the earth move out and away from under them.

This passage uses layers of repetition to build to its syntactic climax. The repeated use of *and* to link the clauses, as well as the chants of *nowhere* and *up, up, up* and *suddenly, scaldingly, holdingly,* and *absolutely* all culminate in the moment when time stops and the earth, metaphorically, moves out and away from under them.

Contemporary novelist Tim O'Brien builds an entire story on a repetition. In *The Things They Carried,* O'Brien reinforces the weight, the routine, the wretched burdens of soldiers in Vietnam. By listing the items the way he does, O'Brien weighs the reader down with words just as the men were weighed down with weapons. The repetition here becomes almost a chant, the eerie chorus of a soldier's marching song gone somehow wrong. The repetition is as inescapable as their gruesome task:

> The things they carried were largely determined by necessity. . . . P-38 can openers, pocket knives, heat tabs, wristwatches, dog tags, mosquito repellant, chewing gum, candy, cigarettes, salt tablets, packets of Kool-Aid, lighters, matches, sewing kits, Military Payment Certificates, C rations, and two or three canteens of water. Together, these items weighed between 15 and 20 pounds, depending upon a man's habits or rate of metabolism. Henry Dobbins, who was a big man, carried extra rations; he was especially fond of canned peaches in heavy syrup over pound cake. Dave Jensen, who practiced field hygiene, carried a toothbrush, dental floss, and several hotel-sized bars of soap he'd stolen on R & R in Sydney, Australia. Ted Lavender, who was scared, carried tranquilizers. . . .

Some things they carried in common. . . . They shared the weight of memory. They took up what others could no longer bear. Often, they carried each other, the wounded or the weak. They carried infections. They carried chess sets, basketballs, Vietnamese-English dictionaries, insignia of rank, Bronze Stars and Purple Hearts, plastic cards imprinted with the Code of Conduct. They carried diseases, among them malaria and dysentery. They carried lice and ringworm and leeches and paddy algae and various rots and molds. They carried the land itself—a powdery orange-red dust that covered their boots and fatigues and faces. They carried the sky. The whole atmosphere, they carried it, the humidity, the monsoons, the stink of fungus and decay, all of it, they carried gravity.

WRITERS CAN ALSO BUILD RHYTHM through the subtle and wavelike effects on the reader of long sentence upon short, of quiet pauses and little breaths—or of strong stops and big white spaces.

Virginia Woolf had an uncanny ability to re-create the pulses and trills of the imagination, of characters' delicate inner monologues, and of the blunt punctuations of outer dialogues. Woolf blended thoughts and actions in a flow of images. Passages like this one, from *Mrs. Dalloway,* though carefully crafted, reflect the mysterious rhythms of the mental stream:

The hall of the house was cool as a vault. Mrs. Dalloway raised her hand to her eyes, and, as the maid shut the door to, and she heard the swish of Lucy's skirts, she felt like a nun who has left the world and feels fold round her the familiar veils and the response to old devotions. The cook whistled in the kitchen. She heard the click of the typewriter. It was her life, and, bending her head over the hall table, she bowed

beneath the influence, felt blessed and purified, saying to
herself, as she took the pad with the telephone message on it,
how moments like this are buds on the tree of life, flowers of
darkness they are, she thought (as if some lovely rose had
blossomed for her eyes only); not for a moment did she
believe in God; but all the more, she thought, taking up the
pad, must one repay in daily life to servants, yes, to dogs and
canaries, above all to Richard her husband, who was the
foundation of it—of the gay sounds, of the green lights, of
the cook even whistling, for Mrs. Walker was Irish and
whistled all day long—one must pay back from this secret
deposit of exquisite moments, she thought, lifting the pad,
while Lucy stood by her, trying to explain how

"Mr. Dalloway, ma'am—"

There's no one way to get to "harmonious prose." If Virginia Woolf mastered the music of the elite drawing room,
Martin Luther King, Jr., mastered the music of street
demonstrations. Writing with power and speaking with
passion, King tailored his style and cadences to his audiences, as on August 23, 1963, when he spoke from the
steps of the Lincoln Memorial. His rhythm and repetition—the *now,* the insistence on being *satisfied,* the *I have a
dream*—swell in an unstoppable tidal wave of feeling. King
put it all together: voice, lyricism, melody, and rhythm:

> We have . . . come to this hallowed spot to re-
> mind America of the fierce urgency of *now.*
> This is no time to engage in the luxury of
> cooling off or to take the tranquilizing drug of gradualism.
> *Now* is the time to make real the promises of democracy.
> *Now* is the time to rise from the dark and desolate valley of
> segregation to the sunlit path of racial justice. *Now* is the
> time to open the doors of opportunity to all of God's chil-

dren. *Now* is the time to lift our nation from the quicksands of racial injustice to the solid rock of brotherhood. . . .

We cannot turn back. There are those who are asking the devotees of civil rights, "When will you be satisfied?" We can never be satisfied as long as the Negro is the victim of the unspeakable horrors of police brutality. We can never be satisfied as long as our bodies, heavy with the fatigue of travel, cannot gain lodging in the motels of the highways and the hotels of the cities. We cannot be satisfied as long as the Negro's basic mobility is from a smaller ghetto to a larger one. We can never be satisfied as long as a Negro in Mississippi cannot vote and a Negro in New York believes he has nothing for which to vote. No, no, we are not satisfied, and we will not be satisfied until justice rolls down like waters and righteousness like a mighty stream. . . .

I say to you today, my friends, that in spite of the difficulties and frustrations of the moment I still have a dream. It is a dream deeply rooted in the American dream.

I have a dream that one day this nation will rise up and live out the true meaning of its creed: "We hold these truths to be self-evident; that all men are created equal."

I have a dream that one day on the red hills of Georgia the sons of former slaves and the sons of former slave owners will be able to sit down together at the table of brotherhood.

I have a dream that one day even the state of Mississippi, a state sweltering with the heat of injustice, sweltering with oppression, will be transformed into an oasis of freedom and justice.

I have a dream that my four little children will one day live in a nation where they will not be judged by the color of their skin but by the content of their character.

I have a dream today.

> I have a dream that one day, down in Alabama, with its vicious racists, with its governor having his lips dripping with the words of interposition and nullification, that one day, right there in Alabama, little black boys and black girls will be able to join hands with little white boys and white girls as sisters and brothers.
>
> I have a dream today.

Cardinal Sins

MAKING TEXT HUMDRUM.

One reason that preachers have an edge when it comes to rhythm is that they are steeped in the cadences of liturgical texts. Books like the Bible, after all, were written to be *read out loud,* and their rhythms lend themselves to regular recitation. Likewise, the traditional Anglican *Book of Common Prayer* was written to be read aloud by a congregation during services. By necessity, its cadences *worked.* But in modernizing the language of the prayer book, revisers forgot to reorchestrate the music. The twentieth century's tin-eared editors forgot about meter and flattened out rhythms. For centuries, the steady iambic rhythm in the last line of the Nicene Creed softened into delicate anapests—"and He shall come again, with glory, to judge both the quick and the dead." But the same line, rewritten in the 1970s to be more contemporary, now lurches from iamb to dactyl to anapest: "and he will come again in glory to judge the living and the dead." Did the revisers deem the wonderfully succinct "quick" too esoteric for modern-day readers? Did they not hear the difference between a dactyl and an anapest?

It's not just clerics who know how to spoil a beautiful phrase. In *What I Saw at the Revolution,* Republican speechwriter Peggy Noonan spoofed staff editors in the White House by speculating about how they would eviscerate that most rhythmic and powerful of presidential speeches, the Gettysburg Address: "Fourscore and seven years ago" would be changed, Noonan jokes, first to "eighty-seven years ago," then to "long ago," then to "sometime ago"; then it'd be deleted altogether. "Our fathers brought forth upon this continent" would end up "our fathers and mothers created here." "Conceived in liberty" would be ditched (the margin screams: "too much sexual imagery—sounds like we're talking about teen pregnancy"), as would "we cannot dedicate—we cannot consecrate—we cannot hallow this ground" ("too negative? Let's talk about what we *can* do!").

"RHYTHM" IS NO DEFENSE FOR SHODDY JOURNALISM.

All this encouragement to build rhythm into your prose requires a caveat. It takes listening and sensitivity (and some talent) to develop an ear for the music of prose. Encouraging "rhythm" is not tantamount to a license for mindless repetition or irritating singsong.

A reporter once refused this editor's request to insert the name of an official in a political story because he didn't want to "mess up the rhythm" of his sentence. Aside from the sheer idiocy of such an excuse, the sentence he was protecting was practically a study in infelicitous meter:

No law enforcement agency has yet proven it needs all these digital trapdoors. "Right now most law enforce-

ment personnel don't have any idea what the NII is"—
this according to one official who appeared on the panel.

That rhythm needs to be scrapped, not saved.

NOT PARALLEL, NOT MUSICAL.

Parallelism builds rhythm, and nonparallelism kills it.
Imagine that Marc Antony had said: "I came for the purpose of burying Caesar, not to praise him." Doesn't exactly roll off the tongue.

Inattentive writers muck up lists badly, throwing im-
balanced cadences together and leaving their sentences
scrambling. The elements of a list should echo each
other in length, number of syllables, and rhythm. "A government of the people, by the people, for the people"
works. "A government of the people, that the people create, for the people" doesn't.

If it's impossible to craft a list of exactly parallel elements, at least try to let the length of the phrases build,
so that you end up with a crescendo, not cacophony:

> Have Jell-O brand gelatin. Because it's cool (like ice
> cream), smooth (like pudding), light (like chiffon pie),
> refreshing (like sherbet), and tastes like fruit.

If you must break your neatly parallel pattern, break it
at the end. Let the longest or most ungainly phrase tum-
ble out last:

> Disney's *The Lion King* is part pageant, part puppet
> show, part parade, with a touch of Las Vegas revue
> thrown in.

THE REPETITION POLICE.

Some editors and copy editors bring their eyes to copy, but not their ears. Tone deaf and too too literal copy editors will remove repetition whenever they see it, ignoring the fact that it is one of our oldest rhetorical tricks. Don't be fooled by an editor's fancy terms when you *want* to keep the repetition in a phrase like, oh, "God said let there be light and there was light." There are editors out there who would argue that "the elegant variation" requires changing the second "light" to "illumination."

Repetition can be a graceful way of changing tack; it can lessen the abruptness of a transition. In a story on San Francisco District Attorney Terence Hallinan, who had attended an infamous birthday party for political consultant Jack Davis, a writer bridged the gap between the end of one section and the beginning of the next with this repetition:

> "It was a great party," Hallinan insisted in an interview months later. "Jack's thing [which featured performers in black leather, mutilation, and urination] was a little like the Tyson fight. You wouldn't do it yourself and it was pretty bizarre, but you're glad you saw it, because it later became the **subject of conversation.**"
>
> Hallinan knows what it means to be **the subject of conversation.** In the nearly two years since he was elected to replace the uncharismatic, almost invisible Arlo Smith, he has frequently made news for behavior that, if not quite bizarre, is still considered strange by D. A. standards.

A clueless copy editor nixed the deliberate repetition, changing the sentence to "Hallinan knows what it means to be talked about."

Tsk tsk.

Carnal Pleasures

Singers and songwriters live at language's epicenter—from ancient bards like Homer, whose epic narratives were told in song, to the jazzman Cab Calloway, whose comic and sometimes profane patter was a foil for the music of his band. (Calloway the wordman registered the Harlem vernacular in a book, *Mister Hepster's Jive Talk Dictionary.*)

Starting in the '60s, Gil Scott-Heron reinvented the notion of jazz patter, his Black Power rhetoric backed by a bongo in songs like "Whitey on the Moon," in which the narrator "can't pay no doctor's bills," even though society's spent billions sending a man to the moon:

> A rat done bit my sister Nell
> With Whitey on the moon
> Her face and arms began to swell
> And Whitey's on the moon. . . .
>
> You know, the man just upped my rent last night
> 'Cause Whitey's on the moon
> No hot water, no toilets, no lights,
> But Whitey's on the moon.

What Scott-Heron is up to is more than just patter. Sure, the blunt language and street syntax makes his story seem uncrafted and conversational. But the repetition of "Whitey's on the moon" (albeit with slightly different phrasing each time) lets him build on his theme with each new utterance. The narrative is more proselike than singsongy, but if you count the syllables in each line, you'll see that Scott-Heron has his rhythm down cold: every other line is close to eight syllables, and the intervening ones are all six.

Folksingers, too, let narrative unfold in bursts of rhythm. Think of all those stories Bob Dylan has told over the years, from "Lonesome Death of Hattie Carroll" to "Not Dark Yet." While some of Dylan's lyrics are pure poetry, some are plainly prosaic. The "music" comes from the rhythm of the words, as in his classic "Tangled up in Blue":

> Early one mornin' the sun was shinin',
> I was layin' in bed,
> Wondrin' if she'd changed at all,
> If her hair was still red.
>
> Her folks, they said our lives together
> Sure was gonna be rough.
> They never did like Mama's homemade dress,
> Papa's bankbook wasn't big enough.
>
> And I was standing on the side of the road,
> Rain fallin' on my shoes.
> Heading out for the East Coast,
> Lord knows I've paid some dues
> Gettin' through.
> Tangled up in blue.

Rap is the latest twist on this tradition of narrative song. Call rap "storytelling with a beat," "sonic brico-lage," or, as one critic prefers, "an endless stream of rhythmic verbal jazz." Into stories of the street, rapping griots mix voice, metaphor, rhyme, and beat.

Hip-hop has gained notoricty for the brutal and misogynistic rhymes of gangsta rap (Tupac Shakur's "William Bennett, Delores Tucker, / you's a mother-fucker; / instead of trying to help a nigger, / you destroy a brother" and Ice Cube's "I'm thinking to myself, / 'why did I bang her?' / Now I'm in the closet / looking for the hanger"). But rappers like Public Enemy's Chuck D churn out authoritative and history-conscious polemics. (Chuck D calls rap "black America's CNN.") Public Enemy's most well-known hit, "Fight the Power," unfolds like a 1989 update of "Whitey on the Moon," and "Louder than a Bomb" takes on subjects like the government's treatment of the black community ("CIA, FBI / All they tell is lies / And when I say it they get alarmed / 'Cause I'm louder than a bomb").

The old-school rap group Grandmaster Flash and the Furious Five was the first to use this musical genre as a gritty medium for serious discourse. Forget correct syntax. Forget iambic pentameter. This is rhyme and rhythm used to pack a point. This is pure language-as-music. In "The Message," every syllable is punched out like an urgent smack on a drum:

> Don't push me, 'cause I'm close to the edge
> I'm try-in' not to lose my head
> It's like a jungle sometimes, it makes me wonder
> How I keep from going under . . .
>
> My brother's doing bad, stole my mother's T.V.
> Says she watches too much, is just not healthy
> *All My Children* in the daytime, *Dallas* at night
> Can't even see the game or the Sugar Ray fight
> Bill collectors they ring my phone
> And scare my wife when I'm not home
> Got a bum education, double-digit inflation
> Can't take the train to the job, there's a strike at the station
> Neon King Kong standin' on my back
> Can't stop to turn around, broke my sacroiliac
> Midrange, migrained, cancered membrane

Sometimes I think I'm going insane,
I swear I might hijack a plane!

Don't push me, 'cause I'm close to the edge
I'm try-in' not to lose my head
It's like a jungle sometimes, it makes me wonder
How I keep from going under . . .

From the King James Bible to the lyrics of hip-hop—you might say we've gone from "sin and syntax" to "sin and syncopation." No matter the genre, all storytellers are engaged in the same struggle: how to use words, grammar, and music to describe the human condition.

"Remember that you are a human being with a soul and the divine right of articulate speech," wrote George Bernard Shaw. "That your native tongue is the language of Shakespeare and Milton and the Bible; and don't sit there crooning like a bilious pigeon."

Sin and Syntax has tried to coax, coach, and cajole you out of biliousness. Of course, there is much more to making memorable prose than linguistic facility. You also need worthy ideas, you need to tell stories with strong plots, and you need to cast and control the right characters. When it comes to developing these narrative skills, though, no book can help you. Experience is the ultimate master.

Ernest Hemingway once advised prose artists to "Write hard and clear about what hurts." It's good advice. But to follow it, you must stop reading.

As anyone who has tried to master French can attest, verb tenses can make even the calmest conjugator—well, tense. Derived from the French (and, before that, the Latin) word for "time," tense is the element of a verb that telegraphs "when" an action occurred.

Tense might be signaled through a verb's spelling (**sing, sang, sung**), through its ending (**singing**), or through the presence of an auxiliary verb (**had sung**).

There are three kinds of verb tenses: simple, progressive, and perfect.

The <u>simple tenses</u>—past, present, future—tell whether something **happened** in the past, **happens** in the present, or **will happen** in the future. The present tense in some ways is the most open-ended of these simple tenses— when does it begin and end? We think of the present tense when we think of something occurring in this instant, today, right now—as in "She clamors for more on tenses." But the present tense is also appropriate for something whose state doesn't change, as in the sentence "Patience with verb tenses is a virtue," or when something happens habitually, as in "He conjugates with abandon!"

The <u>progressive and perfect tenses</u> come into play when we are talking about an action as it is regarded *over time*. The <u>progressive tenses</u> convey a sense of ongoing or not-yet-completed action. The past progressive kicks in for something that **was happening** in some previous time; the present progressive kicks in for something that **is happening** now; the future progressive kicks in for something that **will be happening** in the future—a coming attraction.

The <u>perfect tenses</u> refer to actions that are complete, but that occurred in a kind of "anterior time"—a time frame preceding the overall sentence or context. The past perfect is brought in for an event that transpired before *another* event in simple past: "Melvin **had lurked** for years before he leaped." The present perfect, which straddles the past and the present, is brought in for actions not over and done with: "Melvin **has leaped** into cyberspace determined to forge a new identity." The future perfect is brought in for an action that will have been completed by some future point: "When Melvin returns to meatspace, he **will have** indeed **become** a STUD4XTC."

If you have made it this far without throwing in the towel, pat yourself on the back. Then take a deep breath. Tenses get even hinkier, combining into such hydra-headed monsters as <u>perfect progressives</u>. The following sentence, for example, contains the future perfect progressive tense: "By the time you read this, Melvin **will have been reveling** in ecstasy for five years."

Consider yourself lucky for this verbal flexibility. Our pantheon of verb tenses didn't always exist. As Charles Barber points out in *The English Language,* Shakespeare could—and did—say "my Ladie Hero hath bin falselie accusde," but he could *not* say "she is being falsely accused"; the bard's "as if the garment had bin made for me" passed muster, but "the garment was being made for me" would not have.

How could we bear to be without the following, none of which would have been possible before 1800:

- We were having a blast with verbs before *you* got here.
- Playful punctuation had been developed long before netizens went *nuts* with their keyboards.
- She has been known to disregard logic altogether and lapse into tongues.

A few tips on tense.

Stick to the simple present tense when possible, for it often guarantees strong, direct writing. If the past is required, the simple past is equally compelling. Part of the reason that sentences by, say, Dr. Seuss are so indelible is that they rely on rhythmically bold simple tenses ("The sun did not shine / It was too wet to play / So we sat in the house / All that cold, cold wet day").

Keep your tenses logical and consistent. Within a larger narrative, verbs must live in the same time zone. Don't arbitrarily bob and weave from past to present to future.

Within sentences, several things may each be in different time zones. Don't get flummoxed. Logic it out. Graph it if you have to.

So tense it's taut-o-logical.

Here's the standard way to conjugate *to do* in the major tenses:

	present	**past**	**future**
SIMPLE	he does	he did	he will do
PROGRESSIVE	he is doing	he was doing	he will be doing
PERFECT	he has done	he had done	he will have done

Nonstandard forms of English play fast and loose with tense, but their grammars often have their own loopy logic. In the 1880s, the Warrensburg *Journal* reported these vernacular conjugations of *to do it* (which were in turn recorded for posterity in *Rhetoric Made Racy*):

	present	**past**	**future**
SIMPLE		he done it	he gwyne done it
		they-uns done it	they-uns gwyne done it
PERFECT	he gone done it	he done gone done it	he gwyne gone done it
	they-uns gone done it	they-uns done gone done it	they-uns gwyne gone done it

Verbs are moody little suckers. No doubt you'd already guessed that, but did you know that every verb in every sentence expresses what the grammarians call "mood" or "mode"—the manner or attitude shading the statement? Mood clues you in to the speaker's disposition toward what he or she is saying.

There are three moods in English: the indicative, the imperative, and the subjunctive.

The <u>indicative</u> is the calmest, most neutral, most matter-of-fact. This is the mood of a verb in an ordinary observation:

"The correcting of prose *is* endless, because it *has* no fixed laws; a poem *comes* right with a click, like a box."

(William Butler Yeats was stating what he knew.)

"Languages, while they live, *are* perpetually *changing*. God apparently *meant* them for the common people ... and the common people *will use* them freely, as they *use* other gifts of God."

(Touché to the *Harper's* editor who, in 1886, wrote these sentences using the indicative mood in the present, past, future, and progressive tenses.)

"*Don't* you just *love* the confidence of the prose sages?"

(A sentence can pose a question and also be in the indicative.)

The <u>imperative</u> is the mood of stiff spine and stern expression. It might express a command or make a request—and when the direct order is given to others, the subject "you" is understood or implied:

"*Be* a sport."
"*Say* it isn't so."
(This direct, blunt form of the imperative conveys a sense of authority.)

The imperative might also appear via first- and third-person pronouns and the auxiliary verb *let*:

"*Let* me *tell* you about the very rich."
"*Let* us *go* then, you and I, when the evening is spread out against the sky. . . ."
"If any man objects, *let* him *speak* now or forever hold his peace."
(Call this the kinder, gentler imperative.)

The <u>subjunctive</u> mood is the whimsical one. It expresses wishes, possibilities, and fantasies about conditions or actions that, unfortunately, *aren't.* Rare in everyday speech, the subjunctive has an antique lustre, a linguistic cachet: it can lift mere words to eloquence (or, um, grandiosity).

With most verbs, the subjunctive looks the same as the indicative, with the exception of the present tense, when the third-person singular subject requires a third-person plural verb: *he takes* becomes *he take,* as in "I insist that he take St. John's wort." The subjunctive gets tricky when it involves the verb *to be.* In the present tense, the subjunctive is *be,* no matter the subject (*I be, she be,* and *they be,* not *I am, she is,* or *they are*). Likewise, the past subjunctive is *were* throughout ("If I were," not "If I was," as in "If I were depressed, I'd just jet over to Honolulu, *wikiwiki*").

Here's when it's appropriate to slip into a subjunctive mood:

- In contrary-to-fact statements, or in conditional sentences that start with *if,* include a *would,* and end up expressing something untrue:
  "If I *were* you, I'd be sending out that résumé."
  (Implication: I am not you; *my* job's secure.)
  "If wishes were horses, beggars would ride."
  (Implication: Wishes, unfortunately, don't take you anywhere.)
  As if and *as though* also commonly introduce contrafactual or hypothetical statements and so require the subjunctive:
  "She looked as though she *were going* to stop her harangue with the arrival of the dinner guests. But no."
  (Boor that she is, she dissed me all night long.)
  Do not assume that because a sentence starts with *if* the subjunctive is required. It is only appropriate in statements of contrafactual situations. When, in your clause, you're calling up a fact that is or may be true, no subjunctive is necessary: "If it rains again, my hair *will frizz* beyond repair."

- In sentences introduced by a set of peculiar verbs (including *insist, recommend, pray, urge,* and *ask*) that demand—or merely suggest—something:
  "He urged that the ban on French food *be modified* to allow certain exceptions."

"She asked that I *be offered* anything with chantilly."

"I insist that he *sample* the raspberry soufflé."

"You demand that she *consider* the kugelhopf?"

- In statements expressing a wish for the unattainable:

"I wish it *were* not true."

(Alas, it is.)

"I wish that she *were* my lover."

(Alas, she's my boss.)

- In phrases designed for poetic or rhetorical effect, and in phrases that have become frozen over time:

"Would that I *had* wings!"

"The public *be* damned!"

"Come what *may.*"

"Go ask the powers that *be.*"

"Woe *betide* he who crosses me."

Books on writing are, as Tom Waits would say, as old as dirt. Aristotle wrote the first classics in the genre, *Rhetoric* and *Poetics*. Here is an admittedly subjective list of favorites from among the many books on language written in the past millennium. You've seen many of them referred to in this book; any or all of them would give happy company to your dictionary and thesaurus (you do have a good dictionary and thesaurus, don't you?).

On Language and the History of English

The American Language, Fourth Edition. (New York: Alfred A. Knopf, 1936)

A lifelong project of *Baltimore Sun* journalist and critic H. L. Mencken, this opus comprises a 700-page main volume and two equally long supplements. In it, Mencken traces the ways and wiles of English in its American incarnation, covering pronunciation, proper names, slang, and dialects—from Czech to Chinese. Mencken's passion for the language flashes through, in sentences only he could write: "American is full of what Bret Harte called 'the saber-cuts of Saxon'; it meets Montaigne's ideal of a succulent and nervous speech, short and compact, not as much dedicated and combed out as vehement and brusque, rather arbitrary than monotonous, not pedantic but soldierly."

The Language Instinct. (New York: Morrow, 1994)
Steven Pinker, director of the Center for Cognitive Neuroscience at MIT, argues that language is a human instinct, like web-spinning in spiders. It's not "pedagogical" or "stylistic" grammar, Pinker devotes this book to; it's *mental* grammar: "the brain's program that lets us build an infinite set of sentences out of a finite list of words." Don't miss chapter 12, in which Pinker scraps with "The Language Mavens."

The Oxford English Dictionary. (Oxford: Oxford University Press, 1989)
Most of us don't have the bookshelf space, let alone the 3,000 bucks, for this twenty-volume dictionary-to-end-all-dictionaries. But imagine having 291,500 entries, not to mention usage examples dating back to *Beowolf.* The longest entry (60,000 words) is devoted to one of the shortest words: the verb *set,* with its more than 430 senses. If you have neither a large bookcase nor a savings account dedicated to dictionaries, consider the two-volume tiny-type version, which comes with a magnifying glass. Then there's the CD-ROM: you can search by keyword, etymological origin, or backwards definition. Keep your fingers crossed for the upcoming OED Online <www.oed.com/>. Set to go live in October 1999, the cyberspace version will showcase new entries as they are completed for the third edition, due in 2010.

The Story of English. (New York: Elisabeth Sifton Books / Viking, 1986)

A collaboration among Robert McCrum, William Cran, and Robert MacNeil (formerly of PBS's *Newshour),* this history travels with the Angles and the Saxons across the Continent and over the North Sea, traces the changes in English wrought by Norman invaders and the likes of Shakespeare, and trails Mark Twain and his American successors. If 350-page history books make you fidgety, go to the library and check out videocassettes of the PBS series; you get the same sweep of history, but the accents and dialects are more magical in stereo.

Writing and Prose Style

The Complete Plain Words. (New York: State Mutual, 1987)

Sir Ernest Gowers, the style god entrusted with updating the second edition of *Fowler's,* published the original *Plain Words: Their ABC* in 1954. Among its many entertaining tidbits: George Bernard Shaw going ballistic over split infinitives, Winston Churchill going sarcastic on prepositions at the end of sentences, and (a personal favorite) an Egyptian minister's message to a civil servant, illustrating the value of down-to-earth sentences: "Apollonius to Zeno, greeting. You did right to send the chickpeas to Memphis. Farewell."

The Elements of Style, Third Edition. (New York: Macmillan, 1979)

This is not a book. It's an icon. Originally copyrighted in 1918, it was known as "the *little* book" among the Cornell University students of Professor William Strunk, Jr.

One of those students was E. B. White, whose 1957 *New Yorker* essay on Strunk's gem earned him an invitation to update the book and add a thing or two himself. Watch for another update soon.

And—who woulda thunk it?—Strunk's original is on the Web at <www.cc.columbia.edu/acis/bartleby/strunk/>.

On Writing Well. (New York: HarperCollins, 1998)

William K. Zinsser divides the contents of this eminently wise, eminently readable book into "Principles" (The Transition, Clutter, Style, The Audience) and "Forms and Methods" (Business Writing, Criticism, Humor). Revising repeatedly since 1976, Zinsser boils down his philosophy to four "articles of faith": clarity, simplicity, brevity, and humanity.

"Politics and the English Language" in *A Collection of Essays.* (New York: Harcourt Brace, 1981)

A classic written in 1946 by the author of *1984* and *Animal Farm,* this essay appears in several collections of George Orwell's work. It is short but substantial, and includes this list of rules:

i. Never use a metaphor, simile, or other figure of speech which you are used to seeing in print.

ii. Never use a long word where a short one will do.

iii. If it is possible to cut a word out, always cut it out.

iv. Never use the passive where you can use the active.

v. Never use a foreign phrase, a scientific word, or a jargon word if you can think of an everyday English equivalent.

vi. Break any of these rules sooner than say anything out right barbarous.

Writing Well, Ninth Edition. (New York: Longman, 1998)

> A whopper: words, sentences, argument, mechanics, exercises—it's all here, it's all clear. It does scream "textbook, textbook, textbook," but the effect is mitigated by the insight and erudition of its authors, Donald Hall, a distinguished poet, and Sven Birkerts, a book critic and devotee of reading.

Grammar

A Comprehensive Grammar of the English Language. (Essex: Addison Wesley Longman Limited, 1985)

> Randolph Quirk, the dean of British grammarians, led the team that produced this behemoth, which will tell you everything—I mean *everything*—about grammar. What's a ditransitive verb? Page 54. Not sure about "formulaic utterance"? Page 1,463. When to use a dash? Page 1,629. You may be tempted to use big books only as doorstops. In this case, you'd be better off finding a brick and picking this book off the floor.

The Deluxe Transitive Vampire. (New York: Pantheon, 1993)

> This masterpiece of Gothic humor and racy sentences first came out in 1984 and was made even more fantastic and fantastical when reprinted in 1993. Call it grammar for grownups, or, as author Karen Elizabeth Gordon suggests, "for the innocent, the eager, and the doomed." You will shiver with glee.

Woe Is I. (New York: Grosset/Putnam, 1996)

> A clear-headed stroll through the labyrinth that is English, this book covers all the basics—*that* and *which*, subject-verb agreement, the ins and outs of plurals. Patricia T. O'Conner manages to amuse, too, in chapters with names like "Comma Sutra: The Joy of Punctuation" and "The Compleat Dangler: A Fish out of Water."

Usage

The Careful Writer. (New York: Atheneum, 1977)

> Theodore M. Bernstein first put together this glossary of stylistic snares in 1965, after a long career as an editor at the *New York Times.* Bernstein writes oh-so-cleanly (and with occasional sly humor) about usage, which he calls the "spit and polish" that gives writing precision, accuracy, clarity, and color. If you like Bernstein's style, you'll also want a copy of *Miss Thistlebottom's Hobgoblins,* a guide to "the taboos, bugbears, and outmoded rules of English usage." (Miss Thistlebottom is the archetypal, if apocryphal, eighth-grade schoolmarm.)

Jesse's Word of the Day. (New York: Random House, 1998)

> Lexicographer Jesse Sheidlower sheds light on words like "nerd" and phrases such as "young Turk" and "hoist with one's own petard." But even better than this book is the Web page <www.randomhouse.com/jesse/>, which features a new linguistic oddity every day. What's more, you can ply Jesse with questions about words you hear at the watercooler or the watering hole.

Modern American Usage. (New York: Hill and Wang, 1998)

In tribute to its creator, Wilson Follett, an Ivy League prof and noted editor, this book was edited and completed in 1966 by Jacques Barzun and a "small group of writers and teachers of English" including Carlos Baker and Lionel Trilling. Revised and updated in 1998 by Erik Wensberg, it remains a lucid lexicon true to Follett's original, which aimed to "clear up certain current notions about usage and grammar, purism and poetry."

Modern English Usage. (Oxford: Clarendon Press, 1996)

The idiosyncratic H. W. Fowler first published this, the wordsmith's ur-text, in 1926. The Great Schoolmaster set about to tame the wild edges of English with wit and temerity. Commonly called *Fowler's,* this bible was revised in 1965 by Sir Ernest Gowers and in 1996 by language historian Robert Burchfield. If you really want to flesh out your collection, track down a first edition. Burchfield is ever-so-informative, but not nearly as much fun as Fowler.

Out of the Loud Hound of Darkness. (New York: Pantheon, 1998)

If you're a fan of Gothic grammarian Karen Elizabeth Gordon, you'll want to explore this volume. Call it a fictionary, call it a dictionarrative, this book will set you straight on the difference between *climactic* and *climatic, flounder* and *founder*—that is, if you can keep your attention on usage when characters like Natty Ampersand and Capriccio are making mischief. Other Gordon books worth your while are *The Disheveled Dictionary* (words to die for), *Torn Wings and Faux Pas* (word pairs and style pointers), and *The Well-Tempered Sen-*

tence (everything you ever wanted to know about punctuation).

Wired Style. (San Francisco: Hardwired, 1996)

If you're shaky on the difference between a computer chip and a chocolate chip, this book's for you. My A to Z glossary clarifies the definitions of *Internet, internet,* and *intranet* and separates the geek slang from the gobbledygook. Essays lay out the Zeitgeist according to *Wired* magazine, and a Style FAQ answers all those frequently asked questions. At the risk of shameless self-promotion, I'll tell you that the second edition is due from Broadway Books in fall 1999.

Antiques and Curios

Amo, Amas, Amat and More. (New York: Harper & Row, 1985)

You may want to sprinkle your prose with phrases like *sui generis.* (That's one way to avoid *unique.*) Or you may want to know the difference between *e.g.* and *i.e.* Or you may just want to pronounce your Latin phrases correctly when you brandish them at the office. Whatever your motives, Eugene Ehrlich, editor at the *Oxford American Dictionary,* gives you these and 1,400 other Latin pearls, *in flagrante delicto.* For the same versatility in French, try *Je Ne Sais What?* by Jon Winokur.

History of English Prose Rhythm. (London: Macmillan, 1922)

One of the most influential literary critics of the late Victorian era, George Saintsbury believed in the separability of form and subject matter. He was known for his unsurpassed ear for the felicities of sound and meter, which he

applies to various texts in this book, originally published
in 1912. Let Saintsbury guide you through the literature
of iambs and anapests.

The King James Bible.
Feel free to pick among the many, many contemporary
versions of this translation of the Holy Bible, which hit
the streets in 1611. Its poetry works whether or not
you're a believer, and it resonates profoundly through our
literary culture. If you like this stuff, you may also want
to check out *The Book of Common Prayer.* For musicality,
few texts beat the Prayer of Consecration and the Prayer
of Humble Access in the Eucharist, or some of the Collects (try the First Sunday in Advent, Palm Sunday, and
Trinity Sunday). Look in antiquarian bookstores for a
version that predates the unmusical revision of 1979.

Lectures on Rhetoric and Belles Lettres. (Carbondale, Illinois: Southern Illinois University Press, 1965)
This facsimile reproduction of fourscore-plus lectures by
Dr. Hugh Blair was originally published in 1783 and revised 130 times before 1911. Blair was a well-known
university lecturer, a preacher to a fashionable Edinburgh congregation, an editor, and a literary tastemaker.
He wrote for his age the kind of book Quintilian produced for the first century A.D., and he refers repeatedly
to that Roman as well as to Aristotle, Longinus, and
Cicero.

Letters to a Young Poet. (New York: Vintage Books, 1984)
Originally published in 1934, this is a collection of ten
letters written by the great German poet Rainer Maria
Rilke to a young correspondent. Read it when you're
ready to give up as a writer. Rilke will re-inspire you.

On the Art of Writing. (New York: G. P. Putnam's Sons, 1916)

Sir Arthur Quiller-Couch delivered these lectures in 1913 and 1914, and if you've always wondered what it would be like to go to Cambridge, these erudite essays will give you a taste. (They are also available in an edition published by Folcroft Library Editions in 1978.) Quiller-Couch's essays on jargon are especially edifying. His translation of Hamlet's most famous soliloquy into bureaucratese set the stage for Orwell to revise Ecclesiastes. Here's how Sir Arthur purposely butchered "To be or not to be":

To be, or the contrary? Whether the former or the latter be preferable would seem to admit of some difference of opinion; the answer in the present case being of an affirmative or of a negative character according as to whether one elects on the one hand to mentally suffer the disfavour of fortune, albeit in an extreme degree, or on the other to boldly envisage adverse conditions in the prospect of eventually bringing them to a conclusion. The condition of sleep is similar to, if not indistinguishable from that of death; and with the addition of finality the former might be considered identical with the latter: so that in this connection it might be argued with regard to sleep that, could the addition be effected, a termination would be put to the endurance of a multiplicity of inconveniences, not to mention a number of downright evils incidental to our fallen humanity, and thus a consummation achieved of a most gratifying nature."

Benét's Reader's Encyclopedia. (New York: HarperCollins, 1996)

William Rose Benét based his 1948 encyclopedia (now in its fourth edition) on a similar nineteenth-century reference book by Ebenezer Cobham Brewer. It lists authors, critics, and major literary works; think of it as Leonard Maltin meets the Norton Anthology. What's Madame Bovary's first name? Who was the real George Sand? What did Macduff do in *Macbeth*? All the answers are here.

Rhetoric Made Racy. (Chicago: George Sherwood & Company, 1884)

Doesn't any bookshelf housing a book called *Sin and Syntax* also deserve *Rhetoric Made Racy*?

Write It Right. (New York: Walter Neale, 1909)

"The author's main purpose in this book is to teach precision in writing," begins Ambrose Bierce, "and of good writing (which, essentially, is clear thinking made visible) precision is the point of capital concern." This style and usage handbook (Bierce calls it his "Little Blacklist of Literary Faults") will give you distinctions still worth knowing, like the difference between *literally* and *figuratively* ("It is bad enough to exaggerate, but to affirm the truth of the exaggeration is intolerable"). You'll also see "needless" words gored (if *get married* is correct, why don't we say *got dead*?) Some of the entries are charmingly outdated (Bierce considers the abbreviation of *pantaloons* "vulgar exceedingly" and urges you never to swap "pants" for trousers), but this book—not to mention Bierce's more well-known *Devil's Dictionary*—is worth the bucks if you see it lying around in some antiquarian bookstore.

Index

ABOUT THE AUTHOR

Constance Hale spent her childhood in Hawaii, messing around in the *kapakahi* syntax of Pidgin English. She went on to study English literature at Princeton University and to earn a master's degree in journalism at the University of California, Berkeley. After newspapering for a few years, she landed at *Wired,* where she dabbled in old and new media and wrote *Wired Style: Principles of English Usage in the Digital Age.* She continues to work in print and online, and teaches writing and grammar to grown-ups. Hale lives in Oakland, California, with a guy named Bruce and a dog named Homer (after the Greek poet, not Bart Simpson's father!).